Pragmatics and Its Applications to TESOL and SLA

# Pragmatics and Its Applications to TESOL and SLA

*Salvatore Attardo and Lucy Pickering*

WILEY Blackwell

This edition first published 2021


*Registered Office(s)*
John Wiley & Sons, Inc., 111 River Street, Hoboken, NJ 07030, USA
John Wiley & Sons Ltd, The Atrium, Southern Gate, Chichester, West Sussex, PO19 8SQ, UK

*Editorial Office*
9600 Garsington Road, Oxford, OX4 2DQ, UK

For details of our global editorial offices, customer services, and more information about Wiley products visit us at www.wiley.com.

Wiley also publishes its books in a variety of electronic formats and by print-on-demand. Some content that appears in standard print versions of this book may not be available in other formats.



*A catalogue record for this book is available from the Library of Congress*

Cover image: © Orbon Alija/Getty Images
Cover design by Wiley

Set in 9.5/12.5 STIXTwoText by Integra Software Services Pvt. Ltd, Pondicherry, India

SKY1BA393FF-FDC9-4187-9AEB-F3D0F6F9A974_030521

# Contents

# Tables

# Figures

# Preface

This book started out as a series of guest lectures that Attardo delivered in Pickering's *Pragmatics and SLA* class on Grice, speech-act theory, and presuppositions. We had both taught separately courses on pragmatics, Pickering on the SLA and TESOL connections, Attardo on "Theoretical Pragmatics." Since we were both unhappy with the options for textbooks at the graduate level, besides the venerable Levinson (1983), now almost 40 years old, we started talking about turning the lectures into a book that would be both an introduction to pragmatics *and* a book about its applications to SLA and TESOL.

For obvious pedagogical reasons, the discussion of theoretical pragmatics precedes its applications to SLA/TESOL. However, we want to be very clear that the book was built exactly the other way around: we started from the applications to SLA/TESOL and then proceeded to determine exactly what the students needed to know about the theory in order to understand the discussion of the SLA/TESOL applications of pragmatics.

This decision comes from years of experience teaching these materials in courses structured like this book. Many of the students who need to understand the applications of pragmatics to SLA/TESOL struggle to read the original contributions. Hence the choice of keeping theory to a minimum and keeping the level of the exposition as simple and straightforward as possible.

Related to this was the choice of coverage: we chose to focus on topics which have direct relevance to SLA/TESOL teachers, and of course the materials they need to understand those topics. Another issue was selection: any book of this size, roughly the 15 week US academic semester reading size, requires serious, painful decisions on what to leave in and what to take out. Here our diametrically opposed attitudes served us well: Pickering's restraint provided an effective counterbalance to Attardo's "shiny moving object" expansive approach.

Our treatment of pragmatic theory is both more comprehensive and more in depth than similar books about pragmatics and SLA/TESOL. This is a principled choice. We strongly believe that repeating decontextualized formulations of various parts of pragmatic theories, such as Grice's principle of cooperation (often reduced to its maxims), for example, or of the assumption of rationality in Brown and Levinson's politeness, leads to oversimplification and to missing, if not quite the actual meaning of the theories, at least significant nuances. It is necessary to understand the milieu in which ideas are proposed, what were the scholars who proposed the theories reacting to, why certain ideas prosper and others do not.

In order to enable students to do effective and informed research on the applications of pragmatics to SLA/TESOL they need to understand where pragmatics is coming from and in what direction it is moving, that is, what the future trends are.

This is mirrored in the organization of the text. We begin with an initial chapter on semantics which introduces the basic concepts underlying the idea of meaning as a necessary first step to understanding the history and field of pragmatics, specifically the influence of context on the determination of meaning. These concepts may be more or less familiar to students in a pragmatics class depending on their prior background in linguistics.

Chapter 2 grounds the text very specifically in SLA/TESOL concerns and the audience who inspired this text. It is organized around a series of questions that we have been consistently asked regarding pragmatics and SLA/TESOL over our 20+ year history of teaching this class, and it sets the stage for the remaining chapters that address each issue in more depth. Chapters 3–8 focus on traditional areas of pragmatics. Chapters 3–5 survey speech act theory from its origins in ordinary language philosophy to its development into neo-Gricean pragmatics and rationality-based politeness theories. In Chapters 6–8, we turn to the ways in which contextual information is reflected in discourse ranging from information structure, to social and interactional information. Each of these chapters follows the same organizational structure and begins with a presentation of the theoretical concepts followed by applications to SLA/TESOL and finishes with sample teaching materials to exemplify how these concepts might be introduced in a TESOL classroom. In Chapter 9, we recognize that graduate pragmatics seminars often highlight a student research component as a proposal for a study or a discussion of a replication study. The chapter outlines the typical data collection techniques and research designs that are used in studies that comprise the intercultural, TESOL/SLA-based literature. The final two chapters discuss more recent developments in pragmatics including metapragmatics and some of the cutting edge work such as neuropragmatics and the role of pragmatics in human–computer interactions.

A note on the sources of our examples. We have used a variety of sources: (1) the Godfrey et al. 1992 “Switchboard” corpus. These are quoted by providing the file from the corpus in which the utterance can be found. If we are quoting a single turn, we provide the speaker identification and the turn number in the reference. If we are quoting two or more turns, we provide the speaker identification and turn number before each turn. (2) Invented examples, when useful and when the claim made is not particularly controversial or does not involve features that are below the threshold of consciousness of the speakers.[1] (3) Examples quoted in various sources (generally in a simplified notation, when it was not pertinent to the point being exemplified).

1 Constructed examples have the advantage of being more context-independent and hence more easily grasped, precisely because they are planned to be so. Furthermore, for the same reason, they are more focused on the feature being demonstrated. Finally, they must be realistic: that is, pass an acceptability test in the audience, much like literary texts.

We are aware of the strong preference in some circles for using only naturally occurring data, but the problem with naturally occurring data is that they often need extensive contextualization to be understood and thus appear confusing to the reader. Moreover, they are "messy" as can be seen from looking at any transcription of naturally occurring data. The transcriptions are not always standardized and they impose an extra step to the reader. The pedagogical goal of this text being paramount, we decided to simplify the transcription of the sources, if necessary.

We would like to thank the following people for helping and/or providing us with offprints of their work: Nabiha El Khatib, Nancy Bell, Lachlan Mackenzie, Shigehito Menjo, Salvador Pons Bordería, Francisco Yus, the interlibrary loan staff, and the students who have taken various versions of the Pragmatics and SLA course we taught jointly at TAMUC in the past 10 years, and especially the students in the Spring 2020 version of the course who provided us with invaluable feedback on a draft of the manuscript.

Salvatore Attardo and Lucy Pickering

The Middle of Nowhere Ranch, near Lone Oak, TX

# Typographical Conventions

Numbered examples are set apart, whereas un-numbered examples appear in the running text in italics, as for example *in the present example.* Translations appear in single quotes following the original. Grammatical constructions appear in small caps, for example, LEAVE X ALONE. Mentioned words appear in double quotes: "boy" has three letters. The use/mention distinction

(1) The boy kicked the ball (use/object)
"Boy" consists of three letters (mention/metalanguage)

is parallel to the object language versus metalanguage (see Metalanguage and Object Language section of Chapter 10).

Ungrammatical sentences are marked by a prefixed asterisk (*), whereas pragmatically problematic utterances are marked by the symbol (⁎); contrast

(2) * The children eats breakfast.
⁎ Excuse me sir, would you mind getting out of my face?

Tone units are indicated by double vertical bars, as in the example below

(3) || GRAvy ||

the usual conventions apply:

- CAPS indicate the prominent syllable
- Rising, falling, and level tones are indicated by ⇗, ⇘, and ⇒, respectively.
- Tone markings precede the tonic syllable: || ⇗GRAvy ||

Cross references within the book are given by chapter, section, and subsection: so a cross reference (see 5.3.2) means chapter 5, section 3, subsection 2.

# 1

# Meaning

Let's start from a very simple, everyday situation, a man walks in a donut store and asks for a donut, for example, by saying: "May I have a donut, please?" The donut shop employee turns around, picks up a donut, and gives it to the man. There are many ways of looking at this situation, but we will focus on just one aspect: How did the man and the donut shop employee know that the uttering the word "donut" would cause the transaction to succeed?[1] A simple explanation is that both the man and the employee know that "donut" means a certain kind of pastry made with sweet dough that is deep fried and covered with various glazes, sugar, and/or sprinkles. Furthermore, the man and the employee know that by using the word, they are referring to (i.e., they mean) an object that happens to be in the display case of the shop. However, the word "means" in this explanation is deceptively simple. In fact, a whole discipline, a part of philosophy, deals with the apparently simple idea of "meaning." Within linguistics, which is our domain, many ideas from philosophical semantics have been adopted but a few come from other fields, as we will see.

Semantics is thus the part of linguistics that deals with meaning. We will start out by defining meaning; to do so, we must introduce the idea of the semiotic sign and of code or, to put it differently, explain how it is possible to mean something using something else. We then introduce two major approaches to semantics: the extensional (referential) approach and the intensional approach. Once we have examined these two radically different ways of approaching semantics, we will examine the contentious issue of the boundary between semantics and pragmatics, which is entwined with the idea of context and of modularity. These are big ideas that exceed pragmatics and even linguistics. However, it is important to understand where pragmatics itself as a science is located, within the context of its two older sisters: philosophy and psychology.

1 Of course, many other aspects of the situation have to be just right for the transaction to go off successfully: first, and obviously, the word "donut" appears in the middle of a sentence, and the words and the syntax of the sentence will be a significant part of overall the exchange. Furthermore, the man and the employee must speak the same language, the shop must not be out of merchandise, the man and the employee must share a desire for the transaction to be successful, for reasons that are probably very different, etc. As we said, we are ignoring all these aspects for the time being. They will be considered in other chapters of the book.

*Pragmatics and Its Applications to TESOL and SLA*, First Edition. Salvatore Attardo and Lucy Pickering.

## 1.1 What Do We Mean by Meaning?

Meaning can be a complex and off-putting topic: many students are discouraged by the difficult terminology and symbolism of logic, which is often used in its presentation, or are confused by the fact that there exist many conflicting theories of meaning, unlike the relative simplicity of morphology and phonology. It does not matter that if you scratch below the surface, both phonology and morphology are as conflicted as semantics. Most students never get the chance to enter semantics.

Conversely, others may feel that there's nothing to be studied there: after all, "cow" means "cow" and if I say "cow" I mean "cow" and that's it. What could be simpler? All you would need to teach to a learner of a foreign language would be the vocabulary. Is that a realistic view of language teaching? Of course not. There is much more to speaking a foreign language than plugging in words. In fact, even within a single language, what words convey may change. Consider the sentence: *Nice driving!* The meaning of the words is very clear: "nice" indicates a positive assessment and "driving" refers to operating and specifically directing a vehicle. However, *Nice driving!* could be uttered by a spouse to another who has just driven them to the airport in record time at rush hour, or to a spouse who just crashed the car into a tree, causing significant damage to the car. Note how the meaning of the words "nice" and "driving" is not affected at all by the change in situations. What changes is that the speaker means nice literally in the first situation and ironically in the second. So, even assuming that the meaning of words was simple and straightforward (it is not, incidentally!), the meaning of the utterance could change significantly. So, yes, meaning is complicated.

But, what is meaning, precisely? Meaning is the result of an act of semiosis conducted by an agent.[2] Semiosis is the process of producing a sign. So, to begin with, meaning is associated with signs. We will discuss precisely how in what follows.

### 1.1.1 Semiotics

A sign is the union of a signifier and a signified. The signifier is the mental representation of the physical component of the sign, such as a sound, an image, or an alphabetic symbol. The sequence of phonemes /kæt/, the graphemes "cat," and Figure 1.1 are all possible signifiers of the sign "cat."

The signified is the mental representation of the entity referred to by the sign. When a speaker of English hears the sounds of the word /kæt/ or reads the letters "cat" or sees Figure 1.1, he/she thinks of a cat (has a mental representation, a concept). That thought is the meaning of the word "cat."

So, in a sense, a sign is a tool to connect, via two mental representations, two physical world entities: a group of sounds, that is, the actual pronunciation of a group of phonemes and an actual physical object in the world, the referent (namely, an actual cat, with fur, a tail, whiskers, claws, who has been spayed, goes to the vet on Thursday, etc.). There is no easy way to connect the two without going through a conventional pairing of mental

**Figure 1.1** Image of a cat.

2 Usually, a person, but animals can produce signs as well: the field of zoo-semiotics deals precisely with signs produced by animals and insects: the bee dance is a famous example of communication by insects.

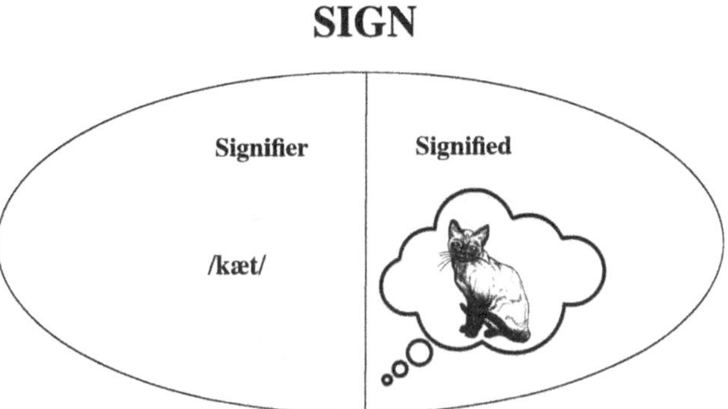


**Figure 1.2** A sign is the union of a signifier and a signified.

representations (of sounds, graphemes, etc. on the one side, and of referents, on the other). If we put all of this into a graphic representation, we get the so-called semiotic triangle, as shown in Figure 1.2. Note how there is no direct link between the sounds and the referent. The job of the sign is to connect the two (sounds and referents).

There is no reason, except social convention, for a cat to be called a cat or a dog a dog. Consider the fact that a dog is called "dog" in English, "chien" in French, "perro" in Spanish, and "gǒu" in Chinese. If there were a good reason for a dog to be called a dog, then that reason would hold also in China and France. Since it obviously doesn't, given the variety of terms just considered, then there isn't one. This is known as the principle of the arbitrariness of the sign.

There are exceptions: iconic signs have a connection with their referent – an arrow points in the direction you want to indicate; the line of a chart goes up in proportion to the increase of the quantity you are symbolizing. Onomatopoetic signs sound like the thing they refer to, for example, "bang," "crash," "hiss." These exceptions are limited and do not affect the principle of arbitrariness of the sign.

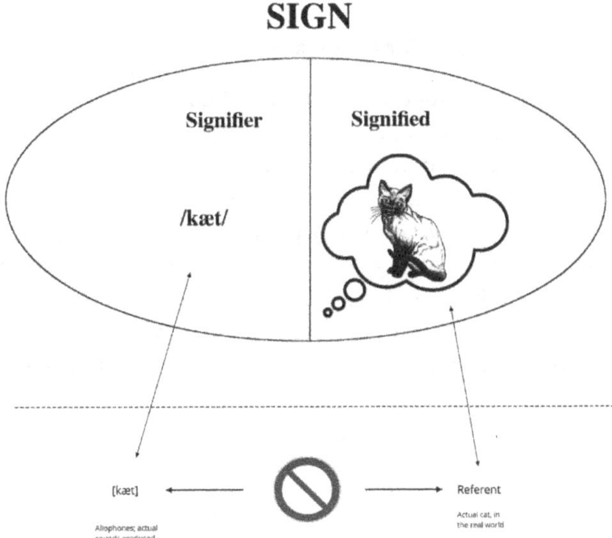


**Figure 1.3** The indirect relationship between the sounds and the referent, mediated by the sign.

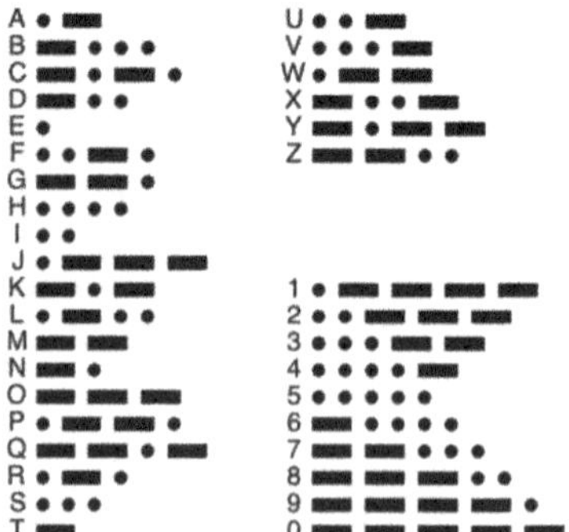


**Figure 1.4** The Morse code.

Generally speaking, signs are conventional: they exist only due to a social convention. Think of money: a dollar bill is just a piece of paper; it is not intrinsically valuable, like, say, gold or a car. The dollar bill is worth something only because we have a convention in our society that anyone will exchange that piece of paper for goods of some kind. When we say that it is a convention, we don't mean to diminish it. Clearly society invests large amount of resources and time to protect this convention: only the state is allowed to print money and if you try to do it on your own, the police will pay you a visit very soon.

A language is then a system of signs. The examples we have used so far, for simplicity, have all been lexical items, but grammatical constructions, word order, intonation, and so on are all signs, which are part of the system. A system of signs is also called a code. Think of the Morse code, which was used in the telegraph, in which to each letter of the alphabet correspond some combination of dashes and dots (Figure 1.4). This system is a code in the sense that to each letter we assign, by convention, a sequence of dashes and dots. Note that just like there was no reason for a cat to be called a cat, there is no reason for the letter A to be "dot-dash," it could just as well have been "dash-dot" (which happens to be the letter N).

### 1.1.2 Extensional and Intensional Semantics

Consider the musical terminology of "largo" (see Figure 1.5). You are probably not familiar with the term, unless you are a trained classical musician. You may perhaps know that it is a tempo, that is, a description of how fast the music is to be performed. You may even be aware of the fact that largo is slower than allegro or andante, so you have some idea of what "largo" means, but until you actually hear a performance of a piece played in a largo tempo, you will not actually know what largo means. The difference is that when you are working with the theoretical definition, and the definition in terms of what "largo" is *not* (i.e., not allegro, not andante, etc.) you do have a meaning in mind, but when you actually hear it performed you have also something in the world that this meaning refers to.

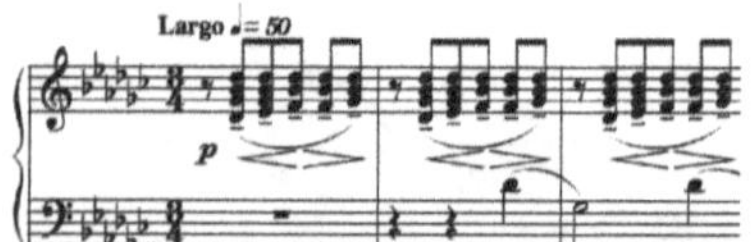


**Figure 1.5** Partition for the beginning of a Rachmaninoff piece with largo tempo.

We thus distinguish two approaches to semantics: the extensional approach that sees the meaning of a word as the thing it refers to and the intensional approach that sees meaning as the relationships that a word has with other concepts. We will consider them both.

**Extensional Semantics**

Most or all of philosophical semantics takes place within the extensional framework. This does not mean that philosophers do not see the difference between sense and referent. In fact, we owe the first clear statement of the difference to Frege, one of the founders of philosophical semantics. However, generally speaking, philosophers are interested in problems of meaning only as a tool to get at truth. The idea is pretty simple: any sentence consists of, at least, a proposition. So, *Mary loves tea*, *The sky is blue*, and *Socrates is mortal* are all sentences, and each of them can be expressed as a proposition. Traditionally this proposition is indicated as "p" (short for "proposition"). Propositions can be true or false, unlike words. A proposition is true if it describes a true state of affairs, and false if it doesn't. So if Attardo says *I am a bachelor* p (= Attardo is a bachelor) is false, as Attardo is in fact married to Pickering. Many linguists have taken the position that "semantics is limited to the statement of truth conditions" (Levinson, 1983, p. 12), thus limiting the scope of semantics to extensional, truth-functional semantics. The name truth-functional comes from the fact that the truth-value of a compound sentence is a function of the truth-value of its constituents: so if *Mary loves John* is true and *Mary loves Bob* is true, the overall sentence *Mary loves John and (Mary) loves Bob* is also true. If either component sentence is false, the overall sentence is also false. This is an important principle, called compositionality, which states roughly that the meaning of a sentence is the sum of the meaning of its components.

Since Aristotle, logic has been preoccupied with determining, given the truth or falsehood of a proposition, how to determine the truth of other propositions that are related to it. The syllogism, which you may have studied in a critical thinking class or in an introduction to philosophy, is precisely one such technique. If one says *Socrates is human* (= p) and *All humans are mortal* (= q), it follows from the truth of p and q that *Socrates is mortal.*

Syllogisms are not the only conclusions that logicians draw. Take the word "bachelor": If one is a bachelor it follows necessarily (logically) that one is not married. It would be a contradiction to say *Bob is a bachelor but he's married.* So, when we have a proposition "x is not married" (q) that follows logically from another (x is a bachelor = p), then we call q a logical inference of p. Note that in common parlance, we use sometimes "infer" differently, as in *the police inferred that the crime happened at 5:00 am.* A logical inference is a technical term.[3]

Another related technical term is presupposition. Let's take again our sentence, *Bob is a bachelor.* As we just saw it follows logically (it is an inference) that Bob is not married. Now consider the negation of *Bob is a bachelor*, namely *Bob is not a bachelor*. If we consider these two sentences together, it no longer follows that Bob is not married, since if he is not a bachelor he must be married. In other words, the inferences are neutralized by the negation of the proposition. So, does anything follow from both *Bob is a bachelor* and *Bob is not a bachelor*? Yes. First, that there is someone called Bob that the speaker and the hearer both know. Second, that this Bob person could potentially be either married or not. If it turns out that Bob is in fact a two-year old baby, both *Bob is a bachelor* and *Bob is not a bachelor*

3 Other terms used are also "entailment" and "implication."

would be odd and inappropriate (although it could be said jokingly). So, presuppositions are inferences that resist negation: if you can draw an inference from a proposition and its negation, those inferences are presuppositions.

The reason inferences and presuppositions are important is that they follow from a given proposition, albeit differently, and thus are part of the overall meaning of an utterance. This is crucial for the definition of pragmatics. Imagine if someone asks *Is Bob married?* and the answer is *Bob is a bachelor.* On the surface, the answer does not answer the question, which is a yes/no question, so technically only a choice of "yes" or "no" is a proper answer. However, when you consider the inferences, that is, if Bob is a bachelor, then it follows that Bob is not married, by logical inference, the answer is in fact quite satisfactory. Recapping: we have the meaning of a sentence, in the form of a proposition, and then other meanings that can be derived from this proposition. That's fairly clear, but it's not the end of the story. There is more to pragmatics than propositions, inferences, and presuppositions.

### Intensional Semantics

Intensional or structural semantics is concerned with the meaning of words and of sentences. Whereas referential semantics posits that the meaning of a word is its referent, intensional semantics is concerned with the sense of the expression. Sense is here defined as the relationship that a given word, for example, has in relation to the other words in the lexicon (the mental dictionary of speakers). So part of the meaning of "good" is that it is opposed to "bad" and related to "better" and "best" by a relation of scalar intensity ("better" is a higher degree of "good"). Another part of the meaning of "good" is that it describes an evaluation on the part of the speaker, relative to its object (so a good child is a child that behaves well, whereas a good donut is a donut that tastes good). Yet another part of the meaning of good is that it can occur as a modifier of nouns ("good boy") but not of verbs (* *I want to speak good*). This part of the meaning is grammaticalized (part of grammar) as the fact that good is an adjective (part of speech) and not an adverb. The adverb of good is "well" and that too is part of knowing how to use "good" in English.

This does not exhaust the meaning of words. Lexical semanticists have figured out that word meanings are stored in the mental lexicon in the form of frames or scripts. Consider the following examples:

(1) a) John stacked the beer in the fridge.
  b) ⁕ John stacked the water in the pool.

A moment of reflection shows that what makes (1.b) pragmatically odd is that pool water does not come in containers, let alone stackable ones. It is hard to imagine that "comes in stackable containers" is part of the lexical meaning of the word beer: most dictionaries define beer as an alcoholic beverage. Some provide the information that it is generally made from fermented cereals and flavored with hops. Few dictionaries provide the information that it comes in bottles, cans, or kegs. This information is considered non-lexical or encyclopedic (i.e., information about the world, not the lexical item). So the idea is that a frame or script contains all the semantic information about a given word: its lexical meaning, its connections with other words, the linguistic contexts in which it can occur (collocations), the extra-linguistic contexts in which it can occur, and of course any encyclopedic information available to the speaker. Frames and scripts are traditionally represented as a

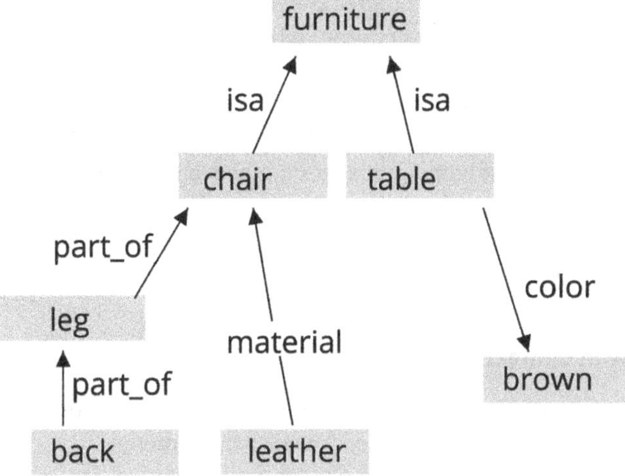


**Figure 1.6** The semantic network of "chair." "isa" labels hyponymy links.

graph, a network of frames/scripts, with each link between two frames/scripts indicated by a labeled line connecting the two. Thus, for example, Figure 1.6 shows a small fragment of the semantic network around the word "chair." "ISA" indicates that the relationship between the two terms is one of hyponymy, that is, *a* chair is a kind of furniture; "part_of" indicates that the term is a partonym (i.e., a part, a component of the item).

Intensional semantics also accepts the principle of compositionality but expands on it with the idea of disambiguation. Consider the word "star." "Star" has at least three meanings:

1. a celestial body, such as the sun, Alpha Centauri, and so on;
2. a prominent individual in a field, usually in entertainment, as in a movie star;
3. the symbol "*" in the ASCII keyboard (also known as "asterisk," after the Greek "aster" = star).

The property of a word (or sign) of having more than one meaning is called ambiguity. Sentences can be ambiguous too. From the standpoint of communication, ambiguity is a problem: how do we know which meaning is the speaker conveying when he/she says: *I found a star*? Here the context in which the sentence is produced (to be discussed more fully later) comes to the rescue: suppose that the sentence *I found a star* is uttered by an astronomer, who is having lunch with a fellow astronomer at the observatory's cafeteria, then the most likely sense is (1); if it is uttered by a movie producer having lunch with another producer, then the sense is probably (2); finally, if two proofreaders are talking about the progress of their work proofing a linguistic textbook, presumably the intended meaning is (3). The process of eliminating the unlikely meanings and narrowing down the interpretation of the utterance to the most likely in context is called "disambiguation." An important point to stress is that disambiguation takes into account pragmatic/contextual factors. As we will see later, this is one of the reasons why drawing a boundary between semantics and pragmatics is so hard.

Disambiguation takes into account not only the context but also the co-text, that is, the rest of the text in which a given word occurs. So if Attardo asks for a cup of coffee, the presence of "cup" will select the meaning of "coffee" as a liquid, rather than as ground beans.

Conversely, if Pickering asked for a pound of coffee, the presence of a weight unit for solids would disambiguate "coffee" to beans or ground beans.

**Convergence of the Theories of Semantics**

In conclusion, who is right? Is meaning intensional or extensional? This may sound a little too pat, but the answer is that both approaches are needed: we need to know what words mean, in the system, and we need to know what they refer to, in the world. We can all use the term "string theory" in the context of quantum theory, for example, but only those with a PhD in mathematics or physics have any real idea of what it refers to.

### 1.1.3 Language in Context

Thus far we have alternated between using the terms "sentence," "proposition," and "utterance." There are deep reasons for doing so. Consider the sentence

(2) I want to eat a donut.

Assume that the speaker is Attardo. We can say that (2) conveys a proposition "Attardo eat a donut."[4] The fact that Attardo wants to eat a donut is the attitude or stance that the speaker has toward the proposition, that is, he wants it to be the case (see Chapter 7 for a more in-depth discussion of stance). However, there is an important missing element: who is the speaker? Where is the exchange taking place? Suppose that the speaker is Attardo who likes donuts very much. Suppose further that the exchange happens in the *Sweetie* donut store adjacent to the university and Attardo is addressing one of the staff. Under those circumstance, most likely the utterance counts and will be taken as an attempt to purchase a donut. Conversely, if Attardo is standing in the middle of the desert, miles away from the nearest donut shop, it will be read as a hopeless wish. So, the context in which a sentence is uttered is very important in determining what the sentence means. A sentence in context is called an utterance.

The context of an utterance is a very broad construct, which involves who the participants are (Attardo vs. a person on a strict diet), where and when the utterance takes place (the donut shop vs. the desert; opening hours of the shop vs. times it is closed), the activity in which they are involved (purchasing a donut vs. hiking), the culture in which the participants operate (in some cultures, if you are a guest, merely indicating an interest in something is equivalent to requesting it), the beliefs of the participants about the situation (donuts are good) and in general about the world (donuts are still good, but some cultures may not be familiar with them), gestures, facial expressions, and generally speaking behavioral cues (e.g., is Attardo smiling or frowning?), the linguistic and cultural backgrounds of the participants (which may not be the same), and the background knowledge of the participants (which may not coincide).[5]

---

4 Note that the verb is an a bare infinitive form, because its tense and mood are not part of the proposition. We will examine this in more detail in Chapter 7.

5 From a different, nonlinguistic, perspective one could describe the situation, for example, as a commercial transaction or as a social event governed by practices of social engagement. The utterance or speech act then becomes more or less irrelevant. These perspectives are not antagonistic to the linguistic one. They merely reflect different interests or areas of research. From a linguistic perspective, the context is what comes "with the text" (con-text) as should be obvious even just from the etymology of the term.

In an intercultural exchange, where speakers come from different cultures and different languages, the cultural background and knowledge of the participants will inevitably differ. That is why sometimes there are problems communicating. For example, in the culture where Attardo grew up, offering seconds of food at the table is a way of showing that one cares for one's guests, and one must politely refuse twice before accepting, or if one refuses a third time, the host assumes that the guest really is full. Pickering, who grew up in a different culture, where food was much less central to the expression of caring, would perceive repeated offerings of seconds to be borderline badgering of guests. Conversely, if someone who shares Attardo's cultural background is offered food by someone from Pickering's background, he/she would politely refuse, only to see the plate being withdrawn.

This is why all these components of context, from presuppositions to shared cultural background, are crucial in understanding and negotiating communication. Note that even the understanding of what is happening, of what activity the participants are engaging in, is affected by their cultural backgrounds: when a speaker refuses an offer of seconds, is she being polite or is she full? There is no way of knowing, unless you know what her cultural background is (and even then, she may be accommodating to the different culture in which she is currently operating). The idea of context is much broader than this short discussion allows. See also Section 8.3 for more detail.

Context is also important from another perspective. Traditionally, the assumption has been that semantics deals with meaning per se and that pragmatics deals with meaning in context. While this is a good first approximation, we will see in what follows that the dichotomy cannot be maintained.

### 1.1.4 The Semantics/Pragmatics Boundary

As just mentioned earlier, one approach has been to argue that semantics is truth-functional, whereas pragmatics would deal with non-truth-functional aspects of meaning, as famously expressed in the formula:

Pragmatics = meaning - truth conditions

This definition has the advantage that it is neat: semantics would be responsible for the literal meaning of a sentence, whereas pragmatics would be responsible for any "extra" meaning. Consider the following example: *The horse is not in the barn.* Setting aside the fact that the notion of literal meaning has itself been seriously challenged, we could describe the literal meaning of the sentence as *The location of the horse is not the barn.* Put it differently, the horse may be anywhere but not in the barn.

What could the pragmatics of the utterance be? It depends on the context: suppose that there are horse thieves roaming in the area. Uttering *The horse is not in the barn* could imply that it has been stolen. If the hearer is a person whose job was to make sure that the horse was put in the barn, the utterance may be a threat of punishment. If the speakers are spies or agents of the secret service, this could mean that a subject has not reached their destination.

The problem, of course, is that the "literal" meaning of *The horse is not in the barn* depends, in part, on the disambiguation of its components. Let's start with "is." "Is" has many meanings; contrast

(3) This is Paul.
The book is yellow.
The book is 5 dollars.
The book is 300 pages long.
It's two hours to Dallas.
Paul is home/in the barn.

In these examples, "is" expresses identity, quality, cost, length, duration, location, and many more concepts. In fact, the verb "to be" does not have much meaning (unlike a verb like "kick") and thus must rely heavily on context to disambiguate it. In the case of our example, which of these meanings applies to "being in the barn"? Probably the location one (compare the example: *Paul is home*). But of course, disambiguation is, at least in part, a pragmatic process. Then there is the problem of the determinative article: it is "the horse" not "a horse," which means it is a horse known to the speakers or such that it can be uniquely identified. Needless to say, "known to the speakers" is a pragmatic notion. So the idea of a neat boundary between semantics and pragmatics seems unlikely.

### 1.1.5 Modularity

Another way of arguing about the boundary between semantics and pragmatics is to resort to modularity arguments. As a teacher, you want your student to "think" in the L2; however, to do so they cannot refer to a rule and figure out what to say based on that, nor can they monitor what they say word by word. All those strategies are way too slow to produce fluent output. The learners must rely on automatic processing. Cognitive psychology has introduced the idea of "fast" and "slow" mental processes. In order to understand the difference between fast and slow processing, we must understand modularity.

Modularity is the idea that some mental processes are "encapsulated," that is, they are based on an input and do not take into consideration anything else. Consider reflexes, for example, blinking when something approaches your eye does not depend on the will of the subject. You cannot will yourself into not blinking. Therefore, we can assume that the blinking reflex is a module, which takes as input the proximity to the eye of an object and is encapsulated, that is, does not consider other inputs, such as the will of the subject not to blink.

Visual illusions are likewise examples of modularity: consider the Müller-Lyer figures in Figure 1.7. Even after you have been told that the two horizontal lines are of the same length, you cannot help seeing them longer and shorter. This tells us the perception of the length of the lines is a module (i.e., is encapsulated), vis-à-vis the knowledge of their length.

Within language, we know that all the meanings of a word get activated when it is first read, albeit for a very short time (about 200 milliseconds, well below the level of consciousness). Later the non-contextually relevant meanings are suppressed, but the activation of the irrelevant meanings cannot be stopped; hence it is a module. While modularity has

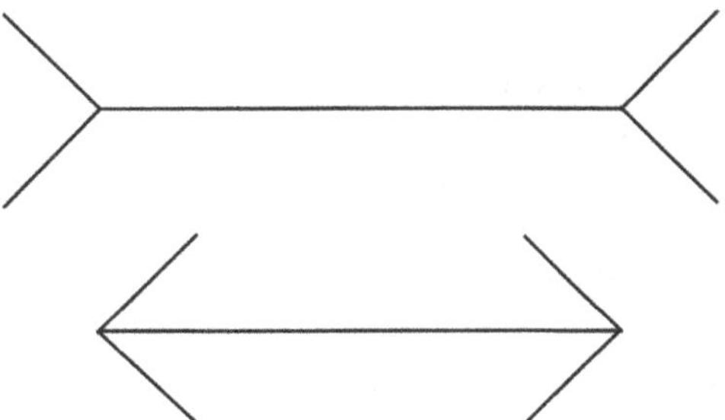

**Figure 1.7** The Müller-Lyer figures.

much to contribute to cognitive science, as a theory of the boundary between semantics and pragmatics, it is a nonstarter (Récanati, 2010, pp. 1–6).

Some theories, for example, Relevance Theory, would see semantics as a code, since it is part of the language system and hence a module, since a code can only consider the information encoded within it. Conversely, pragmatics is the interplay of the semantic code, with contextual information, logical inferences, and pragmatic principles such as Relevance. However, leaving aside Relevance Theory, we know that disambiguation and determining the truth of an utterance rely on pragmatic factors, hence semantics, which deals with disambiguation (i.e., finding the meaning of the sentence) cannot be modular vis-à-vis pragmatics.

Furthermore, even the concepts themselves that are expressed by words are sensitive to context. Consider the word *cut*: we can define *cut* as *sever*, but it is clear that cut in *cut the grass* is rather different from *cut the paper* and *cut his/her finger*: first, in *cut the grass* and *cut the paper*, the severing is complete: at the end of the action, the two parts are no longer attached. In the cutting of the finger, we would need to specify that he/she cut his/her finger off, to achieve full severing. Second, in the cutting of the grass, the use of a lawnmower (or a scythe) requires a largely horizontal motion, whereas paper and finger cutting can happen irrespective of their orientation. So there are "sub-concepts," restricted forms of cutting (completely vs. partially; horizontally vs. omni-directionally). These are called "ad hoc concepts" and are activated by pragmatics (context).

#### Grammaticalization and Pragmatics

Some authors have tried to distinguish between a linguistic pragmatics and a general pragmatics. The idea is that some pragmatic processes are needed to process linguistic components, for example, in the use of T/V pronouns[6] in the Romance languages. If a student chooses to address a professor by the T pronoun, it is the equivalent of addressing him/her by their first name (Lucy), rather than by their title and last name (e.g., Dr. Pickering). The choice is eminently pragmatic (How familiar/informal does the student want to be? How

6 The T/V pronouns stand for Latin *tu* and *vos* as the general term for all pronouns that show the opposition between singular/plural second person and familiarity/lack thereof. See Brown and Gilman (1960) and Section 7.2.3 for further discussion.

much respect and distance does he/she want to show?) and it is encoded directly in the grammar of the language (i.e., grammaticalized).

Other pragmatic phenomena are essentially not linguistic in nature: if one is asked if Mary and Bob are having an affair, and one smiles knowingly, a pragmatic inference can be drawn that it is the case that Bob and Mary are having an affair, that the speaker knows this, and that to some extent they are not that bothered by it. None of these inferential processes is (directly) linguistic.

Another distinction that can be drawn is between grammar and pragmatics. Since grammar is a code, many scholars (e.g., Ariel, 2008) propose to use that as the boundary: in a rough form, the distinction is illustrated in Table 1.1.

The obvious problem is that pragmatics and grammar are in a dynamic relation: what used to be pragmatic inferences become part of the set of conventions of the language and eventually become grammaticalized (i.e., it becomes part of the grammatical system). Consider an example:

(4) Can you pass the salt?

Literally this means "are you capable of passing the salt?" but most speakers of English are surprised by this because the expression has become conventional for "please pass the salt." When a convention becomes so engrained that speakers are no longer aware of its origin, as well as usually phonetically reduced (i.e., loses some of its sounds), it becomes grammaticalized. For example, Old English "willan" (to intend) became "will" (as in "I will go") indicating intention, and eventually it was reduced to "I'll go" indicating future tense. We will return to the topic of the semantics/pragmatics boundary in Section 4.1.7.

It is possible that the reason it is so hard to find a watertight boundary between semantics and pragmatics is that one just does not exist and that there is a continuum of meaning, some more conventional, some less, some grammaticalized, and some not. Ultimately, from the point of view of teaching, the lack of a clear boundary between semantics and pragmatics may be moot: meaning, whether it is semantic or pragmatic, is meaning, and speakers convey it, regardless of the definitions.

However, it is important to understand these distinctions in order to be able to read the literature in the field: what are we to make of the insistence or perhaps obsession in the field with finding a boundary, especially in relation to the idea of modularity? Historically, the idea of modularity was imported from psychology. Likewise, the idea of proposition and the whole idea of truth-functional semantics was imported wholesale from philosophy. The idea that utterances express a proposition that is then "modified" underlies speech act theory, the cooperative principle, politeness theory, and the entire fields of stance and metapragmatics, to use one example. These ideas are now so entrenched into pragmatics

**Table 1.1** The grammar/pragmatics boundary, according to Ariel, 2008.

| | | |
|---|---|---|
| Grammar | Code | Conventional |
| Pragmatics | Inferences (nonlogical) | Not based on convention |

that it is impossible to even talk intelligently about the subject without assuming knowledge of these subjects.

Moreover, increasingly pragmatics is moving toward a more experimental paradigm, in which researchers perform psycholinguistic experiments and draw conclusions from them about the nature of pragmatics. In those types of experiments, which usually involve reaction times or the tracking of the gaze of the subjects as a proxy of their attention, whether semantics is modular is a crucial question, because reaction times will vary depending on that (so far the evidence points to the fact that lexical processing happens in a non-modular fashion).

## 1.2 A Real-Life Application

You might say, all this is fine and dandy, but I am a teacher, what do I care about various theories of meaning? We are glad you asked!

Consider the following two arguments: the main purpose of language is to convey information. Information is meaning. Knowing about meaning is a little like knowing about the engine in your car. Pickering's attitude toward her vehicles is roughly that: what do I care about carburetors and gaskets? All I want is to drive to school to teach my students. When her car caught on fire at an intersection, she realized that perhaps oil changes might have been a good idea (true story, by the way). As a result, she now gets her oil changed and car checked regularly. Knowing about how meaning works, for an English teacher, is like changing the oil in your car: it is not the primary purpose of the activity, and most of the time you can ignore it, but when things go wrong, you end up stranded at an intersection in East Texas, with flames coming out of your hood.

So, when do things go wrong with meaning? Plenty of times, as it turns out. Misunderstandings and miscommunications happen all the time. Consider the following example from an advice columnist:

(5) Annette Richmond (Forbes Magazine, 2013)
One way to avoid misunderstandings with the boss is to make sure you clarify what you think that she means. For instance you might want to say "I understand you want frequent updates. How often does that *mean*? Is it once a week or every few days?" If you're the boss try to be specific. Then everyone will have the same expectations. (our emphasis, SA/LP)

It's easy to imagine a situation in which, two months later, the boss is upset because the employee only provided updates every other week, whereas the boss would have wanted weekly updates. Here, remembering that "frequent" is another scalar adjective along a continuum with "rare," "infrequent," "occasional," "frequent," and "daily" or "constant" might have helped.

Even more frequently, when two interlocutors do not share the same context, background information, or presuppositions, serious communication problems may occur. For example, consider the following situation, discussed in Gumperz (1982). At a British airport, a group of workers (primarily male and British) was found to have a conflictual relationship with the servers of the cafeteria, who were primarily female and East Indian. The men perceived the cafeteria ladies as rude and aggressive, whereas they perceived the men as unreasonable. It turns out that in Indian English the tone distinction between || ↗ gravy || vs. || ↘ gravy || does not exist and so the women were saying || ↘ gravy || (meaning, would you like gravy?) but the men would have expected || ↗ gravy || and so perceived || ↘ gravy || as rude (roughly meaning, it's gravy, take it or leave it). See also Gumperz (1982, p. 173; Pickering, 2018).

So, in conclusion, while it may be OK to ignore the issues around semantics and pragmatics, when communication goes off without problems, as soon as there is a problem, knowing what is happening becomes crucial to finding solutions and even to enhancing social justice. There is a saying that fish know nothing about the water they swim in. Water is so natural to them that they take it for granted. Communication for us is like water for the fish: as long as it's there you can afford to not pay attention to it, but if it goes missing, you are, well, like a fish out of water.

## 1.3 Conclusion

In this introductory chapter, we have outlined some central ideas of semantics. Our treatment is by no means comprehensive, as there are many more theories and approaches to semantics that we might have covered. Our purpose here has been to provide the novice reader with a general understanding of the kind of issues that semantics deals with; for example, the question of "how do words convey meaning?" or the extensional and intensional approaches to semantics. Moreover, we considered how these issues are related to some more specific subjects, such as the idea of context, modularity, and grammaticalization, that can help us define pragmatics. As we have seen, some of the basic definitions of pragmatics assume knowledge of such concepts as "truth function" and thus would be almost impossible to understand without the information provided in this chapter. With the next chapter, on the contrary, we turn to more concrete issues that directly concern the interplay between language teaching and pragmatics.

# 2

# The Language Teaching and Pragmatics Interface

Let's start with an example. Imagine you are an English speaker who is learning Japanese. You will be introduced fairly quickly to the idea of honorific language. This includes the use of specific titles and parts of speech such as pronouns that vary systematically depending on the relationship between the interlocutors and particularly differences in social rank and social distance, such as the T/V pronouns we saw in the previous chapter. Of course, English has words that do similar work such as *sir* or *ma'am*, but the extent of the grammatical differences is far more intricate in the Japanese system. In this case, although the underlying "job of work" from a perspective of pragmatics is the same, that is, to mark the social distance between interlocutors, the way in which it is realized by the two languages is quite different. Cross-cultural or inter-cultural[1] pragmatics addresses these differences, and L2 pragmatics focuses on how they are learned in second-language contexts.

The concept of distance between speakers is both literal and metaphorical in the sense that it can be both physical and social. Within speech communities, because this distance has to be regularly covered successfully, we have developed linguistic conventions that signal our intentions effectively. As L2 learners, we must relearn these conventions. This sounds fairly straightforward, but it is perhaps not quite as easy to bridge these differences as it might seem.

Returning to our Japanese example, Minegishi Cook (2001) reports a study in which 120 American learners of Japanese (JFL) were asked to judge three job applicants for the role of an English-Japanese bilingual clerk in a clothing store. The students were explicitly told that a critical requirement was the ability to speak polite Japanese, that is, to use honorific language as opposed to plain forms. Of the three applicants, Applicant A, who was most qualified in all other respects, used the most pragmatically inappropriate language by using plain language forms and additional negative pragmatic features. Despite this, the JFL students overwhelmingly chose Applicant A (97 out of 120) and appeared to be unaware of the negative impact of the applicant's language choices. The Japanese instructors were "unanimously surprised" by their students' choice as "it was obvious that Applicant A's speech

1 Cross-cultural was originally used in anthropology to refer to a comparative study comparing two or more different cultures. Conversely, intercultural originally referred to the actual interactions between two or more cultural groups (i.e., language contact). Arguably, this distinction has been largely eroded and the terms are now used interchangeably as synonyms.

*Pragmatics and Its Applications to TESOL and SLA*, First Edition. Salvatore Attardo and Lucy Pickering.

style was definitely impolite for applying for a job" (p. 96), and the students had been repeatedly exposed to the correct pragmatic forms as part of their instruction.

So why were these crucial pragmatic features not salient to the learners? One possibility is that the overall language proficiency of the L2 learners was such that they were focused solely on the grammatical presentation of the referential information, and they were unable to process additional information (see, e.g., Ishida, 2007). Another possibility is that they perceived the interaction through their "L1 lens" in which other aspects of the applicant's presentation such as their perceived enthusiasm would be more salient from a US perspective than the grammatical markers. Yet another possibility is that despite the instructors' best efforts, this kind of linguistic knowledge is undervalued in typical classroom curricula and becomes part of the "secret rules" of an L2 (Bardovi-Harlig & Mahan-Taylor, 2003).The investigation of these questions regarding the development of L2 pragmatic skills falls under the area of Interlanguage Pragmatics. Just as the study of interlanguage tells us about the development of learners' grammatical systems, interlanguage pragmatics focuses on the developmental patterns found in all aspects of the acquisition of pragmatics by L2 learners. In the remainder of this chapter, we introduce some of the questions that have been at the heart of the study of interlanguage pragmatics and that we will return to throughout the book.

## 2.1 Are There Universals in Pragmatics That Students Can Bring to Their L2?

The answer is clearly yes in the sense that certain speech acts (apologizing, suggesting, requesting, etc.) are used universally across speech communities (see Section 5.1.4). However, they are often different in both form (pragmalinguistics) and situational use (sociopragmatics) across cultures. Pragmalinguistic knowledge refers to the linguistic resources needed to express the pragmatic message, that is, how something is grammatically encoded. For instance, a request in English may be phrased as an imperative, for example, *Give me that pen*, or by using a modal, for example, *Could you pass me that pen?* Choices made by L1 speakers will depend on the particular context and relationship between interlocutors. One is more likely to use a bare imperative with an intimate, child, or spouse for example; and more likely to use the modal with a stranger or with someone of a perceived higher status. A second-language learner may not possess the pragmalinguistic resources to make all the correct distinctions. In a study of Americans learning German, for example, Wildner-Bassett (1994) found that learners overgeneralized the use of very specific lexical fillers in conversations (*und so* 'and so' and *und so weiter* 'and so on') as they were most familiar with and most comfortable with these forms. We will consider pragmatic markers in more detail in Section 7.3.

Sociopragmatic knowledge comprises a speaker's understanding of what contextual information (Section 1.1.3) needs to be taken into consideration in order to perform a speech act correctly or even at all. For example, in early work as part of the CCSARP Project (Cross-Cultural Study of Speech Act Realization Patterns), Blum-Kulka and Olshtain (1984, p. 209) suggest that coming late to a work meeting may be perceived as a more serious offence in an American setting than in a comparable Israeli one, and thus Americans, as a group, will tend to apologize more intensely than Israelis would expect in this situation. For further discussion of context, see Section 8.3.

A second area of pragmatics that is relevant here is politeness. Traditionally viewed through Brown and Levinson's (1987) politeness theory, three variables

1. social power,
2. social distance, and
3. degree of imposition

are regarded as "universal constraints on linguistic action" (Kasper & Schmidt, 1996, p. 155). We can also assume that some of the strategies used to address these factors may be universal such as the use of indirect vs. direct language or the use of mitigating language. This area also includes the use of interactional discourse markers, semantic formulas, and routines including conventional expressions, for example, those that are frequently used to convey relational goals, such as *nice to meet you*. Wildner-Bassett describes these as "the polite noises we make every day in countless situations, the oil we need to keep the social machine running smoothly" (1994, p. 4). While these "polite noises" are universally expected across cultures, their pragmalinguistic realization and even sociopragmatic context can be very different. In another example from her German as a Foreign Language learners, Wildner-Bassett demonstrates that American English speakers carry over a routine from English, *I'll remember that* into pragmatically inappropriate German ⋇ *ich erinner mich daran* ('I remind myself of that'), as opposed to the correct form *ich werde es mir merken* ('I'll keep that in mind'; pp. 10–11).

Again, although it is clear that these constraints will apply across speech communities, expectations regarding when and how they are expressed can be very different. For example, politeness in interaction would seem to be a fairly straightforward notion and being more polite rather than less polite would be thus a safer option. However, over-politeness, "behavior which is evaluated as too polite for the context" (Izadi, 2016, p. 13), can be just as damaging as impoliteness, as it can be perceived as "mock politeness" or "insincere politeness." Izadi gives several examples from Persian that can be disruptive in cross-cultural contexts including ritualized practices such as perceived over-complimenting or offering food or drink to an adjacent person (who may be a total stranger on an airplane) multiple times. We will look at the field of politeness, which has expanded considerably over the past few decades, in more detail in Chapter 5.

## 2.2 What Do Learners Typically Transfer from Their L1?

To some extent the answer to this is, of course, any linguistic action that is performed in a social context and that the learner may consciously or unconsciously transfer due to their lack of knowledge of the L2. However, research allows us to be more specific in terms of general features of pragmatic development. For example, beginning learners will be limited in terms of both their pragmalinguistic and sociopragmatic strategies. Their grammatical competence is simply not yet strong enough to provide them with the range of linguistic structures that they need to express their intentions. Examples such as *Me no want* or literal translations from the L1 may be the result of underdeveloped grammatical competence. Sociopragmatic strategies are also more likely to be directly transferred. Istifçi (2009) found that intermediate level learners of English from Turkey included the notion of blame in their English apology structure. For example, by shifting blame onto the hearer (e.g., *why didn't you remind me?*). Although this is a sociocultural norm in Turkish, it is not common in English apology structures. She further found that learners at an advanced proficiency in English no longer transferred this aspect of apology structure. Thus, proficiency is one driver of certain kinds of transfer.

There are other possible root causes for transfer effects. Olshtain (1983) proposes that learners may be more or less likely to transfer L1 sociocultural rules depending on their perception of "language specificity or language universality" (p. 233). In other words, given the same situation in both the L1 and L2, in this case different apology situations, some learners believe that the choice to apologize should be based on their understanding of only the L2 pragmatics (i.e., a language specific approach). However, other learners focus only on the situation and believe that an apology is always/never warranted regardless of the particular language in question (i.e., a universal approach). Olshtain reports her results regarding apologies in Hebrew by Russian and English learners by language group and suggests that overall, English learners of Hebrew approached apologies in a language specific way while Russian learners had a more universal approach.

Another possible cause of transfer from the L1 is resistance to the pragmatic norms or the expression of them in the L2 (Iwasaki, 2011; Trosborg, 2010). Siegal (1994, 1996) explores this issue with female learners of Japanese who lived and worked in Japan. Although these second-language learners "were concerned with being polite and not causing offence," there was also some resistance to adopting some of the pragmatic norms when they were considered by the learners to be inappropriate. For example, in the words of Karen, a 25-year-old American English professor and Japanese language student, living in Hiroshima, Japan, (1991):

> I don't think I've found my Japanese persona yet, who I am when I am speaking Japanese? I was listening to this lady speaking on the telephone in a little squeaky voice (imitates voice) it's like no I don't think I can do that, it's not for me – um – I don't know.
>
> (*Siegal, 1996, p. 356*)

Dewaele (2008) further develops this idea of appropriateness and suggests that some learners develop a very keen sense of metapragmatic awareness, which they are willing to adapt to while others have a more "ambiguous attitude" toward adopting different language behaviors. As Dewaele notes, the issue of agency in conscious deviation from the target language also complicates the notion of pragmatic failure. The traditional definition of pragmatic failure is "communication breakdown caused by lack of pragmatic competence" (Matsuda, 1999, p. 40; or see Thomas (1983) for a more detailed definition), which seems to assume a lack of knowledge of sociocultural norms. However, this definition does not seem to allow room for full recognition of these kinds of deliberate choices by learners. We will look further at pragmatic failure in Chapter 8.

## 2.3 Can Pragmatics be Taught through Instruction?

All the research in this area, and there is plenty, shows that the answer to this question is, in general, yes; and, that instruction is preferable to exposure alone (Gharibeh et al., 2016; Rose, 2005). In addition, recent meta-analyses (Plonsky & Zhuang, 2019; Taguchi, 2015) confirm the long-standing findings that instruction may be most effective if it is explicit and includes metapragmatic explanation (Gavamnia et al., 2014) and communicative practice (Gu, 2011). The next obvious questions are what and how, that is, what areas of pragmatics and how best can we teach them? By far the most work has been done with the teaching of speech acts including requests, compliments, refusals, apologies, complaints, and suggestions among others. Explicit instructional techniques have included "awareness-raising" activities such as role-plays, examining natural discourse, or conversation analysis (Gu, 2011; Nyugen et al., 2012; Soler, 2005; Takahashi, 2001). Much of this work is conducted in EFL contexts with limited opportunity to engage in real-life language use with interlocutors other than learners' peers and teachers, and researchers have frequently used video input teaching techniques. For example, Alcón Soler and Pitarch (2013) used examples from the TV series *Stargate* to demonstrate refusal strategies in their successful instructional treatment, and Bagherkazemi (2014) found an improvement in learners' productions of apologies, requests, and refusals following manipulation of materials from the series *Lost* and *Friends* and the movie *Doubt*. Some implicit feedback in the form of recasts has also been shown to be effective in teaching L2 speech acts (Koike & Pearson, 2005; Martínez-Flor & Fukuya, 2005) and also in improving learners' confidence in their pragmatic skills (Martínez-Flor, 2006). To a much lesser degree, other areas of pragmatics that have been investigated with regard to instruction include the use of hedging devices, discourse and interactional markers, indirect speech acts, and implicature. As we address these different areas of pragmatics in the following chapters, we'll look more at what kind of instruction has been used and shown to be effective.

There may also be some drawbacks to classroom instruction. Compared to outside the classroom where learners will engage in multiple roles and relationships with others, the classroom is a far more confined environment with a strict social hierarchy in which much of the discourse is managed by the teacher. This can result in classroom-induced errors (Stenson, 1983). For example, Kitao (1990) reports that Japanese learners rated the request strategy *will you?* as more polite and used it more often than native speakers did and suggests that this is the result of EFL classroom instruction. Wilkinson (2002) found a similar effect with American study abroad students when they were interacting with their French family hosts. She found a number of examples of sequences that mirrored classroom IRF exchanges (i.e., Initiation–Response–Evaluation) that reflected the "omnipresence of instructional norms" (p. 168) despite the homestay context.

There is also a perennial debate as to whether some things, such as cursing or other kinds of taboo language, should form part of a classroom curriculum (see also Chapter 5 on impoliteness). Traditionally eschewed from language syllabi, more recently, teacher-researchers have begun their own debates regarding whether they want to specifically address these things. Mercury (1995) argues for the importance of assisting ESL learners in their comprehension but not necessarily production of obscene language largely for sociolinguistic purposes:

> There is much for ESL students to learn about the social forces behind swearing in English and among English speakers. It is useful still if students only learn to understand for practical reasons why a speaker would choose to use obscenities and when she or he would choose not to.
>
> (*p. 29*)

Dewaele (2008) also adds a note of caution with regard to production. Following his use of a swearword in his L4 that was not accepted by his native speaker interlocutors, he notes that "My first thought was that this was unfair. I later realized that L2 users do not enjoy the same pragmatic freedom as [native speakers]" (p. 252). Horan (2013) discusses some of the same issues in a foreign language learning context and also addresses production by referencing a number of materials that teachers can find to address the topic.

## 2.4 Is There a Developmental Path for Pragmatics?

The gold standard for describing a possible developmental path in pragmatic competence is longitudinal data. Perhaps the most famous early study of this nature is Schmidt (1983) who undertook a three-year study of Wes, a 33-year-old native speaker of Japanese. Schmidt focused on Wes's development of directives (a set of speech acts that includes orders, requests, and suggestions). Initially Wes relied heavily on formulaic utterances or fixed expressions (e.g., *I'll have X, Can I have X, Shall we X*). As his language developed, one way in which it showed was an elaboration of these initial patterns, for example, *OK, if you have time please send two handbag, but if you're too busy, forget it* (p. 154), and he was also more confident in producing face-threatening acts such as complaints, for example, *excuse me, this milk is no good, sour I think* (p. 154). However, issues remained when he began parsing out these formulaic phrases that then led to problematic utterances, for example, *if you back to room, can I bring cigarette?* ("please bring me a cigarette") (p. 155). Although longitudinal studies continue to be rare in comparison to cross-sectional research, more recent studies have agreed with Schmidt's original findings that learners initially stick to routinized utterances and unanalyzed chunks to express meaning (Taguchi, 2010).

With regard to request development specifically, Kasper and Rose (2002) compiled the results of studies to suggest a five-stage development of requests that expands from a formulaic stage to a gradual "pragmatic expansion" in which new forms are added and more complex linguistic patterns are employed and expanded beyond a one-to-one mapping between specific forms and specific functions. Although it is unclear precisely how grammatical and pragmatic competence map onto each other, it seems clear that a certain level of grammatical competence is required (although that can vary considerably, see Bardovi-Harlig, 2013; Yang, 2016). Focusing again on request strategies, Cook and Liddicoat (2002) used a multiple choice questionnaire to assess low- and high-proficiency learners' interpretation of direct and indirect requests. There was a significant difference between the two groups of learners in their ability to process the context and form of indirect requests, and lower proficiency learners relied more heavily on linguistic knowledge (i.e., bottom-up linguistic knowledge) to interpret the requests. That said, the converse does not appear to be true: a higher level of grammatical competence does not guarantee an equally high level of pragmatic competence (Bardovi-Harlig & Mahan-Taylor, 2003; Mirzaei & Esmaeili, 2013). This is particularly the case with pragmatic areas other than speech acts. Exposure to nonliteral meaning such as implicature, for example, has not been shown to necessarily enhance acquisition of this pragmatic concept (Bouton, 1994). We will come back to this in Chapter 4.

Other areas of pragmatic development that have been investigated, beyond speech acts, include a variety of conversational features including adjacency pairs (see Section 8.1.2), topic management, and interactional markers. For example, in a relatively early longitudinal study of interactional markers, Sawyer (1992) traced the development of the Japanese sentence-final particle *ne* by JSL learners over one year in an immersion environment through semi-structured interviews. *Ne* is described as a sentence final particle that indicates very generally a seeking of confirmation from the hearer or a rapport marker signaling expectation of common ground. As with other pragmatic phenomena, it always occurred initially as part of fixed phrases learned as formulaic chunks. However, it was developed later and more inconsistently than other vocabulary items and the success of individual acquisition varied widely. We look more closely at interactional markers in Section 7.3.

A final area to be considered here is the impact of context of use in the development of pragmatics. Traditionally, this has been defined as the difference between ESL and EFL contexts (Rose, 1994); however, more recently it encompasses the manifestation of pragmatic phenomena in English as a Lingua Franca (House, 2010) and the pragmatic development of third-language or plurilingual users (Jordà, 2005). We will come to this in Chapter 11.

## 2.5 Is Acquisition of Pragmatics Different for L2 Child and Adult Learners?

The answer to this is yes, to the extent to which the language acquisition experience of adults and children is always different. On the one hand, Kasper and Rose (1999, p. 87) argue quite rightly that L2 speakers of any age when engaging in a similar action in any language "will rely on the same strategies to perform such an action." For example, an L2 child understands the function of a request and will learn to use the L2 to perform that function as far as their grammatical proficiency allows. However, adults understand the societal value of politeness markers in a way that children do not (Wildner-Bassett, 1994). In other words, they are very aware of the importance of sociopragmatic work and so will piece together routine formulas or coin new ones in order to meet this perceived requirement, for example, *I very appreciate/I never forget you kindness* (Kasper, 2001, p. 509) in ways that children may not unless prompted by an adult.

Perhaps more significantly, children do not routinely perform language functions such as sarcasm, irony, or complex forms of teasing in the way in which adults do. Pexman et al. (2005) suggest that although children can recognize direct (as opposed to indirect) irony at 5 or 6 years old, they do not understand its humorous intent and will tend to identify with the target of the humor as opposed to the speaker's humorous intent. The authors propose that this understanding continues to develop "late into middle childhood" (p. 259) and thus we would not expect these kinds of indirect language functions to develop in a parallel manner to adult learners. We will look at this again in Chapter 4.

## 2.6 Does the Learner Have to Sound Exactly the Same as a Native Speaker?

As Bardovi-Harlig and Mahan-Taylor (2003, p. 38) note "the consequences of pragmatic differences, unlike the case of grammatical errors, are often interpreted on a social or personal level rather than as a result of the language learning process." Does that mean in order not to be misunderstood, an L2 learner must copy the performance of a native speaker? For Bardovi-Harlig and Mahan-Taylor the answer is a clear no. They argue that "the goal of instruction in pragmatics is not to insist on conformity to a particular target-language norm, but rather to help learners become familiar with the range of pragmatic devices and practices in the target language" (p. 38). This may include the use of different but acceptable alternatives to pragmalinguistic formulae such as an L1 transfer of an expression of gratitude, for example, *may God increase your bounty* (Kasper, 1992, p. 14). Both Grosjean (2015) and Eslami-Rasekh (2005) argue that not all L2 learners wish to perform identically to native speakers and suggest that language practices may vary between individuals for a host of reasons that have little to do with underlying competence and more to do with identity construction and distinctiveness as bilingual and bicultural speakers (see also the discussion of resistance to pragmatic norms earlier). At the opposite end of the spectrum, Piller (2002) interviewed adult L2 learners who thrived on "passing" as native speakers and investigated the practices they typically employed in order to do so.

## 2.7 Can Pragmatics Be Assessed in the Classroom?

The answer here is yes. Brown (2001) details a variety of ways in which different pragmatic features can be assessed from multiple-choice tests to role-play tasks. Brown (2008) finds that role-plays assessed by external judges were the most reliable and gave the best discrimination. Tada (2005) and Roever (2005) report good results with multiple-choice tests. Ishihara (2010), however, reminds us that teachers should keep in mind that "pragmatic norms among competent L2 speakers encompass a healthy degree of variation, which is why they are simply norms and not rigid rules" (p. 311). So, it is necessary to exert caution when grading so that one's preferred answer does not become the only 'correct' answer. For example, in response to

(9) Would you like to pet my dog?
  a. Hell, no!
  b. Yes, please.
  c. No, thank you.

clearly (9.a) is pragmatically inappropriate (impolite), but both (9.b) and (9.c) are acceptable.

Practically speaking, what are the best strategies for teachers, especially novice ones? Building a validated standardized battery of multiple-choice questions is probably not cost efficient for the average teacher, but the ease of administration/scoring and the consistency of the assessment recommend this testing approach. However, the artificiality of the setting means that the ecological validity of the data is compromised and that the assessment may not capture actual performance. Role-play may highlight this more effectively and can easily be retooled for assessment; for example, by asking students to perform a given communicative task and then assessing to what degree they were successful in doing so. However, teachers are not limited to those activities. One strategy is the learner as researcher assessment: the students collect their own data and do some degree of assessment on them. Class vocabularies/wikis, building small corpora, and other collaborative endeavors can also be used. Peer-evaluations also fit logically in the learner as researcher paradigm.

Intonation and prosodic choices can be assessed using videos and audio files easily available on the internet. For example, Ishihara (2010) suggests playing a video clip of a conversation and having the students discuss the affect of the situation, gestures, facial expression, and tone of voice. Picture prompts have the advantage that they are extremely easy to produce. They have the added advantage that they will not, as text prompts may, inadvertently bias the learners (Yamashita, 2008).

We note that this is only a brief overview of methods that might be effectively used, and that there are some current collections of essays that include significant attention to assessing L2 pragmatics in the classroom including Alcón Soler and Martínez-Flor (2008), Ishihara and Cohen (2010), and Ross and Kasper (2013).

## 2.8 Conclusion

In this chapter, we have identified some of the key questions that the field of interlanguage pragmatics has focused on. We have done this with a particular view toward the typical questions that TESOL teachers have often asked. There are, of course, a number of other areas of interest that we will address in later chapters such as the experience of multilingual speakers and the specific context of English as a Lingua Franca, as well as the ways in which these findings have been reflected in TESOL materials development.

# 3

# Speech Acts

The reader will recall that philosophical semantics sees reference and truth as the central ideas needed to "explain" meaning. The theory of speech acts is a reaction against the view that language is used only to communicate about the truth of propositions. In fact, the idea is, to paraphrase Austin's inspired title, that one can "do stuff" using words. So, besides describing the world, what can language do? Plenty of stuff as we will see.

We will start out by discussing the Ordinary Language school of philosophy and then focus on Austin and Searle. We will then characterize speech acts in terms of illocutionary force and felicity conditions to understand exactly how they work and this will then allow us to move on to indirect speech acts, the most complex and of course most rewarding concept of speech act theory. We will then pivot to the teaching of speech acts in SLA and TESOL.

## 3.1 Ordinary Language Philosophy, Oxford, and Austin

When considering the work of Austin, Searle, Grice, and their numerous followers, it is always good to remember that their formation belongs to the philosophical movement known as "ordinary language philosophy" associated with Oxford University, in England, and of which Austin was the first proponent. While both Searle and Grice disassociated themselves from ordinary language philosophy and moved on to considerations that are very different from it, there remains in their writings a clear influence from Austin.

Simply put, ordinary language philosophy starts from the assumption that language can tell us a lot about the way "things are." After all, language encodes and reflects the experiences of many generations who have been interacting with reality. It would be very odd if it turned out to be that they had developed a tool to describe and affect reality that turned out to be completely wrong. Needless to say, this does not mean that language is a perfect match for reality, no one has ever claimed that, since after all there are countless examples of language lagging behind the discoveries of science (e.g., we say that the moon and the sun rise and set, which are relics of the Ptolemaic view of the universe with the earth at the center of the universe; whales and dolphins are often categorized as fish, while in reality they are mammals; tomatoes are

*Pragmatics and Its Applications to TESOL and SLA*, First Edition. Salvatore Attardo and Lucy Pickering.

considered a vegetable, while they are scientifically a fruit, etc.). If we move to social constructs such as institutions (kinship, laws, rituals) or beliefs (courage/fear, happiness/sadness, love/hate) that have no (or little) "empirical" existence outside of the social fact, the argument that language can tell us about reality becomes much stronger. Consider our earlier example of money: without the social agreement that we will exchange goods for printed paper of a certain kind, color, shape, and so on, it makes no sense at all to ask ourselves why a 10 dollar bill is valuable. The value of the 10 dollar bill comes from its use within the community as a 10 dollar bill. The meaning of words, sentences, and so on similarly comes from the same kind of social convention.

One of the most significant influences on ordinary language philosophy is the later Wittgenstein of the *Philosophical Investigations*, in which one finds remarks such as "the meaning of a word is its use in language," which are very far from the critical attitude that most philosophers had toward ordinary language, which was seen as the source of error and confusion, to be replaced by the "better" language of logic. Wittgenstein, on the contrary, argues that the meaning of, say, "dog" is just the ways in which speakers use the word "dog," and nothing else. He also introduces in his latter work the concept of "language game" (*Sprachspiel*), which is a type of activity that speakers engage in, such as

> Giving orders, and obeying them–
> Describing the appearance of an object, or giving its measurements–
> Constructing an object from a description (a drawing)–
> Reporting an event–
> Speculating about an event–
> Forming and testing a hypothesis–
> Presenting the results of an experiment in tables and diagrams–
> Making up a story; and reading it–
> Singing catches–
> Guessing riddles–
> Making riddles–
> Making a joke; telling it–
> Solving a problem in practical arithmetic–
> Translating from one language into another–
> Asking, thanking, cursing, greeting, praying.
> (*Wittgenstein, 1953, pp. 11–12; paragraph 23*)

Significantly, Wittgenstein claims that there are "countless" kinds of language games, each with its own set of rules. Searle will directly address the issue of the multiplicity of language games. The notions of speech act and of language game are also found in Levinson's activity type (Levinson, 1979, 1992; see Section 8.3.4).[1]

---

1 There is a little irony here, namely that Wittgenstein was a Cambridge philosopher and apparently Austin did not like his work and claimed not to have been influenced by it (see Searle, 2007). Nonetheless, the similarities are significant, but are probably due to the general cultural context, what the Germans would call the *Zeitgeist*, the "spirit of the times."

### 3.1.1 Austin and Performativity

Austin is most famous for his book *How to Do Things with Words*. The book introduces two crucial concepts of the philosophy of language: performativity and the distinction between locutionary, illocutionary, and perlocutionary acts.

Performativity is at the origin of the speech act theory of language. Essentially, it boils down to the realization that some utterances are neither true nor false, but rather they do something (they perform an action, hence performative). For example, if when Attardo asked Pickering to marry him she had replied "Your utterance is false" (or "true" for that matter), it would literally make no sense. The question is not whether the utterance is either true or false, it is neither, but rather whether it is felicitous or not (i.e., in this case, since it is a question, is it a valid question?).[2] Now consider another example, suppose that in a court of law the bailiff had put on the judge's robe and sat in his/her chair, banged the gavel, and so on and said to the defendant "I sentence you to ten days in jail." Since the bailiff is not a judge, the utterance would be infelicitous. Conversely, if the judge is a judge, in the right court of law, speaking at the right point of a trial, and so on, then the utterance is felicitous. So, performative utterances depend for their felicity on felicity conditions, much like the truth of a sentence depends on truth conditions (see Section 1.1.2).

Performative sentences thus are sentences that make something happen by virtue of their having been uttered (in the right, felicitous conditions): promising, threatening, christening, wedding, betting, sentencing, declaring war, check-mating, calling a player out in baseball, and so on are all examples of performatives.

Austin proposes three criteria to distinguish performatives from constatives (i.e., regular sentences): (1) the presence of an explicit performative verb, such as *I hereby christen this ship the Nautilus*; (2) the presence of felicity conditions vs. truth conditions; and (3) the fact that performatives perform an action, whereas constatives state or describe a state of affairs/event. However, the distinction proved to be too complex to maintain (Austin, 1962, pp. 94, 133, 146–147). Austin concludes that all speech acts are both constatives and performatives. This was his crucial breakthrough: each speech act consists of several different actions.

In the process of assessing the distinction between performatives and constatives, Austin elaborated the speech act theory of language: each utterance consists of three separate actions, which he labels the locutionary, illocutionary, and perlocutionary acts.

- Locutionary act: The act of saying something (so the phonetic production of the sounds, the fact of saying the words, referring to a specific something with them, etc.).
- Illocutionary act: What the speaker is trying to accomplish with the utterance or the way the utterance should have been taken. For example, the fact that saying something commits you to it. Further examples are asking a question, betting, promising, swearing,

2 Suppose that Attardo asked Pickering today if she'll marry him; the question would be non-felicitous, because they are already married and by cultural and legal convention you cannot remarry the same person if you are currently married to them.

advising, and naming; thus, we speak of the illocutionary force of the sentence to mean the interactional purpose of the utterance.

- Perlocutionary act: The effect the utterance has on its audience or the consequences of the speech act. Examples are becoming scared, persuaded, threatened, amused, bored, happy, and so on. Perlocutionatry acts also include the intended effects on the audience (1962, p. 101), meaning that one may succeed or fail to achieve one's intended perlocutionary goal. For example, I may tell a child that there is a monster in the basement with the perlocutionary goal of stopping them from going there, but fail to reach that goal when the child enters the basement out of curiosity.

A clarification is necessary, at this point: as the term "speech act" and the "ordinary language philosophy" moniker indicate, the whole idea of speech acts, performativity, and so on originates very much within a linguistic context. However, there is no reason to restrict speech acts to language. I may refuse an offer or deny a proposition by shaking my head left-to-right (Western culture) or with a chin-lift (Mediterranean cultures). The reader will easily come up with plenty of examples in which a gesture clearly expresses a proposition and hence is a speech act. Even further, actions may convey propositions. For example, opening one's hands to show that they are empty or bidding at an auction by raising a paddle or other gestures.

### 3.1.2 Speech Acts, Searle

The idea of speech acts was taken up by John Searle, who combines it with Wittgestein's idea of "rule following." The canonical presentation of speech act theory is Searle (1969). For Searle, speaking a language is following its rules (1969, p. 12). These rules are conventional (1969, p. 37), which makes them constitutive (1969, p. 36), that is, the activity does not exist outside of the conventional rules (compare playing chess, where the rules are constitutive, with running, where one runs even if one runs regardless of the rules of running competitions). Institutional facts are events that are based on constitutive rules. So, winning a hand at poker is based on and/or makes sense only within the context of the following of the institutional facts, that is, the constitutive rules of poker. If the game of poker did not exist, having four cards that are the same, but in different suits would be meaningless. Significantly, the rules of language are institutional facts (1969, pp. 51–53).

Along the lines of Austin, Searle distinguishes several acts within a speech act. The general form of a speech act is F (p), where F is the illocutionary force of the act and p is the proposition expressed by the speech act. In other words, a speech act consists of at least two separate acts: uttering a proposition and doing so with a given illocutionary force.

Searle lists five types of illocutionary forces; Table 3.1 lists their formal representation (1969, p. 31).

Thus, *I promise I will come* and *I will come* express the same proposition, but differ in illocutionary force, being a promise and an assertion, respectively. Let us consider a different example: take the sentence below followed by its logical representation

**Table 3.1** Speech acts and their formal representation, according to Searle (1969).

| | | |
|---|---|---|
| 1. | assertions | $\vdash$ (p) |
| 2. | requests | ! (p) |
| 3. | promises | Pr (p) |
| 4. | warnings | W (p) |
| 5. | yes-no questions | ? (p) |

(10) The book is on the table.
p = ON(book, table)

The proposition expressed by this sentence is roughly that there is a property of being on something and that a book has that property and the something it is on is a table. When someone says *The book is on the table* they are asserting this proposition, or

$\vdash$ (p) (recall that p stands for ON(book, table))

however, let's assume that we don't know whether it is the case that the book is on the table, we may ask about it, by saying *Is the book on the table?* which corresponds to

?(p)

or we may want the book to be on the table, and so we request that it be so, perhaps by saying *Let the book be on the table,* albeit usually people use polite variants of this, such as *please, could the book be on the table,* which corresponds in Searle's notation as our (p) proposition with the force of a request:

! (p)

Likewise, we can utter (p) with the force of a promise or a warning: *the book will be on the table* (if you do something I want), which corresponds to

Pr(p)

or *The book better be on the table* (or I will do something you do not want), that is,

W(p)

In other words, the force changes with each illocution, but the proposition remains the same.

Searle categorizes speech acts into five large groups,[3] which constitute the kinds of things one can "do with words" or "ways of using language" (Searle, 1979, p. vii)

3 The alert reader will notice that there are some differences between this list and the one from 1969. The reasons for the differences are technical and are discussed in Searle (1979). The Searle1969 list is not meant to be exhaustive and is a list of illocutionary forces; the Searle1979 list is a list of speech acts and is meant as a list of "basic categories" (p. 12) of speech acts.

1. assertives or representatives (assertions, claims and reports, ...)
2. directives (requests, suggestions, commands, ...)
3. expressives (thanks, apologies, complaints, ...)
4. commissives (promises, refusals)
5. declaratives (performatives: the act of speaking itself performs the act: *I sentence you to life in prison*; *Class dismissed*).

(Searle, 1979, pp. 12–19). Thus, Searle directly counters Wittgenstein's claim that there are countless kinds of language games, by reducing them to five very abstract types.

### 3.1.3 Realization Patterns

Every speech act has a set of realization patterns, that is, all the ways a given speech act may be produced. For requests, that set may include the following, among others:

(11) Could you open the window?
I wonder if you could open the window?
Open the window, please.

The actual realizations of speech acts differ across cultures. People request and apologize differently, depending on the culture in which they operate. Needless to say, variation on a cultural basis is not the only type of variability displayed by speech acts. There is also individual variation, that is, a given person may apologize more or less or differently than someone else, while still sharing broad cultural patterns. Another kind of variation is situational: one is more or less likely to apologize to a person depending on the relationship with that person.

Cross-cultural variation in speech act realization patterns can create serious cross-cultural problems, even though speakers may be producing grammatically correct sentences. For example, bald imperatives (e.g., *pass the salt*) are acceptable between intimates in Polish (Wierzbicka, 1985) and Italian, but not in American English, where they may be perceived as rude. We look in detail at the SLA and TESOL applications of cross-cultural speech act differences later in this chapter.

### 3.1.4 How Speech Acts Work

There is substantial agreement that some version of speech act theory is correct and that indeed people do things with words, such as requesting, informing, promising, threatening, and so on. Much of the developments of speech act theory have consisted of establishing a detailed account of the "mechanics" of what makes a speech act work that way. In this section we consider the components of illocutionary force and felicity conditions. As we will see, they both help answer the question, what makes a promise, a promise (a request, a request, etc.).

#### Seven Components of Illocutionary Force

Searle and Vanderveken (1985) have identified seven components of illocutionary force. They are detailed here.

- Illocutionary point: This is the purpose of the speech act. For example, promising has the point of committing the speaker to doing some action stated in the proposition. The point of a threat is to dissuade the hearer from doing something. The illocutionary point of a speech act is necessarily achieved by successfully performing the speech act. So, for example, I may have threatened my neighbor to keep him from shooting at the deer, but he may ignore my threat and keep shooting. However, if I successfully performed the threat I have successfully threatened the neighbor, regardless of whether the threat worked. Whether the neighbor stops shooting or not is a matter of perlocution, not of illocution.
- Degree of strength of the illocutionary point: Two speech acts may have the same illocutionary point but with different strengths. Searle and Vanderveken use the examples of

  - request vs. insist
  - suggest vs. solemnly swear
  - express regret vs. humbly apologize

  However, we should not assume that only two-way oppositions exist, consider

  (12) tell vs. state vs. assert vs. attest

  which encode increasing strength and formality of the assertion (Searle & Vanderveken, 1985, p. 183; they do not analyze attest, but the extension is straightforward).
- Mode of achievement: In some cases, an illocutionary act requires a "special set of conditions" for a felicitous performance of the act. For example, a witness in a trial may make a statement (an assertive) when asked if they would like a glass of water, but will be *testifying* when asked under oath if, say, they recognize the defendant. In this case, being the witness, being sworn under oath, being questioned by a lawyer or the judge, and so on constitute the mode of achievement. One cannot stand on the corner of the street, on one's own, and testify (in the legal sense).
- Content conditions: In many cases, the illocutionary force of the speech act will put restrictions on the proposition that the utterance must convey. For example, if one makes a promise, one cannot make it about an event that happened in the past. It would be odd, to say the least, to say *I promise that if you are good, we will have eaten ice cream last week*. Likewise, an apology must refer to something the speaker is responsible for:[4] the utterance *I apologize for the sum of the squares of the other two sides of a triangle being equal to the square of the hypotenuse* is clearly odd or humorous (Searle & Vanderveken, 1985, p. 16).
- Preparatory conditions: These conditions are the conditions that must obtain for the speech act to be both successful and not defective; for example, you can only successfully promise something if both the speaker and the person receiving the promise think that what is being promised is positive. Thus, it would be a defective promise to say *If you behave today you will have to do all your chores tomorrow*. Obviously, if the addressee

4 There is a use of the expression *I am sorry that X*, which is intended to convey solidarity but can be taken as an apology. It is not, because the apology would be infelicitous. We have both witnessed speakers respond, *You don't have to apologize, it's not your fault.*

believed that doing chores was a great privilege, this would be a successful promise. However, generally speaking, people do not like to do their chores.

- Sincerity conditions: A successful speech act requires that the speaker perform the assertion, request, and so on sincerely, that is, that he/she be in the "psychological state" required by the speech act: so if the speaker is stating a fact, he/she must believe it is true, if they are requesting something, they must want it, and so on.
- Degree of strength of the sincerity conditions: Much like the illocutionary point can occur with different strengths, so can the sincerity conditions. As Searle and Vanderveken (1985) put it, one can make a request ("ask"), but if the speaker "begs, beseeches, or implores" (p. 19), then they are expressing a stronger desire than a request.

### Felicity Conditions: An Analysis of the Speech Act of Promising

Searle provides a worked out example of the kinds of constitutive rules that define a prototypical, idealized speech act, using the example of "promise." The analysis is painstaking, but worth considering in detail, if one wants to understand how speech acts actually work. It consists of several felicity conditions, starting with the assumption that the speaker is making the promise to the hearer:

1. Normal input/output conditions. Output is generally speaking, and input is hearing, but appropriate changes can be made for writing, sign language, and so on. This is a very broad category, which includes that both speaker and hearer are capable of and competent to speak the language (e.g., they are not sick, drunk, or otherwise impaired), that they are "seriously" and "literally" engaged in speaking. This stipulation rules out not only "parasitic" (1969, p. 57) uses of language, such as "play acting, teaching a language, reciting poems, practicing pronunciation" (1969, p. 57n1) but also joke telling (1969, p. 57) and nonliteral uses, such as metaphor, irony, and sarcasm.
2. The speaker expresses a proposition p. As we saw, this allows the analysis to decouple the illocutionary force (the promising) from the locutionary aspect (the proposition, or to put it differently, what gets promised in the act of promising). We may add that if the speaker did not express a proposition, the act of promising would be very strange, as witnessed by the following imaginary conversation:

   (13) A: I promise.
   B: What?
   A: Nothing, I am just promising.

3. The promise must regard a future act performed by the speaker. One cannot sincerely promise to do something one has already done, for example. Nor can one promise someone else's action (although one can promise that one will make someone else do something, but then the promise is that the speaker will coerce the other party). To put it differently, one can only commit one's will, not someone else's. Searle stresses too that the future act may be a non-act (as in promising not to do something).
4. The promised act must be viewed positively by the hearer and the speaker must share this belief. If the hearer believes that the promised act is to be viewed negatively, then the promise is not a promise but a threat.

5. The speaker was not going to perform the act independently of the promise. One cannot sincerely promise to go to work the next day, if one was going to do that anyway. In fact, saying *I promise to go to work tomorrow* presupposes that there is at least a possibility that one may not go to work the next day.
6. The speaker intends to perform the act promised. According to Searle, the distinction between sincere and insincere promises lies in the fact that the speaker does or does not intend to perform the action. Searle also notes that the sincere intention to perform an act presupposes one thinks it is feasible to do so.
7. The speaker intends to incur into the obligation to perform the act promised.

What happens if S produces a speech act but violates one of the aforementioned felicity conditions? We are then faced with a "defective" performance of a speech act (Searle, 1969, p. 54). What does it mean that there was a defective performance? The act was still performed, but one of the felicity conditions is not satisfied. Searle notes that this does not destroy the speech act entirely: if one promises to sing a song, while in fact not intending to do so, they have still performed a speech act of promising, only it was an invalid one. Searle notes that this is directly related to Austin's concept of infelicity. We will return to this in Chapters 9 and 10.

### 3.1.5 Indirect Speech Acts

The analysis of speech acts discussed earlier has a significant gap: it is possible to perform a given speech act by performing a different one instead. Recall that speech acts need not be linguistic, so it should not surprise us to find that one can perform more than one speech act at a time. Searle explains this as an "indirect speech act." Consider the simple example:

(14) Can you pass the salt?

literally this is a question concerning the capacity of H to perform an action (passing the salt). However, the illocutionary force of the utterance is that of a request to pass the salt. Simplifying a little we have two paraphrases for (14) depending whether we look at the conventional meaning (sentence) or at the meaning in the situation (utterance).

(15) Are you able to pass the salt? (sentence force = question)

(16) Please pass the salt. (utterance force = request)

Searle argues that four components are needed to explain indirect speech acts

1. the theory of speech acts
2. the cooperative principle (see Chapter 4)
3. mutually shared background information
4. an ability to make inferences (1979, p. 32).

This is particularly significant because often the last two components are ignored.

Searle thus explains indirect speech acts by arguing that S performs one speech act at the sentence level, but using the principle of cooperation produces an inferential path whereby H can reconstruct another speech act, relying of course also on the mutually shared background of knowledge that S and H share, thus performing another speech act at the utterance level. Searle notes that the conclusion (i.e., the indirect speech act performance) is always "probabilistic" (1979, p. 35). This is due to the fact that all inferences based on the cooperative principle (implicatures) are probabilistic, as we will see.

Searle identifies some general classes of indirect speech acts. Thus, for example, one can perform an indirect request by asking whether a preparatory condition (see Section 2.1) for the speech act obtains. This is the case of passing the salt, if you cannot pass the salt, say because the salt shaker is out of your reach on the other side of the table, then I cannot properly request you to pass it. Conversely, if the salt is within your reach, and no other impediments exist, then by asking whether you can perform the action I indirectly ask you to perform the action. Another example is performing a directive by stating or asking whether the propositional content holds, for example,

(17) Will you stop making that noise?

where literally, at the sentence level S is merely asking whether H will or will not continue to make the noise in question, but at the utterance level, S is telling (i.e., directing) H to stop.

Indirect speech acts tend to conventionalize, which is why different languages have different ways of asking indirectly, for example. Once the forms have become idiomatic, they are preferred by the requirement to speak idiomatically (Searle, 1979, p. 50). Finally, Searle observes that the driving force for indirectness is the desire to be polite (p. 48).

Some recent research on indirect speech acts has gone in the general direction of the field (see Chapters 7–8 and 10–11), that is, toward more attention to the context of the performance of the speech acts. For example, in Mey's (2001) idea of the pragmeme, that is, a speech act in context, in which the "interpretation" of the situation is based not just on the speech acts performed and the social negotiation of meaning but also on the situation and its affordances, that is, the interpretations/readings it favors. The idea has attracted some attention (e.g., Allan et al., 2016).

### 3.1.6 Public Commitment for Speech Acts

We have seen that a mutually shared background is necessary for indirect speech acts. There is also another way in which speech acts build on a complex (and generally tacitly assumed) background of social convention. Consider the earlier example of promising. Let's say that I promised ice cream to the children if they behave. Recall that one of the felicity conditions is to "incur into the obligation to perform the act promised." In what sense am I obliged to provide the ice cream? The children are probably too little and weak to physically coerce me into doing so and barring special circumstances cannot retaliate effectively. One may argue that I am morally bound to do so, because a righteous person would not falsely (or infelicitously) promise something. Another argument would be that hurting the feelings of the children is again morally or ethically reprehensible. However, these and other appeals to ethics, morality, or kindness do not constitute an obligation.

The obligation is a social one: we live in a culture that values commitment, so much so that it has been institutionalized in the idea of contractual obligation. Entering into a contract means assuming an obligation that is enforceable legally by society. Even if you cannot go to jail for infelicitously promising ice cream to your children, your social status (a.k.a., face, see Chapter 5) will be diminished. Note that this is a different case than the one in which we rescind a promise, that is, we notify the recipient of the promise that we are no longer in a position to fulfill the promise.

Likewise, just as a promise is a commitment made in front of a social group, speech acts "involve intentional undertaking of a publicly accessible commitment" (Green, 2017): it is not enough to have the intention of buying the ice cream, one has to publicly state so (albeit, not necessarily linguistically; recall the bidding by raising a paddle example). This is because a promise is a commitment in front of the speaker's social group.

There are other approaches to commitments, of course. One approach is to say that one enters in a commitment by voluntarily assuming an obligation. In other words, I am committed to doing something because I want to be committed to it. It is my choice. This approach is rather weak, as it does not distinguish commitments from intentions, except perhaps in terms of length of the commitment. The other approach is to say that one is committed to an action if one's moral values, goals in life, and so on make it necessary to follow a course of action. So we might say that a Mennonite refuses to serve in the military and becomes a conscientious objector because he is committed to certain religious beliefs. However, speech acts, as we saw, require a public commitment, in order to establish their force as such. Note in passing that internal commitment (what one thinks) and external commitment (what one makes explicit) may differ, for example, in the case of lies or hypocrisy.

Recent work on speech acts has focused on debating the nature of the constitutive rules of speech acts. In other words, are speech acts linguistic or social conventions, much like the rest of linguistic signs (recall the arbitrariness of the connection between signifier and signified), or are they based on the speakers' intentions (if the speaker intends to perform an act and their intentions match a set of felicity conditions, then they have made a promise, e.g.), or on the functions for which they are used in conversation, or are they expressions of a state of mind of the speakers, or are they constituted by social norms? Norms are more stringent social requirements than conventions: for example, it is a convention that people should line up at check out registers, but it is a norm that one cannot drive on the left, in the United States. Violating the former will get you nasty looks, violating the latter will result in a hefty fine.

Another interesting approach is based on the idea of "conversational score" or the "common ground" shared by the speakers (see Section 8.3). When someone utters a sentence, the audience updates the conversational score with the content of the proposition of the utterance, but also of its presuppositions, and implicatures. So, for example, Attardo uttering *My favorite painting by Vermeer is "View of Delft."* both updates the conversational score with the fact that Attardo's favorite painting by Vermeer is *View of Delft* and that Vermeer is a painter. In other words, both facts are now publicly accessible, as well as the fact that Attardo uttered the sentence and so he is committed to its truth, under normal circumstances (e.g., he is not being ironical). The idea of a common ground or a conversational score that is accessible to all participants turns out to be an important one that will recur in the discussion of context (Section 8.3), of the definition of what is old and new information in a sentence (Section 6), and of course of Grice's definition of nonnatural meaning (see a short discussion in Section 4.1.6). An excellent summary of the discussion can be found in Harris et al. (2018).

## 3.2 Conclusion

In this chapter, we have presented an approach to pragmatics that is in a sense antagonistic to the truth-functional approach to meaning seen in Chapter 1, since it sees the purpose of language as "doing things." However, from another perspective it is totally compatible with it, given that it sees an utterance as expressing a proposition along with an illocution, that is, the speech act. As we will see in Chapter 7, this is a common approach to the description of stance. We have considered in detail the mechanisms that make speech acts work, that is, felicity conditions and indirect speech acts, that is, the ways in which a speaker says one thing but means another one. This required us to introduce the concept of "implicature," which will be a central topic of the next chapter. However, before we turn to this subject, we need to address the ways in which research in speech acts has been applied in teaching and SLA.

## 3.3 Speech Acts in SLA and Applications to TESOL

The investigation of speech acts in SLA and its applications in classroom instruction is one of the successes of the story of pragmatic instruction in TESOL. This is in part because it is "low hanging fruit" compared to many other aspects of pragmatics. As we noted in Chapter 2, every language develops ways to request something or apologize to someone because they are ubiquitous acts in human interaction, but not every language may develop highly ritualized uses of honorific particles, for example. In addition, because of the pervasive nature of speech acts, their expression is highly conventionalized as we noted earlier. For example, in American English, apologies typically comprise three parts:

1. the reason for the apology (e.g., *I'm so sorry I'm late*);
2. explanation of responsibility (e.g., *the bus was late/You know me, I'm never on time*); and
3. offer of repair/promise that it will not happen again (e.g., *I'll catch up with Tom regarding the meeting/This won't happen again*; Blum-Kulka & Olshtain, 1984).

There are also expected sociopragmatic contexts in which they are performed (e.g., coming in late for a meeting) and standard pragmalinguistic formulas with which they are expressed (e.g., *I'm so sorry, I want to apologize*). Any one of these three facets of speech act production can change cross-culturally. We can demonstrate this using the speech act of complimenting.

In American English, Herbert (1986) suggests that a compliment structure is a two-part routine, and the response to the initial compliment will be one of three choices:

1. Agreement (e.g., *thank you, I love it!*);
2. Nonagreement (e.g., *it's just an old shirt*); or more unusually,
3. Other interpretations (e.g., an offer such as *would you like to borrow it?*).

In Chinese, however, Chen (1993) suggests that Rejection or Nonagreement is a far more common response. From a sociopragmatic perspective, compliments in American English tend to appear in interactions between people of equal status such as between friends or colleagues, whereas in Japanese, speakers are more likely to compliment people of a higher social status than themselves. Finally, pragmalinguistically, Chen (2010) suggests that compliments in American English typically take the structural form NP IS/LOOKS REALLY ADJ (*Your blouse looks really beautiful*), or I REALLY LOVE/LIKE NP (*I love your car*) (p. 79), while in Arabic, a common response is a formulaic utterance of offering, for example, *I proffer it to you; It's all yours* (p. 93)

As we noted in Chapter 2 much of the research in SLA has focused on examining how these differences are learned in a second language, and a number of syntheses of interlanguage speech act studies (Kasper & Rose, 1999; Plonsky & Zhuang, 2019; Taguchi, 2015; Takahashi, 2000) give us a clear picture of the development of this field. Early studies were typically experimental in nature and used elicited data such as dialogue completion or roleplays; see Chapter 9 for a detailed discussion of these designs. One effect of this line of research noted by Kasper and Rose (1999) is that low-proficiency learners may not have sufficient overall language competence to engage in these kinds of language activities; thus, primarily intermediate and advanced learners are investigated. A consistent finding across these studies is that similar to native speakers, learners control a wide range of strategies with which to enact speech acts; for example, they use both direct and indirect strategies and they understand the necessary components for effective speech act performance such as offering repair in the case of apologies. In contrast, their pragmalinguistic choices differed from native speakers. This would not be unexpected as the language used in these contexts may be idiomatic in nature (e.g, *got a light?*). Blum-Kulha and Olshtain (1986) found a bell-shaped development curve in the use of modality markers such as hedges, supportive moves, or intensifiers (see Section 7.1, for discussion) used with speech acts where they were initially under-supplied at lower-proficiency levels, and then oversupplied at higher levels before they reached a more nativelike distribution. The use of modals also developed over time from an overuse of *(I) want* or bare imperatives (e.g., *give me*) toward more nativelike uses of may *(I), would (you) and could (you)* (Hill, 1997).

Later research focused on how sociopragmatic and pragmalinguistic features might best be taught. Overall, studies showed a clear, positive effect for explicit intervention suggesting that Non-Native Speaker (NNS) pragmatic competence can be positively impacted through classroom instruction even in EFL environments. For example, Eslami-Rasekh et al. (2004) administered a multiple-choice awareness test to both a control and treatment group of Iranian learners following 12 weeks of metapragmatic instruction in requests, apologies, and complaints for the treatment group, and a significant difference in performance was found between the two groups. Rose and Ng (2001) report a similar finding for deductive instruction of compliments and suggest that it may be particularly effective for increasing learners' sociopragmatic knowledge. These findings regarding the effectiveness of explicit treatments of speech acts have been further confirmed by the most recent studies that have come to similar conclusions particularly within EFL contexts (Eslami-Rasekh, et al., 2015; Nguyen et al., 2015; Sarab & Alikhani, 2016; Zaferanieh & Eslami-Rasekh, 2016). Investigation of the effectiveness of different instruction techniques also continues to expand. Most recently, Taguchi and Kim (2016) investigated the potential benefits of task-based teaching and collaborative dialogue between students. Following instruction, two groups of EFL learners in South Korea developed their own request dialogues: One group developed them collaboratively in pairs and the other group worked on them individually. Language produced during the collaborative task and in the immediate post-test showed an advantage for the collaborative group; however, in a delayed post-test conducted one month later both groups performed alike.

### 3.3.1 Speech Acts in the TESOL Classroom: Materials

Having assessed through ongoing research that instruction in pragmatics is both possible and meaningful, we can look at how this is typically addressed in classroom materials. Although traditionally the teaching of pragmatics has been underrepresented in TESOL textbooks, the exception is the presentation and practice of speech acts which are often taught under some form of the idea of "the functions of English" (e.g., Jones, 1981).

Speech acts that are typically represented are many of those we have covered in this chapter such as requests, apologies, complaints, suggestions, and so on. However, when we look more closely at pedagogical presentations, we find that they often suffer from our perceptions of what we think we do rather than what we actually do. This applies to both the acts themselves and the way in which we express them. Wolfson (1990), for example, describes an early study focused on invitation-giving (Wolfson et al., 1983) in which "native speakers of American English described themselves as using forms which were rarely or never heard in observations of actual interactions, and expressed strong disapproval of forms which they were heard to use all the time" (p. 2). Boxer and Pickering (1995) focused on the presentation of direct complaints in textbooks (e.g., *Excuse me, we've been waiting here for 15 minutes, are we ever going to be served?*) vs. indirect complaints (ICs). ICs are typically used as a form of commiserating or complaining between interlocutors (including strangers) in which a negative evaluation is expressed about someone or something that is not the addressee's fault. For example:

(18) Two female graduate students in a departmental library.
A: They never have what you need in here. You'd think they'd at least have the important books and articles.
B: They didn't have what you were looking for?
A: No.
B: That's typical. (Boxer & Pickering, 1995, p. 45)

They are far more common than direct complaints in daily interaction and are often used as a form of relationship-building or phatic communion (see Functionalism Section 6.1.1) between speakers; thus, they are an important area for language learners. Despite this,

Boxer and Pickering found a universal presentation of direct complaints across the seven texts that they surveyed and only tangential treatment of reactions toward attitudes or emotions. Vellenga (2004) noted that not much had changed in a decade. Speech act presentations in ESL and EFL textbooks remained problematic comprising decontextualized examples with little or no discussion of register and formality and a continued focus on speech acts that may be less relevant to learners. With regard to direct complaints, for example, she notes "imagine the pitfalls for a population of learners who think direct complaints are the norm in English!" (p. 16). And nearly two decades later, investigations of the presentation of speech acts in EFL texts for Vietnamese students (Nguyen, 2011) and Chinese students (Ren & Han, 2016) reported the lack of a justification as to when and how speech acts were introduced in the texts and very traditional pedagogical presentations that continued to lack contextual and metalinguistic information.

More recently, there has been a movement toward using corpora of naturally occurring discourse to identify key language that should be addressed in these kinds of textbook presentations (see, e.g., Simpson & Mendis (2003) study of idioms in academic spoken discourse; and Cheng's (2010) study of thanking). Jiang (2006) compares the presentation of making suggestions in 6 ESL textbooks with recordings of natural discourse between professors and students and in student study groups. A key finding was that LET's X? was by far the most commonly used phrase to make suggestions in the naturally occurring data yet the form appeared in only one of the textbook series that she examined. She notes that "the limited selection of certain structures, and not others, is not well supported by real-life language use, as reflected in the corpus materials" (p. 51).

A second approach to establishing contextualized examples that can be used to create more appropriate materials is classroom- or institution-based research. E-politeness or e-etiquette has become a growing area of research particularly in academic contexts. Economidou-Kogetsidis (2011) examined NNS email requests sent over several semesters in English at an English-medium university in Cyprus. She collected 200 e-requests from students sent to 11 professors at the institution; these were then judged by NS lecturers from universities in the United Kingdom. Overall, the strategies used by students failed to "observe [expected] deference principles and tend to assume compliance on the part of the addressee" (p. 14). This was at least in part because a popular strategy in the requests was a please + imperative structure (e.g., *please answer me as soon as possible*), which instructors felt sounded like an order or a demand. There was also a lack of sufficient mitigation (e.g., *I was wondering if*) and often a lack of an opening/closing salutation, both of which irritated many of the instructors. A study like this contains a great deal of information that can be used to create more nuanced pedagogical materials that can respond directly to the perceived pragmatic failures typical in this specific context.

In a similar study, Cheng (2017) investigated instructors' perceptions of both online and spoken apologies given by both NS and NNS university students. Overall, NS apologies were rated more highly than those by NNSs, and Cheng includes examples of both highly rated and poorly rated student apologies, which is extremely useful for building pedagogical materials. For example, the qualities of the highly rated email apology in example (19) (e.g., willingness to take responsibility, acknowledgment of the importance of the instructor's time, careful presentation, and opening/closing salutations) can be directly contrasted with their absence in the poorly rated apology shown in example (20):

(19) Hello Dr. Smith, I am so sorry about missing our appointment earlier. I would still like to talk to you about this matter but I understand if you do not wish to schedule another appointment. I will stop by your office during your office hours. Again, I apologize for missing our appointment. Thank you for your time, Mary. (p. 15)

(20) Hi Mr. Smith how are you? hope you have a nice day. i really email you because i have missed an important lecture and as you know the next two weeks we will start the final exams. i seen all my friends and nobody was taking notes or anything else. Would you mind repeat the lecture again or give me a brief summary for the lecture. Because I really need it as soon as possible to study it for the exam. (p. 17)

Cheng discusses a number of pedagogical strategies that could be used to address these issues in ESL classes including both explicit and implicit instructional techniques and provides an excellent list of basic concerns that teachers can discuss with students when focusing on this high stakes area of pragmatic instruction (see Cheng, 2017, p. 21).

### 3.3.2 Sample Teaching Materials

In this final section, we look briefly at two sample lessons that can be used as models for a variety of speech acts. The first is a suggested lesson plan to address ICs from Boxer and Pickering (1995, pp. 52–55) and follows a presentation to practice model.

#### Lesson Plan 1: IC Lesson Plan

1. Present and discuss typical IC sequences taken from natural discourse. These can be as short as a routine that might occur in a supermarket check-out:

   A: I feel like I've been standing here forever.

   B: They never seem to have more than about two registers open and they have about 20!

   Discuss the three most likely responses to ICs: Agreement, reassurance, or commiseration.
2. Present examples of ICs without responses and ask students to discuss possible responses, for example, "Boy, this line is so slow!"(p. 54)
3. Present examples of IC responses and discuss with students what might have prompted them, for example, "Female friends at home discussing adolescent children: 'They're so difficult, these issues!'"(p. 54)
4. Present short conversations that focus on an IC in a jigsaw exercise that students have to arrange in the correct order to be followed.
5. Practice and feedback: Provide roleplay situations that students can perform on videotape (e.g., "A female receptionist at the dentist's office complains to a male patient about how they are tearing down all the historical buildings in the neighborhood" (p. 55)) and then playback and discuss appropriateness of responses.

The second is from an excellent resource for teachers, Tatsuki and Houck (2010) *Pragmatics: Teaching Speech Acts* from the TESOL Classroom Practice Series published by TESOL Press. This volume contains ideas for teaching multiple speech acts. Houck and Fujimori focus on advice-giving also using a presentation to practice model.

#### Lesson Plan 2: Advice-Giving Lesson Plan

1. Use a diagnostic worksheet to determine students' current advice-giving strategies. For example, you are walking down the street and meet Mr. Suzuki, your principal. You talk for a minute or two. He looks very sick. What would you say? (p. 97)
2. Use examples to present three advice-giving strategies: direct (*you should*), softened (*you might want*), and indirect (no modal) and practice understanding using prerecorded dialogues.
3. Provide controlled practice activities such as responding to short scenarios (e.g., a five-day holiday is coming up. Your oral communication teacher, who recently moved to the area, is planning to drive to a vacation spot. You know the highways will be very crowded (p. 101)).
4. Practice using open-ended roleplays in which students can practice the speech act and provide feedback (p. 94).

# 4

# Grice's Principle of Cooperation

## 4.1 Gricean Pragmatics as Rational Cooperation

The idea of cooperation and the cooperative principle (CP) was introduced by Grice in his 1967 William James lectures. The lectures were widely circulated as mimeographed transcripts, and then in a series of papers starting with the classic Logic and Conversation (Grice, 1975) and then collected as part of Grice posthumous *Studies in the Way of Words* (1989). Grice's account of the CP and more precisely of the idea of implicature has been extremely influential in pragmatics, since it is relevant, among other things, to indirect speech acts (see Chapter 3), the classical rational theories of politeness (see Chapter 5), and the discussion on the boundary of semantics and pragmatics (see Chapter 1), not to mention that relevance theory (RT) is also inspired by Grice's CP.

Grice sees human beings as rational beings, that is, they are endowed with a capacity to evaluate things, choices, decisions, and pretty much anything on the basis of a set of values. Rationality can be defined as choosing the most efficient and least expensive way of achieving your goals: minimize costs and maximize benefits. The goals of speakers get evaluated from a rational viewpoint as well. Suppose you want to eat a donut. The rational (i.e., most efficient) way of doing so is to go to a place where they sell donuts (donut shop, general store, supermarket, etc.) and purchase one, typically for about $1 per donut and in a very limited amount of time. Alternative plans in our goal to eat a donut could involve cooking your own, which would require securing flour, eggs, milk, sugar, and so on and crucially large amounts of boiling-hot oil, which is expensive, time-consuming, difficult to do, and even dangerous. Other, even more far-fetched approaches to securing a donut involve holding up a donut store, begging patrons who leave the store to give you one of the donuts they have purchased, marrying the owner of the donut shop, and so on in increasingly absurd plans to eat a donut. The point to the facetious escalation of plans-to-eat-a-donut is that there is a most efficient way to accomplish this goal, which becomes the standard way of doing it, and other substandard (less efficient) ways of achieving the same goal.

### 4.1.1 Conversational Cooperation Is Rational

Gricean cooperation is commonly taken to be motivated by niceness or by a sense of duty. Some authors (e.g., Pratt, 1986; Sampson, 1982) have assumed that Grice is committed to the view that speakers are motivated by goodwill in cooperation. Moreover, to further add to the confusion, the CP was worded as a set of maxims, phrased as imperatives. This has led many scholars (e.g., Margolis, 1979; Taylor & Cameron, 1987) to interpret the CP as prescriptive and its mandate of cooperation as moralistic. In fact, this is not the case, as we will see later. In Grice's view, cooperation in communication, far from being altruistic, is rational. This is a very important point and we will return to it in the rest of the chapter.

Grice's wording for the CP was

> Make your contribution such as it is required, at the stage at which it occurs, by the accepted purpose or direction of the talk exchange in which you are engaged.
> (*Grice, 1989, p. 26*)

In its general wording, the CP is clearly rational: the speaker is enjoined to adapt his/her contribution to the requirements of the exchange and its purposes (i.e., goals). Grice further explicates the CP into four maxims, some of which have submaxims:

> Maxim of Quantity
> Make your contribution as informative as is required (for the current purposes of the exchange).
> Do not make your contribution more informative than is required. (1989, p. 26)
>
> Maxim of Quality
> Supermaxim: Try to make your contribution one that is true.
> Submaxims:
> Do not say what you believe to be false.
> Do not say that for which you lack adequate evidence. (1989, p. 27)
>
> Maxim of Relation (Relevance)
> Be relevant. (1989, p.27)
>
> Maxim of Manner
> Supermaxim: Be perspicuous.
> Submaxims:
> Avoid obscurity of expression.
> Avoid ambiguity.
> Be brief (avoid unnecessary prolixity).
> Be orderly. (1989, p. 27)

As we said, the wording of the maxims consists of imperatives (e.g., "be relevant") but nonetheless the CP and its maxims are not prescriptive. Recall that for Grice cooperation is rational action: it is more efficient to cooperate if you want to achieve your goals. The speaker is free to cooperate or not, but to do so is more efficient (nets more benefits) than not doing so. Suppose Attardo walks into a donut shop wanting to eat a donut and, having decided not to be cooperative,[1] he asks for a cinnamon roll. He will receive a cinnamon roll and thus fail in his goal to eat a donut. Not following the maxim of quality (he lied about his wants) cost him a positive outcome (i.e., he did not maximize his benefits). Or suppose that when asked *How can I help you?* he responds: *I slept like a log last night.* Not following the maxim of relevance also would cost him the donut. So we see that following the CP is not an obligation, it is the rational thing to do. This is similar to a situation in which someone asks for advice on how to get to the Dallas airport and is told *don't go at rush hour*: obviously the speaker is not forbidding or obliging the hearer not to go. The speaker is giving them advice. It would be odd for the hearer to respond, *who are you to tell me where I can or cannot go?* While worded as an imperative, (good) advice is just that, advice and can be paraphrased as *If I were you, I would not drive to the airport at rush hour.* Likewise, it is an easy exercise to reword Grice's formulation of the CP as advice.[2]

Summing up, Gricean pragmatics is rational because it assumes a rational agent (speaker) who does what is in their best interest to achieve their goals. This is why the CP, while couched in prescriptive language, is in fact not prescriptive: one should be clear or relevant, not because it is a morally or socially good thing to be clear or relevant, but because if one is clear or relevant one stands a better chance to achieve one's goals. One does not cooperate out of altruism, but out of self-interest.

### 4.1.2 Implicatures

The significance of the CP in linguistics comes from the fact that it sheds light on an otherwise inexplicable phenomenon. From what a speaker says, we can derive other meanings, called "implicatures," that were not in fact said and were merely implied. In fact, it is possible to derive implicatures both from following and from not following the CP. That requires some explanation. Consider the sentence

(21) I have read many books by Chomsky.

Literally, (21) states that the speaker has read an unspecified number of books by Noam Chomsky. We cannot guess exactly how many, but probably more than three or four, at

1 Many of our students were confused by this example, presumably because it is hard to conceptualize someone not cooperating with oneself. However, there are many reasons why speakers may not want to say what they want, for example, shame, fear, embarrassment, and so on. For example, in Stephen Vizinczey's novel *In Praise of Older Women* the protagonist is embarrassed about his lack of sexual control, and so, when asked by a young woman he is attracted to if he wants to go home with her, he answers that he'd rather finish reading his book. She takes offense and leaves. Needless to say, he later regrets not telling the truth. The point of the examples is that if we do not state truthfully, clearly, and so on what we want, we will probably not get it. Note also that in the donut example, Attardo did not change his mind and decide he wanted another pastry, because then he'd be rationally following the CP. The example is supposed to show what happens if one is *not* rationally following the CP.

2 Grice does *not* present it as advice. Grice presents behavior following the CP as "quasi-contractual," "expected," and "habitual." The point is that Grice does not present it as an obligation.

least (since the plural implies at least two). We can call this the literal meaning of the sentence; Grice's term for this was simply, "the said." However, you should also get another meaning, and namely that the speaker has not read all of Chomsky's books. Now, this meaning is different from the previous meaning we called literal or "the said." First and foremost, the sentence never actually says anything about all of Chomsky's books. In fact, all it says is that Chomsky wrote books, that there are many of them, and that the speaker read a large number of books by Chomsky. The sentence does not say anything about all of Chomsky's books. So, why would it mean that the speaker did not read them all? This is where the CP kicks in. We will call this extra, nonliteral meaning conveyed by the utterance of (21) a figurative meaning.

Essentially, what the CP does is guide our interpretive analysis of the meaning of the sentence in context (i.e., the utterance) to extract an extra figurative meaning, called an implicature. How does it work? Assume the hearer hears (21) in a context in which the speaker is trustworthy and behaving normally. Then the hearer reasons as follows: the speaker has told me that they have read many books by Chomsky. I assume they are following the CP, so this is a true and relevant statement. I also must assume that the statement follows the maxim of quantity and therefore that the speaker is giving me just the right amount of information. If they had in fact read all of Chomsky's books, then they would have told me so; therefore, I conclude that they have not in fact read all of Chomsky's books. Consider now another example. It would be inappropriate for Attardo to say

(22) I have read many books by Grice.

when Attardo has read three books by Grice and Grice has published three books overall. In order to follow the CP, Attardo should have said: *I have read all of Grice's books* (i.e., provided the strongest statement possible).

So, is this how language works? Is there always an implicature? Always a literal and a figurative meaning? Is it always through the CP? The answer to these legitimate questions is, somewhat surprisingly, yes. All utterances by speakers trigger implicatures. Of course, not all of them are interesting and worth processing. Take an example:

(23) A.2 4: [ Our, + our ] kids are grown up.
A.2 5: We don't have any grandchildren yet.
(Switchboard corpus: sw_0015_4877)

Here speaker A, by uttering turn 5 triggers the implicature is that they want grandchildren: why say "yet" unless one expects or wishes that in the future one will have grandchildren? The "interesting" sort of implicature is the kind that usually gets taught in pragmatics classes. However, turn 4, *our kids are grown up*, also triggers several implicatures: the speaker has more than one child (also an inference) but probably not more than 3 or 4 (a not *un*usual number of children; had A had 13 children, they would have said so, per the maxim of quantity). Another implicature is that A is middle aged. This latter kind of implicatures[3] are usually not noticed, unless they suddenly become relevant (and indeed RT will

3 Searle (1992) calls these "background assumptions."

make much of this; see later). It also seems odd to call "we don't have more than 3 or 4 children" a "figurative" meaning, but technically any nonliteral meaning has to be figurative.

### 4.1.3 Scalarity and Implicatures

Humans tend to organize some aspects of their knowledge of the world in relative terms: is x bigger/better/more useful than y? The comparative and the superlative degrees of adjectives in English and many other languages are a good case in point: *Mary is taller than Jane* means that on a scale of tallness, Mary occupies a higher place, echelon, ranking, and so on than Jane. This tendency to conceptualize the world in scales can be utilized to draw implicatures.

Consider the following scale:

a few < some < many < most < all

it is clear that this scale ranks the degree to which a given set is in relation to another set: for example, I can say I have met one of Mary's children, or a few of Mary's children or all of them. Likewise, I can say I have read one of Chomsky's books, a few of them, most of them, or all of them.

The point is that if I affirm a level of the scale this generates the implicature that I cannot affirm a stronger level of the scale. If I have read most of Chomsky's books, I have not read them all. If I have met a few of Mary's children, I have not met most of them. These scales are known as "Horn-scales," after Larry Horn who studied them. However, scalarity also exists outside of conventionalized scales such as quantifiers.

The "let alone" construction is instructive in this regard, as it creates more or less arbitrary scales. Consider this example:

(24) "I've never been much of a fan of coffee, let alone tiramisu but this was heavenly."
source: my.openrice.com/gourmet/userdetail.htm?userid=566021&SubmitYear=2016&SubmitMonth=11

This example establishes an improbable, but obviously real to the writer, "coffeeness-scale" in which tiramisu, which is made with biscuits soaked in coffee, among other ingredients, occupies a higher level than coffee, so that the scale would look like: coffee < tiramisu. It is easy to construct examples that show the versatility of the construction:

(25) Lucy does not ride 5 year old horses, let alone mustangs.
*5 year old < mustang; scale: "difficulty in riding horses"*
John has not read *Ulysses*, let alone *Finnegan's Wake.*
*Ulysses < Finnegan's wake; "accessibility of Joyce's novels"*
Mary does not eat vegan, let alone macrobiotic
*vegan < macrobiotic; scale "restrictiveness of diet"*
Sal does not exercise, let alone do cross-fit.
*exercise < cross-fit; scale "strenuousness of exercise"*

So the construction let alone carries the implicature that the left-hand item of the equation is at a lower level of the right-hand element on a scale-to-be-determined contextually. Thus, we can predict that if a science fiction writer produced the following sentence:

(26) "The ship's shields could not handle a photon torpedo, let alone a neutrino missile"

they intend the reader to understand that a neutrino missile is worse (more destructive) than a photon torpedo.[4]

### 4.1.4 Flouting and Implicatures

As we mentioned earlier, following the CP is not the only way to get an implicature. In fact, there is a completely different way of getting implicatures that is based on not following the CP, at least on the surface. We turn to this process, called "flouting," next.

So far we have looked at what happens if we follow the principle of cooperation. However, there are many situation in which we do not do so. The most obvious example are lies. Consider the following example, which took place when Attardo's daughter was about 4 years old:

(27) Father to child, whose face is covered in chocolate. "Did you eat the chocolate?"
Child: "No."

Setting aside the ineptitude of the child's technique at effective lies, there can be no question that she was not, at the time, following the principle of cooperation, insofar as the maxim of quality goes. Since her intention was to avoid getting in trouble for eating the chocolate and she was hoping that her audience did not find out about the lie, this is a case of violation.

The speakers may have any number of reasons for violating a maxim. These reasons may include

- the desire to exit the communicative exchange altogether; think of the "no comment" expression;
- the right not to incriminate oneself (taking the fifth amendment in a US trial);
- the speaker may be unable to fulfill the maxim's directions, for example, because they lack the information to answer a question;
- politeness: Attardo: *Do these leather pants look good on me?* Pickering: *Sure*;
- lying: the speaker may want to mislead the hearer (see the chocolate example).

However, we are interested in a special case, in which, while there is a violation, it is not covert (hidden, as in lies or politeness[5]), but on the contrary it is overt, that is, clearly detectable.

Consider the following example of dialogue:

4 Because it hits you *before* it's been fired.
5 If the speaker announces that they are lying or being polite, or even if the hearer figures it out on their own, the speaker's goal for lying or being polite is defeated. *I don't really like these pants on you but I am saying so to pacify you* seems to be actually worse than saying *They don't look good.*

(28) A.1 I don't like the idea of people being able to kill me with very little effort. Um, and, uh, guns are very symbolic of them having that power over me.
B.2 **Well, me being from Texas,**
A.3 Uh-huh.
B.4 I hope you're ready for this.
(...)
B.8 So I don't have a fear of fire arms in any respect.
(Switchboard Corpus. sw_0402_2634)

Here turn B2 (bolded) is clearly not directly relevant to the point, made by A's first turn, that he/she is uncomfortable around guns. So, we can say with a fair degree of confidence that B is violating the maxim of relevance, since A was not talking about regional origins. However, it is also clear that B is not somehow trying to hide the fact that they violated the maxim of relevance. So, deception is not likely the intention behind B's violation. At this point, the CP "kicks in" again and the hearer (A) may reason along these lines: if B is obviously violating the CP and he/she wants me to be aware of this violation, then he/she must have a reason for doing so and the CP is going to give me a clue in what direction to search for the answer. Since B mentioned Texas, what are the salient features of Texas that might be relevant/pertinent in this setting? Texas is associated with the far west, cowboys, and carrying guns. So, if B were trying to imply that he/she is not bothered by guns because he/she is from Texas, his/her apparent violation of the CP would be "redeemed" or reconciled with the assumption of communication in the CP. Or to put it differently, the violation would be found to make sense after all. Hence, assuming B is trying to communicate and has not lost his/her mind, or has checked out of the conversation, or is not incapacitated, then the hypothesis that he/she is trying to convey an implicature must be correct. Indeed, the rest of the conversation clarifies that this guess was correct, because after A's noncommittal reaction in turn 3 ("uh-huh"), B comes out and explains what he/she meant (turn B8).

So, the general model of an implicature produced by a flout is that

1. the speaker obviously and blatantly violates any maxim of the CP;
2. the hearer assumes that the speaker is still wanting to communicate and is not incapacitated, unable to communicate, and so on;
3. the hearer then reconstructs, based on the CP, a probable implicature that would explain away the violation;
4. the hearer then assumes that the implicature is what the speaker meant to communicate.

Apart from the initial process of blatant violation of the CP, flout-generated implicatures share the same characteristics (defeasibility, probabilistic) of implicatures generated by following the CP.

### 4.1.5 Difference between Inferences, Presuppositions, and Implicatures

The reader will recall that in Chapter 1 we introduced the idea of inferences and presuppositions. Inferences (also called "entailments" or "implications") are propositions that follow logically from a sentence, whereas presuppositions are inferences that resist under the negation test. In this chapter, we have introduced the idea of implicatures. One may thus reasonably ask what is exactly the difference between the inferences and presuppositons and implicatures. In a nutshell, we can say that implicatures are probable but not necessary inferences. The technical term for this is "defeasible." Consider the following example:

(29) Mary married John on the 18th May, at St, Mary's Church in Sutton Mallet, Somerset.

From (29) the following inferences follow (among others):

(30) Mary is no longer single.

(31) John is no longer single.

(29) and (32)[6] imply (33) and (34).

(32) Mary did not marry John on the 18th May, at St, Mary's Church in Sutton Mallet, Somerset.

(33) Mary exists

(34) John exists

(30) and (31) are inferences and (33) and (34) presuppositions. All are logically necessary. For example, it is contradictory to say

(35) Mary married John on the 18th May, at St, Mary's Church in Sutton Mallet, Somerset, but she is still single.

Let us now consider an implicature, from (29) and namely that

(36) Mary and John live together.

Given (29) and what we know about our society (and the Sherlock TV show), (36) is very likely to be true. However, no law of logic would be violated if we said

6 Example (32) is actually a naturally occurring utterance: (https://bakerstreet.fandom.com/wiki/Mary_Elizabeth_Watson Accessed January 23, 2019). The example is reproduced verbatim, including the grammatical and punctuation errors.

(37) Mary married John on the 18th May, at St, Mary's Church in Sutton Mallet, Somerset, but they don't live together.

This may be a big problem for Mary and John, or a twist in the plot, but it is not a logical problem. Many people are married and do not live together. Hence, (36) the implicature is not logically necessary as it can be "defeased," as we just did in (37). There are other tests for implicatures (Grice, 1989), but this is the strongest.

### 4.1.6 Developments of Grice's Theory

The reception of Grice's ideas on cooperation was mixed: on the one hand, most scholars acknowledge the significance and originality of his ideas. Obviously, Grice was not the first to recognize the importance of cooperation or its effect on linguistic behavior (see Horn, 1973, 1990), but "it was Paul Grice who put it all together" (Horn, 1990, p. 463). Furthermore, Grice's theory of implicatures and the CP have been extremely influential, across the field of pragmatics, for example, in speech act theory, discourse analysis, and politeness theory. On the other hand, his principle of cooperation and its maxims have been subject to a range of criticisms, to which we turn next.

#### Some Criticisms and Misconstruals of Gricean Pragmatics

There have been many criticisms of Grice's CP. Here we will limit ourselves to the most significant ones. First, we will address the claim that people simply do not follow the CP: the CP is either an idealization of human behavior or it is prescriptive. Second, we will consider the criticisms that the CP ignores the issue of power. Third, we will address the claim that the CP is not psychologically realistic. Finally, we will consider the claim that the CP's claimed universal status is refuted by cross-cultural variation.

The most obvious criticism is that the whole idea of having a principle of cooperation must be mistaken because people don't always cooperate and so the idea of a CP must be an idealization or grounded in unwarranted optimism. Chapman (2005, p. 190) provides a good sampling of these critiques. However, these objections disappear entirely in light of our prior discussion of the rational nature of cooperation. The fact that Grice's views have been presented in a fragmentary manner is most likely responsible for this error in perspective. Indeed, Grice's work on rationality appeared fully only posthumously, so the rational nature of the CP was obscured. A related criticism is that the CP is prescriptive, which as we also have seen above, is mostly due to the unfortunate imperative wording chosen by Grice.

A more serious criticism is that the CP ignores power imbalances and other social factors. For example, those in a position of power often do not feel the need to be cooperative, whereas those who are not often find themselves forced to be cooperative. These criticisms are more on target, but they too are easily addressed.

However, before addressing power imbalances, we need to distinguish a duality within the CP: Grice's wording of the CP does not distinguish between, on the one hand, linguistic cooperation finalized to furthering the conversation itself and, on the other hand, cooperation finalized to helping the interlocutor(s) achieve their extra-linguistic goals. Consider the following example: suppose that A needs to go to Brighton and is currently in Victoria Station in London. A asks a person wearing a British Rail uniform, "What platform does the train for Brighton leave from?" An answer that does not provide the relevant information (say, "Platform 2") would be noncooperative. Now, imagine a situation in which there is a strike and so the trains are not running; answering "Platform 2," while relevant and truthful, would be noncooperative because it does not further the goal of getting to Brighton. An extra-linguistically cooperative answer would be "You'd better take the bus, the trains are on strike." Thus, we need to acknowledge that the CP is not always the ultimate goal of the speakers. Speakers have many other goals, also ruled by rationality. So, in situations in which other goals override cooperation, the speakers will feel free to be noncooperative at the linguistic level, and, provided they are cooperative at the extra-linguistic level, the hearers will not mind in the least.

We now can turn to power imbalances. Consider a standard teacher/student situation. If the teacher asks

(38) What is two plus two?

the student cannot reply

(39) Why are you asking me? You know the answer to the question!

which is most likely true. However, the situation, the classroom setting, allows for "fake" questions (technically called "pedagogical questions") in which the speaker knows the answer (which would violate the felicity conditions of a normal question speech act, see Chapter 3) and is asking to check if the student knows the answer. Furthermore, the student cannot answer

(40) I'd rather not talk about this

let alone

(41) I refuse to answer

which would both be appropriate answers in different contexts. The teaching situation is clearly a setting in which the power, as far as the pedagogical experience goes, is largely if not entirely in the hands of the teacher. So, how does this map onto cooperation? When the teacher asks a question, the students' decision to answer is likely not governed by the desire to be cooperative, but rather by the desire to avoid punishment, that is, the coercive force of the imbalanced situation. However, this is in fact not a problem for Grice's theory, in light of the recognition that cooperation is not the ultimate goal of the speakers. Obviously if one is in an imbalanced situation, one needs to do whatever one considers tactically and strategically necessary, regardless of its cooperative nature. This reasoning explains away many of the objections that the CP is unrealistic or blind to power imbalances.

A different criticism directed at the CP was that it was not psychologically accurate. If one considers Grice's proposal as a psychological theory, some predictions may be extrapolated: for example, since an implicature requires a more complex inferential path than the "literal meaning" of a sentence, one would expect that it would take longer to process a sentence that requires a flout than one that does not. This was called the "standard pragmatic model," and attributed to Grice. However, Grice himself never stated that he was presenting a psychologically realistic model of processing. Grice makes it clear that he is presenting a rationalization of how the speaker *could* reason. So, according to Grice, the hearer does not actually go through the actual reasoning. Most of the processing is subconscious and never makes it to above the threshold of consciousness, so a Gricean rational speaker would not have the opportunity to consciously choose to follow the CP. This is similar to driving a car: you don't consciously choose to brake if you see a child run in the street. However, you can model the situation as an algorithm along the lines of "if you see a child crossing the street → brake."

A group of psycholinguists (e.g., Gibbs, 1994) performed experiments that showed that sentences requiring a flout, for example, irony, in some cases, were processed faster than literal ones. Clearly, this is incompatible with the standard pragmatic model. So, Gibbs and others argued for a direct access model, in which speakers accessed directly the implied meaning (say, the irony) without first accessing the literal meaning. A different interpretation of the results and other experiments (e.g., Giora, 2003) provided a two-stage explanation: speakers would access the most salient meaning first and the less salient one later, regardless of which one was the so-called literal meaning. This debate contributed to the birth of experimental pragmatics, an approach to pragmatics based on psycholinguistics, which cannot be discussed in this context, but see Schwarz (2017) and Noveck (2018), for example.

We now turn to considering the claim that Gricean pragmatics is refuted by cross-cultural differences. We will examine one of the best-known arguments that have been brought to support this idea, the management of information by Malagasy speakers. Elinor Ochs Keenan, an anthropologist at UCLA, examined the communicative practices of the speakers of Malagasy, an Austronesian language spoken in Madagascar, in relation to this apparent violation of Grice's CP. She found that

> they [the speakers of Malagasy] regularly provide less information than is required by their conversational partner, even though they have access to the necessary information.
>
> (*Ochs Keenan, 1976, p. 70*).

If correct, this would be a significant blow to the assumption of rationality of the CP. Likewise, it would be a significant blow against the claim of universality, since all human cultures are equally rational, that is, base behavior on a cost/benefit analysis. So let us consider some concrete examples.

Among the Malagasy there is a "virtual taboo" against referring to children by their proper name; nicknames or Christian names are used. People refer to children and also to adults since the taboo diminishes with age, but does not disappear, as "person," "boy," "girl," and so on. If asked when a given ritual will take place they will say "In a bit" or "around September" even if an exact date has been set. They will, however, reveal the exact date when they are absolutely sure that the event will take place, for example, only a few days or hours before or "at the last moment" (Ochs Keenan, 1976, p. 71).

These examples, and others provided by Ochs Keenan, seem indeed quite problematic for the CP, as they are in direct violation of the maxim of quantity. However, when we dig a little more, it appears that the situation is more complex. First, when the information is trivial, it is provided readily: Ochs Keenan mentions that if you ask someone who is cooking if the meal is ready you will get an accurate answer. Conversely, if the information is meaningful and important the speakers will be more reticent. Second, the closer the relationship between the speakers, the more likely is the information to be provided: so two siblings or two members of the same clan will share information between them that would not be shared with a stranger. These differences point us in the direction of the solution to the apparent problem. It is not the case that "conversational implicatures differ in these societies" (Ochs Keenan, 1976, p. 75) but simply that the Malagasy speakers attribute value to information slightly differently than Western society does. On the surface, information such as the name of a person or the time of an event, in Western society is considered more or less "free goods", that is, something with a negligible cost of production that can therefore be given away freely (think, e.g., of freely accessible web pages on the internet). However, also in Western culture, not all information is free goods. While we freely tell people our children's names, CEOs of companies will not disclose information about imminent drops in price of their company's stock, and bank managers do not reveal the time and date of the arrival of the armored truck carrying cash to the bank. The point here is that valuable information does not always get disclosed. Obviously, different cultures will decide what counts as valuable information: the Malagasy clearly place a high price on information. Other cultures may be more liberal with it.[7]

One might object that this nonetheless refutes Grice's CP's contention that one should provide complete information, regardless of cultural variation. This is however not the case. As we saw earlier, the CP is not the only principle governing speakers' behavior. Without getting too far into this under-explored area, it is obvious that speakers may choose not to be cooperative, for example, by lying, if they judge that it is in their interest. So, for example, a child wanting to play videogames will falsely tell his/her parents that they have done their homework. This does not refute the CP. It simply shows that the child's self-interest overrules the injunction to cooperate. Cooperation is not necessarily our top motivation, it is only one of the principles driving human behavior.

### Revisions of Grice's CP

Many authors, while generally accepting the idea of a CP, felt the need to amend it. We have done so ourselves above, in order to show that despite its wording the CP is not a prescriptive principle. However, by far the most common line of revisions of the CP was to either add to the maxims or, conversely, to reduce the number of the maxims.

---

7 There is no need to travel to Madagascar to find examples of groups that value information differently. In France, the inhabitants of the Normandy region are famous for their "evasive" answers, with the expression *P'têt ben qu'oui, p'têt ben qu'non* ("maybe yes, maybe no") having acquired proverbial status, indexing precisely this regional origin (Section 10.2).

Some authors have added maxims: John Searle adds a submaxim of Manner: "speak idiomatically" (Searle, 1979, p. 50); Leech (1983) adds several other maxims, including a politeness maxim (see Chapter 5); one of us (Attardo, 2000) proposed a maxim of appropriateness, enjoining the speaker to say things that are contextually appropriate. These ideas will be taken up again in Chapter (5). Others have argued that the number of maxims should be reduced. We will review these approaches later.

### Neo- and Post-Gricean Theories of Pragmatics

A classification of pragmatic theories one is likely to encounter distinguishes between neo-Gricean and Post-Gricean theories. Neo-Gricean approaches can be characterized as using and adapting, often critically and with significant revisions, as we have seen earlier, Grice's fundamental insights. Post-Gricean pragmatics consists mostly of RT, which claims to have gone beyond Grice's insights and to have essentially discarded them (Clark, 2013, pp. 83–84). Other authors postulate other principles or the replacement of cooperation by other principles.

Two prominent neo-Gricean approaches take a different direction from the proposal to expand the CP seen earlier. Both Larry Horn and Stephen Levinson have argued that the CP should be replaced by fewer maxims. Horn (1984) argues that the CP should be replaced by two principles:

1. Q principle: Make your contribution sufficient; say as much as you can.
2. R principle: Make your contribution necessary; say no more than you must.

The names are meant to recall Grice's quantity and relevance, but clearly the principles are inspired by the principle of least effort and maximum differentiation familiar in historical linguistics. Speakers tend to minimize effort, which leads to reduction of sounds in the direction of ease of pronunciation; however, this is counterbalanced by the desire to make processing easier as well, and thus the need to differentiate between excessive similarity. On the principle of least effort, see Zipf (1949); on maximum differentiation, Martinet (1955).

Levinson argues for three maxims: Q, I, and M, explicitly modeled after Grice's and Horn's maxims.

1. Q principle: Make the strongest statement consistent with what you know (Levinson, 2000, p. 76).
2. I principle: "Say as little as necessary" (p. 114).
3. M principle: Use marked linguistic expressions to indicate "abnormal, non-stereotypical situations" (p. 136).

Levinson (2000) proposes a theory of generalized conversational implicatures, an intermediate category between the said and the particularized conversational implicatures, to be derived by the revised maxims. What is the difference between the two? Both types of implicatures derive from the CP: whereas particularized conversational implicatures can derive both from following the CP and flouting it, generalized conversational implicatures only come from following the CP. Furthermore, generalized conversational implicatures are "coded" by the linguistic system and are context independent, whereas particularized conversational implicatures are completely context dependent.

### Relevance Theory

RT was developed by Sperber and Wilson (1986); it is conveniently summarized in Sperber and Wilson (1987), which we will follow in our exposition. Sperber and Wilson's starting point is ostensive communication defined as communication which makes manifest the intention to communicate something. This is indebted to Grice's definition of nonnatural meaning, which crucially involves the intention of having one's intention to communicate recognized. This intention is called the "M-intention" (Grice, 1957; Sperber & Wilson, 1987, p. 698).

RT derives the principle of relevance from the need for a speaker to produce something worth listening to, that is, justifying the cognitive effort invested in it. So, what the speaker says has to be the most relevant thing they could have said (because they are costing the hearer effort to process their utterance). So, in conclusion, "Every act of ostensive communication communicates the presumption of its own optimal relevance" (Sperber & Wilson, 1986, p. 158) relative to the "speaker's abilities and preferences" (Wilson & Sperber, 2012, p. 65). Thus, RT redefines the idea of relevance, which is no longer a maxim, but its own principle. RT definition of the relevance of a phenomenon is as follows:

- Condition 1: A phenomenon is relevant to an individual to the extent that the contextual effects achieved when it is optimally processed are large.
- Condition 2: A phenomenon is relevant to an individual to the extent that the effort required to process it optimally is small (1986, p. 153).

The reader may have recognized, in the duality of the definition of relevance, Zipf's (1949) "minimal effort" law, reflected in the need to justify the cognitive effort of processing, and Grice's maxim of quantity, reflected in the need to say the "most relevant" thing one can say. Nonetheless, RT's relevance is radically different from Grice's maxim. First and foremost, relevance is an exceptionless principle (1987, p. 704), which cannot be flouted, for example. Second, RT defines relevance as optimal relevance, that is, both the stimulus that is least effortful and most rewarding (worth listening to).

The contextual effects that determine whether the processing has been worthwhile are inferences and implicatures, which can be weak or strong (i.e., implied more or less explicitly). An important consequence of these definitions is that communication becomes "a matter of degree" (Sperber & Wilson, 1987, p. 700), namely that one can make some assumption more or less strongly manifest and hence communicate it more or less strongly. Stating explicitly is an example of strong manifestness, implying is a weaker case.

One may wonder, in relation to RT but also the reductionist Neo-Gricean models of Horn and Levinson, how these models account for the maxim of quality. All these approaches postulate that adherence to the truth is somehow presupposed by the communicative situation at large and need not be incorporated in pragmatic principles. For example, Sperber and Wilson claim that an "assertion comes with a tacit guarantee of truth" (1986, p. 49). However, see also Wilson and Sperber (2012, pp. 47–83). According to Levinson, the maxim of quality "plays only a background role" (2000, p. 74) in his model. RT has been very successful and has been applied broadly, including to SLA. We will review some of the applications of RT to SLA later in the chapter.

### 4.1.7 Modularity in Light of Gricean Pragmatics

The reader will recall that in Section 1.1.5 we discussed the idea of modularity and of the boundary between semantics and pragmatics. Recall that Grice introduces a distinction between what is said and what is implied by an utterance. This looks like a good place to place the boundary between semantics and pragmatics. While semantics would handle the said, pragmatics would handle the implied. While it is tempting to identify the said and the literal meaning, it is now generally assumed that the concept of literal meaning is not tenable in its naive formulation, that is, the proposition conveyed by the sentence. It would be impossible to summarize the highly technical discussion, but in a nutshell, pragmatics is inextricably enmeshed into semantics and even such stalwarts of logical meaning such as determiners (*a, the*), quantifiers (*all, none, at least one*), and connectors (*and, or*), not to mention negation, are affected by pragmatics. In other words, in order to calculate the literal meaning of a sentence, one needs to resort to pragmatics under several guises (the CP or other such principles, context, goals, etc.) so that it makes little sense to try to distinguish between a hypothetical pure semantics and one that incorporates pragmatics.

Various proposals have been put forth to distinguish intermediate categories between the said and the implied, such as explicatures, enrichments, and implicatures, to which we turn next. A related concept is Levinson's Generalized conversational implicatures, which we saw earlier.

*Explicatures* are introduced by Sperber and Wilson (1986) as "developments" that can be inferred by information explicitly said in the sentence (and in this they differ from implicatures, that are not said explicitly). They augment the proposition literally stated in the sentence. Consider the following exchange:

(42) Leona: "Thank you for hiring Regina. I appreciate it."
Justin: "I hired her because she's good, not because you asked me to."
Leona: "Okay, then I don't appreciate it."
(Russell Andrews, 2005. *Midas*. p. 175. New York, NY: Warner books.)

It is clear from the co-text that "it" refers, in both instances to "hiring Regina." This fact is derived from the said of the sentence and does not require accessing any implicit meaning, just resolving the attribution of the referent of the pronoun, in this case. Other related, but distinct terms are *enrichments* (which derive from "I have not had breakfast" → "I have not had breakfast this morning" lest one means one has never had breakfast in one's life and from "I don't drink" → "I don't drink alcoholic beverages"; Récanati, 1989) and *implicitures* (note the spelling), introduced (Bach, 1994) to indicate an intermediate level between the literal meaning of the sentence, which is purely compositional, and implicatures, which are not.

The proliferation of intermediate levels between the literal or propositional meaning of the sentence and its figurative meanings (implicatures) shows that the position that pragmatics is non-truth-conditional meaning (Pragmatics = meaning - truth conditions formula we saw in Chapter 1) is an oversimplification and ultimately untenable. Of course, this makes determining the boundary between semantics and pragmatics difficult, if not impossible, and likewise makes the position that semantics and pragmatics are independent modules untenable. Other approaches, such as Default Semantics (Jaszczolt, 2005), completely abandon the idea of distinguishing a propositional meaning, determined just by syntax and lexical semantics, and instead postulate a "primary" or default meaning, derived in part pragmatically, meant by the speaker as the starting point of inferential work.

## 4.2 Conclusion

Gricean pragmatics has been extremely influential and has in fact helped define the field of pragmatics itself. The basic idea that figurative meaning (implicatures) are derived by reference to some cognitive principles is no longer questioned. The discussion has moved on to the nature of the cognitive principles (relevance, rationality, cooperation) and their components (maxims). The existence of a boundary between semantics and pragmatics is now seriously questioned, due to the intrusion of pragmatics in what was previously thought as the domain of the semantic, so much so that Levinson speaks of a conception of meaning as a "composite notion" (2000, p. 21) and of semantics and pragmatics as "being component processes that offer their own distinctive contribution to a single level of representation" (p. 9).

## 4.3 Applications to SLA

### 4.3.1 Grice in SLA

When we look at the history of this part of the field, in comparison to work on speech acts (Chapter 3), there is far less in SLA and TESOL in relation to the cooperation principle and implicature. This has been particularly true of English language teaching textbooks where Bouton (1994) has argued that "little attempt is made in the ESL/EFL classroom to make learners aware of implicature as a tool of communication or to give them practice at using it in English" (p. 157). Bouton's own work in the area has formed the foundation for the way in which implicature has been approached in both SLA and TESOL so we will begin there. Much of the later work that we discuss is based on his research designs.

Bouton conducted a series of studies spanning the decade from 1988 to 1999. He was interested in whether L2 learners derived the same conversational implicatures in English as native speakers did and believed that in order to do so, L2 learners must have a common perception of (1) the utterance from which the implicature is to be derived; (2) the roles and expectations of the participants in conversation; (3) the context in which the utterance occurs; and (4) the world around them as it pertains to their interaction (1994, p. 89). In an initial study (1988), Bouton focused on developing the materials that he (and many others) would use to test learner understanding in the absence of any specific instruction in the area. Four examples are given here that target different kinds of implicature. In each case, learners are asked to decide what the speaker means:

1. Understated/indirect criticism:

(43) Two teachers are talking about a student's paper
Mr. Ranger: Have you finished with Mark's term paper yet?
Mr. Ryan: Yes I have, I read it last night.

Mr. Ranger: What did you think of it?
Mr. Ryan: Well, I thought it was well typed

2. Sequence of events:

(44) Two friends, Maria and Tony, are talking about what had happened the night before. They had had dinner with Sandy, a friend of theirs, in a little town just outside Philadelphia. Then after dinner Sandy had left. Now, this morning, Maria and Tony are trying to figure out what Sandy did after he left them.
Maria: Hey, I hear Sandy went to Philadelphia and stole a car after he left us last night
Tony: Not exactly. He stole a car and went to Philadelphia.
Maria: Are you sure? That's not the way I heard it.

3. The POPE Q implicature (e.g., Is the Pope Catholic?)

(45) Fran: My mother wants me to stay home for a while, so I can be there when our relatives come to visit us at the beach
Joan: Do you have a lot of relatives?
Fran: Are there flies in the summertime?

4. Irony:

(46) Bill and Peter have been good friends since they were children. They roomed together in college and travelled Europe together after graduation. Now friends have told Bill that they saw Peter dancing with Bill's wife while Bill was away.
Bill: Peter knows how to be a really good friend.

Bouton then conducted longitudinal studies in which the same research method was used to test learners at 17 months, 33 months, and 4.5 years. Although at all levels they performed significantly differently to NSs, there was a gradual improvement over time. At 17 and 33 months, the four types shown earlier continued to be problematic for learners, although relevance-based implicatures such as the following one showed improvement:

(47) Frank wanted to know what time it was, but he didn't have a watch.
Frank: What time is it, Helen?
Helen: The postman has been here
Frank: Okay. Thanks.

At 4.5 years, although there was still a significant difference between the performance of learners as compared to native speakers, the learners had lessened the gap particularly in relation to the kinds of implicatures exemplified above.

Bouton's early work established that culture played an important role in predicting NNSs' ability to derive implicatures. In 1988, he tested English language learners of roughly equal proficiency from seven different groups: German, Spanish/Portuguese, Taiwan Chinese, Korean, Japanese, and Mainland Chinese. All groups of language learners differed significantly both from NSs and from each other. German and Spanish speakers performed most similar to the native speakers and Japanese and Chinese speakers the least.

More recently, studies have addressed the role of learner proficiency and, in general, find that higher proficiency does result in increased comprehension of implied meaning (e.g., Garcia, 2004; Taguchi, 2005). Taguchi (2002) included both responses to the kinds of dialogues created by Bouton and introspective verbal reports with the experimenter in which they explained their choices, for example,

(48) Jim: Hi Mom, I'm home
Mom: Hi Jim. Didn't you get the report card today? How were your grades this semester?
Jim: You know mom, I don't think the teacher grades fairly.
Q: Did Jim get good grades this semester? (p. 171)

Although the higher-proficiency learners did significantly better than the lower-level learners, the introspective protocols showed that this was largely due to an issue of confidence. Lower-proficiency learners had, in fact, often derived the correct meaning; however, they chose the *I don't know* option in their responses. In addition, she found that while both groups of learners used multiple contextual cues to recognize implied meaning, the high-proficiency group reported more use of global strategies, while the low-proficiency group used more background knowledge and keyword inferencing. Kim (2012) also documented the reasoning of high-proficiency learners as they attempted to retrieve implicatures. The participants were Korean EFL teachers who had degrees in English and Kim used some of the scenarios created and tested by Bouton. Two hundred and thirty responses were collected and, although 72% were correct, when learners' explanations were reviewed, it was clear that only 56% of the implicatures were actually understood. This was particularly true of the kinds of implicature that Bouton had previously found to be problematic for learners such as the Pope Q implicature. An example is shown here. The dialogue task is as follows:

(49) Frank is a big sports fan.
Jim: Did you see the game last week?
Frank: Is the Pope Catholic?

(a) Frank saw the game
(b) Frank did not see the game
(c) Frank wants to know if the Pope is Catholic
(d) Frank is more interested in religion than sports. (p. 76)

In the following two responses, the learners correctly picked (a) Frank saw the game; however, their step-by-step reasoning revealed that they started from a far more literal meaning:

Response #1:

Step 1: When people take part in the Pope Catholic's ceremony they can feel it's too long or peaceful, boring
Step 2: Because Frank is a big sports fan, he saw the game and disappointed the game was boring

> Response #2:
>
> Step 1: Frank is a big sports fan
> Step 2: So Frank see all the sorts games if it's not prohibited
> Step 3: Frank thinks only Pope Catholic and prohibit seeing the sports game. (pp. 66–67)

Finally, research has also addressed the role of instruction in the classroom in this area and unanimously found it to be beneficial. Kubota (1995) divided Japanese EFL learners into three groups. Using materials based on Bouton, the first treatment group had explicit instruction in which rules were given by the teacher; the second treatment group was given implicit instruction using consciousness raising tasks; and there was a third control group that received no specific instruction. In post-tests, both treatment groups performed significantly better than the control group. More recently, Cignetti and Di Giuseppe (2015) found that explicit instruction had a positive and significant impact on Argentinian learners' ability to recover implicatures in an EFL context.

### 4.3.2 Relevance Theory and SLA

There has been a substantial interest in RT within SLA. We will follow a few of the strands of research later. For further discussion, see Jodloviec (2010), Culpeper et al. (2018), and Taguchi and Yamaguchi (2019). For a complete bibliography on the subject, see the RT online bibliography.[8] Generally speaking, most RT-inspired work is located within the communicative competence framework. There is also work on pragmatic markers and some aspects of grammar, but we will not examine those in this context.

An early and influential study was Carroll (1995), which pointed out, using RT, that learners when confronted with negative evidence (corrections, recasts, requests for clarification) are faced with a relevance problem, that is, figuring out what, if anything, went wrong. After all, it may just be a problem of, say, ambient noise, and not a linguistic problem. The issue is further discussed in Carroll (2001).

We will begin our review by considering some of the arguments put forth in Foster-Cohen (2000), which helpfully reviews the 1995 second edition of Sperber and Wilson's seminal *Relevance Theory* (1986) and highlights the points of contact between RT and SLA. Foster-Cohen argues that since the learners construct their interpretations of what happens in interactions, logically enough, from their subjective perspective,"RT predicts hearers turn to a metalinguistic interpretation of correction only as a last resort" (2000, p. 84). Foster-Cohen (2000, p. 80) further notes that RT suggests that students will "notice" (Schmidt 1990; Van Patten, 1996) forms based on their quest for maximally relevant input. This is elaborated upon by Nižegorodcew (2007), who, on the one hand, acknowledges that "Relevance Theory cannot answer directly the questions asked by SLA theory concerning the usefulness of L2 classroom input for

8 The bibliography is maintained by Francisco Yus and is categorized by topics, which include a separate "second language acquisition" section. https://personal.ua.es/francisco.yus/rt.html#second

language acquisition" (pp. 20–21) while, on the other hand, she claims that it can be useful because "it elucidates the question of input interpretation" (p. 21). She sees the role of the teacher as that of a "manager" of classroom discourse, and as such "the teacher's input communicates its own optimal relevance in a given function of classroom discourse" (p. 20). Practically speaking, by drawing attention to the formal aspects of discourse away from meaning or vice versa, the teacher can achieve focus on form or on meaning. However, Niżegorodcew advocates a balance between communicative and form-oriented input (pp. 149–150).

Foster-Cohen (2000) further argues that even results that are prima facie antagonistic to an RT approach may be reinterpreted in RT terms. Thus, the finding that repetition and redundancy facilitate understanding (Pica et al., 1987) flies in the face of maximal relevance (since the processing cost of redundant and repetitious information is obviously higher than the processing cost of nonredundant and non-repetitious information, as the present sentence exemplifies). However, if we assume that the NNS is willing to invest extra effort in the hope that full comprehension will yield more contextual effects (i.e., implicatures), then the apparent contradiction is explained away. While Foster-Cohen does not say so, we may add that the NNS may not be in a position to have a choice as to whether they will process redundant information if, for example, their employment depends on understanding a given piece of discourse.

Foster-Cohen (2002) adds further areas in which RT may be useful to SLA. For example, she argues, using developmental evidence from children, that within testing, irrelevant questions relative to a context, redundant information (e.g., repetition), and information organization that does not follow relevance, may cause poor performance. In De Paiva and Foster-Cohen (2004), RT is applied to Bialystok's model of analysis of knowledge and control of processing (1993, 1994) and Schmidt's "noticing hypothesis" (1990, 1993), that is, the idea that one must pay attention to something before they can learn about it ("the conversion of input to intake" 1993, p. 209) and more specifically in the case of pragmatics to form, function, and context. According to De Paiva and Foster-Cohen, RT can contribute "a plausible theory of cognition and communication which operates with a notion of internal context" (i.e., context is a mental representation of the speakers, not an external situation). For more discussion of context, see Section 8.3.

Taguchi's work on the "conventionality effect" (for a full list of references, see Taguchi & Yamaguchi, 2019) has shown that conventionality facilitates processing, because it requires less integration of (multiple) cues from the context in the search for relevance. However, the conventionality effect does not apply to multimedia input, because presumably the multiplicity of inputs dilutes the effect.

Padilla Cruz (2013) extends to L2 pragmatics the concept of epistemic vigilance (Sperber et al., 2010). Epistemic vigilance can be defined as a cautious attitude toward new information. Rather than blindly accepting anything that another speaker says, an epistemically vigilant hearer will be more careful and subject new information to some degree of scrutiny. According to Padilla Cruz (2013, p. 122), "instruction in L2 pragmatics should contribute to the development of learners' epistemic vigilance towards communication in the L2 in order to create in them an alertness to the risks of communication, but more importantly, to the flaws and mistakes that can affect their comprehension and eventually hinder understanding." The idea of epistemic vigilance has gathered significant support; see, for example, recent work by Madella and Romero-Trillo (2019) that applies it to pragmatic processing of yes/no responses interpreted using prosodic, gestural, and facial cues.

Furthermore, we can also mention that RT has been applied to idioms (Bouherar, 2017), Korean learners' difficulties in calculating explicatures and implicatures (Cook, 2012), and finally that Infantidou (2014) claims that explicit instruction helps the acquisition of L2 pragmatic competence. In conclusion, it is fair to say that RT has proven to be a productive application of pragmatic theory to SLA and that it has contributed an original perspective to the field.

### 4.3.3 TESOL Classroom Materials

As we have already noted, in the sense in which they are discussed earlier, implicatures have traditionally remained unaddressed in the TESOL classroom. Thus, coverage has typically depended on individual teachers, the materials that they choose, and how they use them. Bouton (1994) reports some success in an early pilot study in which a small group of students were introduced to several kinds of implicature and then discussed similar examples in their own languages, for example, in China: *Does the sun come up in the west*? Or in Puerto Rico, *Will you have poinsettias at Christmas time?* (p. 102).

Armstrong (2007) suggests that teachers employ consciousness-raising activities in the classroom in which implicature is directly presented and discussed using classroom materials that are already in use. In the example here, the first version is taken from a textbook (*Side by Side*, Molinsky & Bliss, 2002), and the second adapts this example to include a specific implicature:

(50) Version 1:

A: Did you live in Tokyo for a long time
B: Yes. Five years.

(51) Version 2:

A: Did you live in Tokyo for a long time?
B: Yes, an eternity! (Implying that she did not like living in Tokyo) (p. 91)

Abdelhafez (2016) presents a comprehensive example of how effective such classroom presentations might be. Using some of Bouton's test materials, he created consciousness-awareness raising materials that were presented and discussed in 12 4-hour sessions over 3 months. In post-testing, students showed a statistically significant gain in their ability to recognize and interpret some of the traditionally more problematic implicatures such as understated or negative evaluation. An example is shown below:

(52) Lee has spent a lot of money on a new sweater and he asks his friend, Sandy, about it

Lee: How do you like my new sweater?
Sandy: It's an interesting color.

What does Sandy mean?
a. She does not like the sweater
b. She is interested in the color of the sweater
c. She thinks it is a bore to discuss the sweater
d. She thinks Lee is color-blind. (pp. 459–460)

In an initial test, only 11.5% of the participants correctly chose (a); in fact, most of the participants (80%) chose (b), suggesting they were parsing the meaning of the sentence literally. In the post-test, 77.8% of the participants chose the correct answer.

Example (53) focuses on irony:

(53) At a recent party, there was a lot of singing and piano playing. At one point, Matt played the piano while Brian sang. Jill was not at the party, but her friend Linda was.

Jill: What did Brian sing?
Linda: I am not sure, but Matt was playing "Yesterday."

What does Linda probably mean?
a. She was only interested in Matt and did not listen to Brian.
b. Brian sang very badly
c. Brian and Matt were not doing the same song
d. The song that Brian sang was yesterday

As with the previous example, instead of the expected answer of (b), in the initial test the sentence was interpreted literally and most learners chose (a). The post-test showed an improvement from 3.8% to 81.5% correct interpretations.

### 4.3.4 Sample Teaching Materials

In this final section, we will look at two sample lessons that can be used as models for the teaching of implicatures. The first is suggested by Murray (2010) and follows a presentation to practice model. The second is a 90-min lesson plan proposed by Blight (2002), which he created for Japanese learners.

#### Lesson Plan 1: Implicature Lesson Plan (Murray, 2010)

1. Have students reflect on the ways in which overall context influences language use, for example, using prompts such as "Why are we sometimes indirect in the way we say things? Why might the amount we say be important?" Responses may include "If we say very little it might seem unfriendly or rude; Sometimes we lie because we don't want to hurt the other person's feeling" (p. 298)
2. Present dialogues that includes a variety of contexts and different levels of directness, for example, At home:

   A: Tell me what you think of Ali
   B: He's not exactly what I expected

In a university seminar:

A: So what do you think of my approach?
B: I don't like it; it's too direct and I think you're on the wrong track completely
(P. 298)

3. Discuss the differences in the responses and what the speakers' intentions may be in their choices; compare this to learners' L1 language and culture.
4. Practice using role-plays.

### Lesson Plan 2: Implicature Lesson Plan (Blight, 2002)

- Stage 1 (20 min): Present Grice's Cooperative Principle and the four maxims
- Stage 2 (20 min): Provide sample model conversations with multiple possible responses and have students assess the appropriateness of each. For example,

  A: Go anywhere today?
  B: Yes, we went down to Como
  A: Anything to see there?

  Possible responses:

  1. B: Yes
  2. B: It's got a big stone cathedral
  3. B: A city

- Stage 3 (20 min): Discuss each of the responses presented and work through the interpretations of each answer in terms of most likely violations of the CP (e.g., a response of *yes* would violate the Maxim of Quantity).
- Stage 4 (20 min): Expand the discussion to include different examples of conversations and what the most "useful" implicatures might be in each case (e.g., more than one implicature may be possible but as we noted earlier in the chapter, some are recognized as not worth processing).

# 5

# Politeness

## 5.1 Theories of Politeness

We should start with a distinction: it is fairly obvious that there is plenty of non-linguistic politeness, or politeness performed without using language: opening doors, letting people go first, surrendering one's seat for elderly people on public transportation, and many other actions more or less codified. The boundary between politeness and common decency is fluid: is it polite to help someone carrying a large object by opening a door for them or is it just a small kindness? Activities such as letting people go first, helping old ladies cross the street, not mocking people with disabilities, sending holiday cards, and so on likewise may or may not be considered polite, but they are part of a category of pro-social behaviors; the stereotypical nature of these behaviors is deliberately emphasized by our choice of "typical" polite behaviors.

Several areas of demeanor are socially codified (and show the same arbitrariness of linguistic codes: yawning, sneezing, coughing, belching, etc. are defined as "rude" gestures in Western societies). Etiquette, such as table manners, the position of silverware, the sending of flowers, and so on were, at least in some social groups, heavily codified and are still a marker of socioeconomic privilege.

We are interested in and will primarily deal with linguistic politeness, which is not the same thing as politeness at large, despite Lakoff's (1973, p. 303) claim that the rules governing both of them are the same. This point should be kept in mind while reading the rest of the chapter. Ultimately, politeness, like many other such categories, such as irony, madness, game, or leisure, is a "folk-concept" not to be confused with its scientific definition. For example, "madness" has no scientific or legal standing in the United States, where the courts use the term "insanity," which is defined in the penal code. As for psychology, they use the terms "psychosis" and "psychopathology." So the folk definition of politeness should not be confused with the scientific definition of politeness. In order to distinguish between the folk concept of politeness and its scientific definition, they have been relabeled Politeness1 and Politeness2, respectively (Eelen, 2001; Watts, 2005).[1] In this chapter we will

1 Of course, it is quite clear that Politeness1 influences the definition of Politeness2 (Terkourafi, 2011).

*Pragmatics and Its Applications to TESOL and SLA*, First Edition. Salvatore Attardo and Lucy Pickering.

deal primarily with Politeness2, and so we just refer to it as "politeness," but the reader should keep in mind that ours is a treatment of the theories of politeness, not of Politeness1.

### 5.1.1 Classical Politeness Theories

The linguistic interest in politeness is relatively recent and coincided with the birth of pragmatics as a discipline. The first theories of politeness that were developed share some significant features: they are all formulated within a broadly understood Gricean framework and specifically they share the rationalist and universality stance of Gricean pragmatics. Among the classical theories, the three we have chosen to present garnered the most following. Broader reviews of theories can be found in Kasper (1990), Held (1992), and Eelen (2001).

**Robin Lakoff (1973)**

Lakoff's approach to politeness is explicitly based on Grice's cooperative principle, which had been circulating in mimeographed form since its first presentation in 1969. The influence of Grice can be seen even in the formulation of the theory that consists of two rules, the first of which is Grice's CP, renamed as a "rule of pragmatic competence" under the heading of "be clear" (Lakoff 1973, p. 296). Lakoff explicitly states that the "be clear" rule follows from Grice's CP (p. 297). The second rule is "be polite," with three further specifications, which yields the following schema:

- Be clear (from the CP; Grice 1975)
- Be polite
  - Don't impose
  - Give options
  - Make H feel good, be friendly.

Lakoff sees politeness as a flout of the CP governed by a "politeness rule," which the speaker chooses rationally: if one wants to merely communicate, then one just follows the CP; however, if one wants to "navigate (...) among the respective statuses of the participants" (p. 296), then one's goal is no longer clarity but politeness, which Lakoff describes as the "opposite" of clarity. Politeness, in most cases, "supersedes" clarity (p. 297).

This may seem counterintuitive, but is in fact quite correct. Consider the following advice from an etiquette website:

(54) Compliment the host[...] if you like the food, but don't voice your opinion if you don't.
https://www.thespruce.com/table-manners-and-dining-etiquette-1216971

Suppose now that you did not like the food and that the host asks you: "How did you like the food?" If you want to follow the advice in (54), you should remain silent, which is of course not good advice, since it would inevitably be followed by even more pressing questions. So your best option is to either flat out lie (which is of course against Grice's CP) and say "I loved it," or obfuscate, for example, by saying that you have never eaten anything that tasted quite like it. Lakoff is quite right then that politeness is the opposite of clarity or the CP at large: the point of politeness is not to be truthful, clear, and to the point, but rather to obscure and hide one's true feelings or to display feelings one is not experiencing, as in greeting someone one doesn't particularly care for. This type of talk is often called "phatic communion" (see Section 6.1.1).

Lakoff's stance is universalistic, that is, the rules listed earlier are present in every culture, but their ordering may differ, and so some cultures may emphasize one strategy over another: American culture notoriously leans toward camaraderie (make the hearer feel good), whereas European cultures tend to lean toward distance (don't impose). An example of this can be found in a depressing anecdote: during the Korean war a British officer found himself and his men surrounded by overwhelming force and reported the situation to his UN superior, an American general, as *Things are a bit sticky, sir,* ("don't impose"), which led the general to assume that things weren't that bad and therefore not to send reinforcements or have them withdraw. This caused a major battle in which thousands were killed. According to other officers, if the British officer had reported the situation as *all hell breaking loose here, sir* (camaraderie, directness), the American general would have appreciated the severity of the situation (Ezard, 2001).

**Penelope Brown and Stephen Levinson (1978/1987)**

Brown and Levinson's theory of politeness has had the most success in terms of influence and widespread adoption. Indeed, it is also the most theoretically developed one and so we will examine it in more detail than any other theory in this chapter. Brown and Levinson's discussion has two starting points: Goffman's idea of face and Grice's rational cooperation.

Goffman's notion of "face" (1955) is central to Brown and Levinson's discussion, so we need to elucidate it in some detail. Let us start by saying that, "face" has nothing to do with facial expression. Face, for Goffman,[2] is the "image of [the] self," a "positive social value," a "good showing," or the "impression" others have formed of the speaker (1955, p. 222). So, the definition of face is a self-image one claims and negotiates in public. An individual may "have," "gain," "lose," or "maintain" face. In short, Goffman introduces both the conceptual apparatus of face and the terminology adopted by Brown and Levinson of face-work (p. 226), face saving, and threats to face (p. 227).

Concerning Grice's rational conversational model, we will not repeat the discussion in Chapter 4, so we will limit ourselves to noting that Brown and Levinson see face-work as rational (Brown & Levinson, 1987, pp. 64–65) and predicated on a means/ends strategy and specifically including a capacity to optimize, that is, capable to determining the best option. In other words, they see politeness as part of a theory of actions, governed by a rationality principle (pp. 84–91) in which agents make choices, albeit not necessarily conscious ones, predicated on their assessment of the cost/benefits of the choices and their foreseeable outcomes.

Brown and Levinson expand on Goffman's distinction between"presentational" and "avoidance" rituals (Goffman, 1967, p. 62) with the concepts of positive and negative face. Positive face is anything that builds up the ego or the social standing of the speaker. It corresponds to the desire to be well-regarded or even admired or "to have [one's] wants to be

2 A somewhat broader discussion of Goffman's influence on interactionist sociolinguistics and pragmatics can be found in Section 8.1.1.

desirable" (1987, p. 62) to the other agent. Conversely, negative face is the desire not to have one's time and attention impinged upon, or as Brown and Levinson put it, "the want (...) that his[/her] actions be unimpeded by others" (p. 62). Negative face could be also paraphrased as the desire to be left alone and to act as one pleases. As such, compliments, displays of interest in the other, and small gifts and generally showing care attend to positive face, as they have the goal to make the recipient feel good about themselves, while apologies, displays of deference, and preemptively offering options that include making excuses and even that of refusing a request, all tend to negative face, since they tend to minimize the imposition on the other.

Brown and Levinson introduce the idea of the "face-threatening act" (FTA). An FTA is any action that causes a potential damage to the face (positive or negative) of a speaker. For example, asking for something is an FTA because it is an imposition on the hearer who has to either deny the request (thus having to engage in an FTA) or grant it and thus go against his/her desire not to be imposed upon. While asking for something may not necessarily be an FTA, for example, if the hearer was well disposed to giving it anyway, as, for example, the stereotypical grandparent doting on their grandchild will gladly provide sweets to said grandchild. Others are inherently face threatening, such as correcting errors or rejecting a potential romantic partner.

The point of politeness then is to minimize the risk faced by a speaker who has to produce a face threat (p. 60). Note that Brown and Levinson say that politeness minimizes and not eliminates face threats. Some FTAs are such that the damage to the hearer's face cannot be avoided. To put it simply, there is no sufficiently polite way to say to someone either "you are wrong" or "I don't find you attractive" such that it will erase the stigma of the act.

When faced with the need to produce an FTA, the speaker has a number of strategies available, which Brown and Levinson summarize in a decision tree (Figure 5.1).

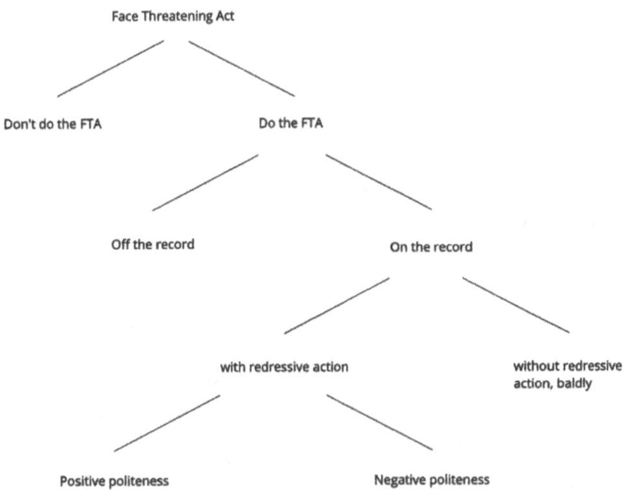


**Figure 5.1** FTA strategies; adapted from Brown and Levinson (1987, p. 69).

Essentially, the agent can choose to forgo the FTA entirely, if they judge that the cost/benefits ratio is not favorable and obviously that is the less risky strategy or they may do the FTA on or off the record. On the record is explicitly stating or very strongly implying the FTA, for example, saying *Can you loan me $50?* is an on the record FTA, because the speaker explicitly mentions the loan. This is the riskiest strategy, which involves no reduction of risk. Conversely, an off the record FTA would be hinting at one's financial problems: *Damn, I am out of cash, I forgot to go to the bank today* (Brown & Levinson, 1987, p. 69). On the record FTAs may be performed "baldly," that is, without trying to lessen the face threat. The stereotypical expression: *Dad/mom, can I borrow the car?* uttered by American teenagers in the age of single-car families is an example of bald on the record FTA, probably motivated by the assumption that the parents will readily acquiesce. The other option is for the speaker to perform the FTA using either positive or negative politeness. Positive politeness tends to the positive face of the addressee; consider example (55)

(55) stockme43: Red flags? Since you [overachiever] are the expert and seem to have insight!

which comes from the investing website InvestorsHub. "Red flags" is stock trading jargon for "reasons of concern" about a company's financial stability. So the user stockme43 is asking the user overachiever, who had written a previous post about a penny stock company, for any signs of risk (everything is relative, penny stocks are dangerous to begin with and that particular one had been delisted from the stock market, which is a pretty big red flag). In order to mitigate the FTA of asking for evidence, stockme43 points out the expertise and knowledge of overachiever. This has also the side effect of minimizing the imposition, because experts are supposed to have much knowledge and hence are more likely to impart it freely (*noblesse oblige*).

Negative politeness, as one would expect, tends to negative face. Mostly that consists in giving people an out, that is, "escape" options to avoid the FTA. Consider the following example,

(56) A.83 (...) and so I don't use drugs any more.
B.84 Oh, what kind of drugs did you use, if you don't mind? (Switchboard corpus: sw_0053_2184)

which comes from the Switchboard corpus; recall that these phone conversations took place between strangers. It is widely considered intrusive of one's privacy to inquire into one's drug habit (past or present), so speaker B literally gives A a way out, using the conventionalized formula *if you don't mind*, which, formally at least, leaves the door open to speaker A to say: *As a matter of fact, I do mind, sorry*. As Brown and Levinson point out, to a large extent these exchanges are formulaic and ritualized, or as they put it, it "pay a token bow to the negative-face wants of the addressee" (1987, p. 71).

The rest of Brown and Levinson's book is dedicated to reviewing various strategies and their interactions with social factors in three languages: an important point to note, in light of some of the criticisms leveled at the Brown and Levinson model, which will be examined in the next section, is that the theory relies on extensive data collection in English (British and American), Tzeltal, a Mayan language spoken in Chiapas (Mexico) and South Indian Tamil. While it is a very rich and interesting discussion, we cannot follow it in any detail, due to space limitations. Nonetheless, if one is to sum up Brown and Levinson's contribution to the research on politeness, one cannot but agree with Sifianou and Antonopoulou's (2005) observation that "despite valid or invalid criticisms, Brown and Levinson's theory has served and still remains a significant springboard for research on politeness phenomena" (p. 263).

#### Geoffrey Leech (1983)

Leech posits a Politeness Principle (PP), obviously modeled on Grice's CP, down to the maxim couched as imperatives format, stating that the speakers should "minimize the expression of impolite beliefs" (p. 81), and its converse, albeit "somewhat less important" (p. 81), maxim enjoining the speaker to "maximize the expression of polite beliefs."

For Leech, the PP is on a par with the CP and has the same capacity to generate implicatures, so in the following example

(57) A: We'll all miss Bill and Agatha, won't we?
B: Well, we'll all miss Bill (Leech, 1983, p. 80)

Leech argues that B could have provided a more informative statement to the effect that they will not miss Agatha, but "only at the cost of being more impolite" (p. 81) and that therefore B chose to follow the PP and provide a less informative but more polite statement.

The PP has six maxims, here slightly rephrased for clarity:

1. tact: minimize cost to other and/or maximize benefits to other
2. generosity: minimize benefit to self/maximize cost to self
3. approbation: do not criticize others/praise others
4. modesty: minimize self praise/maximize self-criticism
5. agreement: minimize disagreement/maximize agreement
6. sympathy: minimize antipathy and maximize sympathy with other (Leech 1983, p. 132).

Leech's theory is significantly weakened by the theoretical profligacy of adding principles and maxims to account for various behaviors: besides the maxims already listed, Leech considers a few more politeness maxims, including a phatic maxim (p. 141) "avoid silence/keep talking." Besides politeness, his model calls for

1. An Irony Principle (p. 82) and a Banter Principle (p. 145), which describes a sort of second-degree irony in which one uses ironically and ironical utterance, thus in fact intending to communicate the non-ironical meaning of the utterance.[3]
2. An Interest Principle: "say what is unpredictable, and hence interesting" (p. 146), which accounts for over and understatements (*I told you a million times* is clearly more interesting than *I told you four times*).
3. A Pollyanna Principle "prefer pleasant topics of conversation to unpleasant ones" (p. 147).

3 This is the "double negation affirms" principle at work. Irony scholars live short, brutish lives.

The reception of Leech's approach almost universally has been negative and his proliferation of principles, which are often redundant, even in their wording, has been ridiculed. This is unfortunate, because his approach, and especially his treatment of politeness, has much to be recommended. For example, the duality between self and other orientation of politeness is unquestionably on target.

Finally, let us note that Leech notes that cross-cultural differences in politeness have not been sufficiently addressed (recall that he writes in 1983), but that his framework may help this investigation by showing that different cultures rank some maxims higher than others: for example, Leech claims that English-speaking cultures give more prominence to the maxim of tact and the irony principle, whereas the Mediterranean culture places more emphasis on the generosity maxim.

**Indirectness**

Besides the theoretical underpinning of the Grice-Goffman rational model of the polite agent, the classical theories share a focus on indirectness as both an indicator and a tool essential to "doing" politeness: when Lakoff notes that being unclear is better than being impolite, or Brown and Levinson note that performing openly an FTA is the least polite way of doing so, they end up equating politeness with indirectness. Indeed, this is quite an attractive stance. Consider the following options to request a book:

(58) Give me the book.
Please, give me the book.
Could you please give me the book?
Would you mind giving me the book?
Would you consider giving me the book?

in which increased indirectness conveys increased politeness/face repairs. The same can be said of mitigation; for example, *Could you give me the book* **for a minute**? where the **bolded hedge** minimizes the request: the speaker will return the book after a short time; hence, the imposition is minimal.

### 5.1.2 Second Wave Approaches (1990 and Forward)

Despite or maybe because of the significant accomplishments of the rational theories of politeness and especially Brown and Levinson's face-based model, around 1990 a number of criticisms started to coalesce into a set of significant challenges to the conceptualization of politeness, which ended up amounting to calls for a new paradigm. This new paradigm has been referred to as the "postmodern" or "discursive" approach (e.g., Kadar & Culpeper, 2010), because of its emphasis on interactional discursive data, as opposed to fabricated or decontextualized examples.

However, Eelen (2001) is probably the discussion that had the most impact on the re-evaluation of theory of politeness, even though Kasper (1990) already includes an explicit discussion of impoliteness and distinguishes between politeness as rational strategic reduction of conflict and politeness as social indexing, which are precisely some of the issues that Eelen will focus on a decade later.

According to Eelen (2001), what we have here defined as classical politeness theories, and in fact quite a few other theories of politeness that we have not considered for reasons of space, suffer from a set of fundamental problems. These are as follows:

1. A confusion between folk-theories of politeness (Politeness1) and scientific theories of politeness (Politeness2). Politeness1 is what the speakers say is polite, Politeness2 is a theory, produced by a researcher. Politeness1 is always evaluative, whereas Politeness2 shouldn't be, for example (p. 44). Often, researchers confuse these levels.
2. The almost exclusive focus on politeness and the corresponding neglect of impoliteness. In other words, researchers talk about politeness but ignore the equally interesting and important notion of impoliteness, which is reduced, a priori and without appropriate examination, to simply the negation of politeness (p. 95).
3. The focus on the speaker's following maxims or more generally norms and the corresponding neglect of the hearer's role in recognizing and evaluating politeness (p. 98).

Eelen proposes replacing the underlying theoretical mechanisms (maxims, principles, etc.) of the classical theories with a more sociolinguistic approach, based on French sociologist Pierre Bourdieu and especially his notion of *habitus*, that is, a "disposition" inculcated in the speakers' minds by a lifetime of practice of the cultural rules prevalent within their socioeconomic (i.e., class-related) conditions in a given society (see Section 10.4.1). This approach has, in Eelen's view, the advantage of handling directly ideas such as power and class as they relate to politeness.

Held (1992) notes that the focus on face and indirectness in the classical theories has led to the neglect of other areas of politeness, such as (social) status relations, the observation of social rules and conventions (*wakimae*, see Section 5.1.2), politeness as "supportive" relations, conflict avoidance, and the emotive aspects of politeness. Furthermore, Held notes that an aspect neglected by the classical theories is the degree of formulaicity and ritualization of politeness. As we will see, this aspect will be taken up in more detail in the third wave theories of politeness (e.g., Terkourafi, see Section 5.1.3). The problematicity of the concept of face is further brought to light by the work of Locher and Watts (2005) who argue that face is only one aspect of a broader concept of politeness (see Section 5.1.2) and that Brown and Levinson have produced a theory of face work, not of politeness at large. For example, Culpeper, when dealing with impoliteness (see Section 5.1.3) adopts a broader scope than face and considers all the "work done by speakers to tend to their relationships."

The discursive approach to politeness is openly antagonistic to the classical theories, essentially arguing that one should focus on discourse (interpersonal interaction), rather than on politeness, or as Watts puts it:

> a shift in emphasis away from the attempt to construct a model of politeness which can be used to predict when polite behaviour can be expected or to explain post-factum why it has been produced and towards the need to pay closer attention to how participants in social interaction perceive politeness.
>
> (*Watts, 2005, p. xix*)

The reliance on the assessment of the speakers, as it happens in discourse, yields a "data-driven, bottom-up approach" (Locher and Watts, 2005, p. 16). Note incidentally how this is consonant with Eelen's criticism that classical models of politeness privileged the speaker. The focus on the discursive interaction also allows us to account for variability of judgments of politeness across culture but more importantly within cultures. It is often the case that two participants to the same exchange may disagree on the politeness evaluation of a given exchange. This is a major problem for theories based on general cognitive principles, as all speakers should be equally aware of these principles. Hence, the focus on the negotiation of the politeness status of the utterances.

However, there is a price to pay for this emphasis on the perception of the speakers in the discourse situation. Haugh has presented a critical review of these claims. He concludes that the criticism of the discursive approach to politeness theory essentially ended up throwing away the baby with the bath water. While a focus on naturally occurring conversational/interactional data always good practice, Haugh argues as early as (2007) that there is a basic problem: if one does not have a theory of politeness to guide one's decisions of what counts as polite in the data, then one inevitably will end up basing that decision on one's opinion or practice. This problem is mirrored in the discursive turn theorists' rejection of politeness2 theories entirely: "The essence of the discursive challenge, then, is that a theory of politeness is neither necessary nor desirable" (Haugh, 2007, p. 297) and likewise abandons "any attempts to develop a universal, cross-culturally valid theory of politeness altogether" (Haugh, 2007, p. 297). Indeed, Watts (2005) ends up defining politeness as "a slippery, ultimately indefinable quality of interaction" (Watts, 2005, p. xiii).

Related to the desire to produce analyses closer to the participants perceptions and just as critical of the classical theories Mills (2003) is, a feminist criticism of the politeness theories, firmly rebutted in (Holmes, 2005; Holmes & Schnurr, 2005), who is also critical of the discursive turn, along the same lines.

#### Surplus vs. Appropriate Politeness

Locher and Watts (2005, but see also Watts, 1992) broaden the scope of politeness to relational work, which they see as broader than face work, as it includes the negotiation of any interpersonal relationship (2005, p. 10), and not merely of the public image (face) of the speakers. Locher and Watts (2005) note that the dichotomy polite/impolite, and the consequent assumption that all that is not polite is impolite, is an oversimplification. Behavior may be polite, impolite, or neither. The intermediate status is not-polite but "politic" or "appropriate" (on appropriateness, see also Section 5.1.2). For example, in an East End pub a request worded as

(59) A pint of lager.

would not be perceived as impolite, but merely as appropriate. Excessive politeness, such as the following request, still in the same setting

(60) Could I bother you for a pint of lager?

would be considered as over-polite and thus mocking (Locher & Watts, 2005, p. 12). So, there are in fact four types of (im)polite behavior, summed up in Figure 5.2. Note how over-politeness borders with impoliteness.

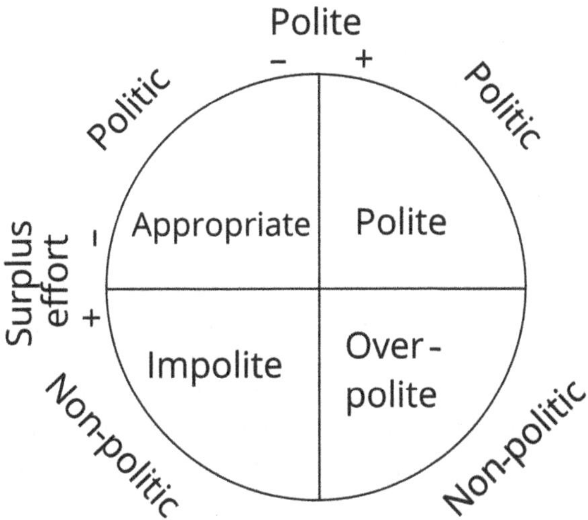


**Figure 5.2** Degrees of (im)politeness and types of polite/politic behavior.

Classical theories of politeness only consider the "Positive Politeness" side, whereas relational work broadens the scope of (im)politeness studies to all four categories.

Thus, politeness is seen as marked and a surplus of effort vis-à-vis unmarked politic behavior, which is merely appropriate. As we saw, excess of politeness, for example, a very formal request among close intimates, is perceived as inappropriate and hence as either impolite or ironical:

(61) Father to his teenage daughter: "Would you consider straightening up your room, if it's not too much effort?"

which is clearly inappropriate and marked, vis-à-vis the normal

(62) Clean your room!

On the opposite side of the spectrum, the other non-politic and inappropriate behavior is open aggression/rudeness. Consider the following extract from an interview between Jon Stewart, Paul Begala, and Tucker Carlson on the Crossfire show, hosted by Begala and Carlson. Stewart is the guest.

(63) STEWART: It's not honest. What you do is not honest. What you do is partisan hackery. And I will tell you why I know it.
CARLSON: You had John Kerry on your show and you sniff his throne and you're accusing us of partisan hackery?
STEWART: Absolutely.
(CNN Crossfire, Oct 15, 2004) https://www.youtube.com/watch?v=ZjgZ_Vr_K2E

The exchange comes after several turns with the argument becoming increasingly heated. Stewart accuses the Crossfire hosts of being dishonest and partisan hacks and

Carlson counters by accusing Stewart of being too soft on the democratic candidate (Kerry). "Sniff his throne" is obscure, but is probably a synonym for brown-nosing. What is significant here is that Stewart first explicitly attributes two negative qualities (dishonesty and hackery) to his interlocutors and when challenged, "antes up," so to speak, by saying that he is doing so "absolutely" rather than deescalating the conflict. Both attributing negative characteristics and escalating conflict are impolite, socially inappropriate, and hence negatively marked and non-politic.

**Cross-Cultural Validity**

One of the major criticisms of the classical theories is the lack of cross-cultural validity of their claims. We can start from the easily discerned fact that folk-theories of politeness (Politeness1) vary across cultures (e.g., Sifianou 1993) and even subcultures: consider how politeness rituals may be different at your local tavern and on the floor of your state legislature. Various studies, for example, Blum-Kulka and Olshtain (1984) and Blum-Kulka et al. (1989), compared different realization patterns (see Section 3.1.3) for apologies and requests. The cultural and cross-cultural differences in realization can still be analyzed in terms of face-work, relativized to the culture in which the exchange takes place. For example, as we saw in (Section 3.1.3), in Polish (Wierzbicka, 1985) and Italian it is acceptable when talking to close associates to use a bare imperative to request something, so a teacher may say to a student, *Give me the book.* In American English, this is considered impolite and a mitigated form, such as *Please, give me the book* must be used. One can argue, for example, that Polish and Italian value directness and familiarity more than negative politeness (do not bother the interlocutor).

However, there have been claims that cross-cultural differences cannot be reduced to face-work and need other concepts. One such concept is the idea of norms. The classical theories can certainly be reworded as injunctions to follow a socially established norm. The example of relativizing the use of imperatives with or without mitigation is essentially that. Proposals involving centrally the idea of norms are Gu (1990) based on Japanese culture and Lakoff and Ide (2005).

**Individual vs. Community-Based Societies**

Another claim of incompatibility of cross-cultural politeness practices with the face-based classical theories is the difference based on cultures that are based on the idea of the individual (such as Western cultures) and cultures that are based, on the contrary, on the ideas of a social-self. Among these theories, Ide's work has enjoyed particular prominence.

Ide popularized the concept of *wakimae* ( わきまえ ; Ide, 1989, 1992) a Japanese term that can be paraphrased as "discernment" (1992, p. 298) or "linguistic politeness" (Ide, 2012, p. 121). Crucially, *wakimae* is defined in terms of "appropriateness" to a society (1992, p. 298). Hill et al. (1986), who introduced the concept in Western discussions of politeness, define it as "the almost automatic observation of socially-agreed-upon rules" (p. 348) and note that it extends to non-linguistic politeness. Ide stresses that wakimae is not merely observation of social norms, it is "intrinsically obligatory" (p. 299). *Wakimae* consists of a repertoire of obligatory choices, much like in English one has to necessarily mark the tense of the main verb as past/non-past (present) (Ide, 1992, p. 301). These markers, called "honorifics," are clearly organized around a distinction between an ingroup and an outgroup. According to

Ide (2012), the ingroup/outgroup distinction in Japanese is different from the similar distinction in English, insofar as the ingroup overlaps in part with the self in Japanese, whereas there is a clear boundary between self and ingroup in English (p. 128).

The system of Japanese honorifics is very complex, but an example is given here:

(64) *Taro ga byooki da*
Taro is ill

which contrasts with

(65) *Taro ga byooki desu*
Taro is ill (polite)

Note the form of the copula *da/desu*. In other words, what is strikingly different here from English or other Indoeuropean languages is that the morphology of the copular verb grammatically encodes the distinction between neutral/polite. The example clearly shows that honorifics are used in Japanese also outside of FTAs, as there is nothing face threatening about either (64) or (65).

#### Forms of Address

There is no question that there is a significant difference between the individualistic cultures of the West and the community-based cultures of China and Japan, for example. However, one can question whether the differences are so radical. After all, some Western languages have a similar set of distinctions in the pronominal system. In the Romance languages the so-called T/V pronouns convey a familiarity/solidarity vs. formality/distance social dynamic (Brown & Gilman, 1960; T/V is short for Latin *tu/vos* taken to be representative of the set of pronouns. There are some differences in individual languages). English, having lost the thou/you distinction, resorts to other means to encode the same dynamic, using forms of address: thus First Name (FN) vs. Title + Last Name (TLN) encodes more or less the same meanings. Different cultures privilege the solidarity/familiarity side over the formal/respectful/distance side. Another personal anecdote will convey the cultural differences involved: when Attardo first met his advisor, Victor Raskin, he obviously addressed him as Dr. Raskin (TLN). Upon being informed by Raskin that his preferred mode of address was FN, Attardo proceeded to avoid addressing him at all for about a year, despite almost daily interactions, because he felt uncomfortable doing so informally and therefore disrespectfully, in Attardo's eyes.

#### Conclusion: The Second Wave's Critical Stance

Summing up, we can identify a few common instances of the postmodern/discursive approaches to politeness: first and foremost, the second wave approaches criticize or flat out reject the classical rationalist, face-based approaches because of the excessive emphasis on the speaker's intentionality. Instead the second wave theories put an emphasis on the evaluation of the hearers, in a "relational shift" (Kádár & Haugh 2013, p. 50) and focus on relationships (rapport/emotions) among speakers. A related criticism is the emphasis on negative face in the classical theories, with the consequent neglect of the positive face strategies (make people feel better). Even further, they advocate for "disentangling" of face and politeness: Not all face has to do with politeness (Kádár & Haugh, 2013, p. 51). Furthermore, the artificial, decontextualized examples, the stress on individualism (politeness is an individual choice by an agent) that is associated with a Western bias, as other cultures, such as the Chinese or Japanese put more stress on the social communal good. Finally and possibly the most widespread criticism is the assumption of universalism of the classical theories, which comes under widespread criticism and which we address in what follows.

### 5.1.3 Third Wave Theories: Ritualization and Norm

Terkourafi (2005a) explicitly positions her work as a synthesis between the first and second wave of theories of politeness and at the same time as going beyond both, by proposing a theory based on frames and contextualization. Terkourafi starts out by rebutting most of the second wave theorists methodological claims. Essentially, Terkourafi concludes that by the second wave theories' own standards, the second wave theories fail to produce a new theory of politeness and in fact seem content with mere descriptive work (see also, Haugh, 2007, for a similar assessment). Terkourafi's work is based on a corpus of naturally occurring conversational data, but the regularities are investigated using frames (cf. Section 1.1.2).

Returning to the idea of norms, Terkourafi notes that

> On the one hand, traditional theories assume the existence of norms a priori, hence they do not bother engaging in quantitative analyses of the data. On the other hand, post-modern theories challenge current understandings of norms, pre-empting the value, or indeed the possibility, of quantitative analyses.
>
> *(2005a, p. 246)*

Unlike the classical and the postmodern theories, the frame-based theory she proposes generalized norms from the statistical occurrence of patterns in the data (p. 247).

In other words, the polite nature of a given expression emerges from the data, thus answering one of the main concerns of the postmodern theories, concerning the confusion of levels between politeness1 and 2; furthermore, by noting the acceptance of the expression by the interlocutor, evinced by the lack of challenge, the frame-based approach addresses the other concern of the prioritization of the speaker. In Terkourafi's approach, the hearer is given equal status theoretically:

> the regular co-occurrence of particular types of contexts and particular linguistic expressions as unchallenged realizations of particular acts that creates the perception of politeness. Politeness resides, not in linguistic expressions themselves, but in the regularity of this co-occurrence.
>
> *(Terkourafi, 2005a, p. 248)*

Of note also is the claim that the linguistic expressions per se are not polite or impolite, but it is the regularity of the association, hence a social process, that makes them so. This stance allows Terkourafi to bring back the idea of rationality, since the speakers can perform a given act of politeness/impoliteness only if they expect their interlocutor to recognize it and hence ratify it, which means that they rationally must choose those expressions, idioms, and so on that are socially accepted. Or as she puts it:

> the speaker's *individual* rationality is constrained on this occasion by a *societal* rationality which has pre-cast, so to speak, for him/her the universe of possibilities into a range of concrete choices.
>
> (*Terkourafi 2005a, p. 249; emphasis in the original*)

In other words, politeness is just as socially constructed as are language and, crucially, conversations. Therefore, in her view, politeness is not so much a matter of calculation, but rather a matter of norms and frames, which store the expressions, and their associated values of politeness, this becoming the embodiment of Bourdieu's *habitus* (cf. Section 10.4.1). See also Terkourafi (2005b).

Thus, in conclusion, Terkourafi successfully combines elements of the classical theories (face and rationality) with the concerns of the postmodern theories (reintegration of the hearer's perspective, negotiated social interactionist perspective, the idea of *habitus* and norms). She also incorporates novel ideas, such as the emphasis on idiomaticity and the idea of frames that store the various expressions and their associated politeness levels.

#### Impoliteness

I'm taking pride in telling you to fuck off and die
*(F.O.D., Green Day, 1994, Dookie)*

As we saw, one of the major criticisms of the classical theories of politeness was their neglect of the idea of impoliteness. Because of the significance of the issue, we deal with it in a separate section. What little explanation there was in the classical theories consisted in the idea that if one was not polite, then one was impolite, that is, a derivative definition based on the lack of politeness. More recent theories instead focus more on impoliteness as an active behavior. For example, there can be no question that the quote from the Green Day song used as the epigraph of this section is extremely rude and impolite, as it references sexual intercourse and wishes for the death of the hearer. It is simply impossible to consider this as *lack of* politeness. The speakers of these and similar expressions are actively, cheerfully even, engaging in aggressive, impolite behavior.

Taboo language (see, e.g., Jay & Janschewitz (2008); Beers-Fägersten & Stapleton (2017) on swearing) has obviously strong negative connotations, but the situation is further complicated by the fact that native and non-native speakers use of taboo forms (expletives, swearing, etc.) is perceived differently (Dewaele, 2004, 2010).

Culpeper (1996) was the first major study of impoliteness. He begins by noting that some behaviors are inherently impolite, such as drawing the attention of a driver who has left their windshield wipers on despite the lack of rain, to this fact (p. 351). The reader will recall that some FTAs also end up being inherently impolite insofar as no amount of politeness can eliminate the inherent threat to the face of the hearer. However, a more interesting angle is to examine situations in which one participant has more power than the other, such as an employer/employee relationship. Clearly the employer enjoys a greater freedom from having to respect the face wants of the employee, especially in the negative politeness side, that is, the employer by definition will tell the employee what to do. The lack of capacity to retaliate make these situations power-asymmetrical. Culpeper examines an interaction between a soldier and two sergeants, in which the sergeants bully, intimidate, and insult the private soldier, who remains mostly silent. When taking place between equals, situations such as exchanges of insults or open face threats may escalate easily, up to physical violence.

While innovative, this study still remains largely within the Brown and Levinson classical face-work framework. Culpeper (2010, 2011) shows that impoliteness is much more complex and depends on a host of factors that include among others, the intention of the speaker, the perspective of the person who is offended, the relationship of both relative to the ingroup/outgroup dynamic (e.g., it is acceptable for a member of the ingroup to disparage humorously the ingroup, but not for a non-member; in simpler terms, Attardo can tell jokes about Italians, but Pickering cannot, and vice versa), cultural expectations, the severity of the infringement on rules, and much more. Culpeper (2010) looks at formulaic impoliteness, expanding Terkourafi's work on formulaic politeness to impoliteness.

Despite this, as Culpeper (2015) acknowledges, the study of impoliteness has suffered from remaining tied to the idea of impoliteness-as-not-polite. There have been attempts to link impoliteness to the transgression of norms in a community of practice (Mills, 2005), but the most promising approach is that of considering impoliteness in interaction. Bousfield considers impoliteness in interactions taken from British reality-TV shows (2007), he notes that

1. impoliteness is triggered by what is perceived to be a threat to some aspect of the impoliteness utterer's face (p. 2190)
2. responses to what is considered here an *offending situation* can also be, themselves, considered as *offending situations* (p. 2195; emphasis in the original)
3. conclusions, which may include the submission of the aggressed party, compromises, standoffs, in which neither party succumbs, or withdrawals, in which one party abandons the communicative exchange entirely, usually by leaving the scene.

The following is an example of withdrawal, from Bousfield (2007, p. 2212), in which a corporal has been addressing recruits in the barracks about their poor performance:

(66) S1: IT'S NOT GOOD ENOUGH [storms out slamming the door]

Bousfield describes the final turn as "withdrawing in a manner which indicates that he's not entirely happy" (p. 2212), which is another example of British understatement (cf. Section 5.1.1).

### 5.1.4 Universality of Politeness

Lakoff and Ide (2005) point out that any generalization of universality should be made very carefully and tentatively. This is true of all universal claims, but perhaps more so for politeness, because the phenomena relative to politeness can only be fully appreciated from a cultural insider perspective. This is a fair point. However, the classical theories of politeness come with a built-in claim at universality, that is, that they are founded on the rationality of human beings, which is a universal trait.

There is a healthy debate, which is far from being settled, on the existence of universal politeness. Probably most scholars will agree that the existence of politeness itself is a universal. The question then becomes, are there different politeness systems in different cultures?

On the one hand, some scholars believe that there are different culturally bound systems of politeness, for example, Matsumoto (1988); Ide (1989); Gu (1990); Spencer-Oatey and Jiang (2003), and so on. We will look at this in more detail in the rest of the chapter. On the other hand, some major dissenting voices are Leech (2005) and Brown (2015) who argue that, on the contrary, the underlying principles of politeness are universal (e.g., face work).

While there are real theoretical differences between these proposals, it is possible that the disagreement is in part a matter of emphasis: we need to distinguish between "surface" politeness (culture specific) and "deep" politeness (universal or very broadly applicable). Consider the example of thanking behavior. Gratitude is widely believed to be universal (Bonnie & DeWaal, 2004; Sidgwick, 1907; Taylor, 1989). We can thus assume safely that expressing gratitude, that is, thanking, is very widespread across cultures, if not a universal. However, there are many ways of thanking someone, not the least by saying something, such as *thank you*, *merci*, *grazie* , *danke*, and so on. Let us however focus on gestures.

Consider Figure 5.3 and contrast it with Figure 5.4

**Figure 5.3** Thanking gesture in Indian culture.

**Figure 5.4** Thanking gestures in other cultures.

The gesture used to express the idea of gratitude may be different in Western, Indian, and other cultures, much like the lexies vary across languages, but the idea of thanking is roughly the same. Thus, when discussing the universality of politeness, we must distinguish between a deep politeness trait, say "respect for the elders" and the ways in which it is expressed (reserved seating, deference). An intercultural anecdote may well convey the "feel" that different cultures have in this respect. Attardo once collaborated with a Chinese visiting scholar who was much younger than him (she could easily have been his daughter). At some point, she presented him with an idea. Attardo responded that the idea was probably wrong, but that if she wanted to test it out anyway, a good way to do so would be such-and-such a test. A few weeks later, the visiting scholar came back with a set of results, which, upon analysis, showed that the idea was entirely correct. Attardo praised the visiting scholar's ingenuity and concluded: "You were right." This, to his surprise, the visiting scholar vehemently denied, arguing that Attardo had been right. After trying to convince her otherwise for a while, Attardo ended up giving up when he realized that most likely culturally imposed respect for the elders or for teachers was motivating her refusal to admit that Attardo had been wrong and she had been right. The difference here seems to be a matter of degree: Western society certainly mandates some degree of respect for the elders, but obviously a Chinese/Confucian 孝 (xiào) does so to a much greater extent.

Many of the results in cross-cultural studies of politeness can be explained as cultural differences in emphasis: for example, Fukushima and Sifianou (2017) find that Greek and Japanese female students use the same concepts to describe politeness (consideration of others and appropriate behavior; p. 534) , but in different proportions and that only the Japanese students mention honorifics. The fact that honorifics are mentioned by Japanese subject is not surprising, since Japanese morphologically marks honorifics, whereas Greek does not; Greek behaves like other Western languages in this (see Section 5.1.2).

### 5.1.5 Sociopragmatics and Power

An aspect of politeness, which has received less attention than such concepts as face or norms, is the inherent in-group/out-group function of politeness and its connection with power and, in Western society, with the opposition between the people (*vulgus* → vulgar) and rural inhabitants (*villa* → *villano*; "uncouth" Italian), on the one side, and the inhabitants of the "of the cities, or of the court," in short, the moneyed elites, on the other. Politeness is associated with the upper class and their behavior as opposed to the vulgarity of the poor people.

Scholars, primarily Western scholars, have tended to see politeness as a positive social force facilitating interactions and smoothing social life. However, a different point of view is also possible, closer to the scholars that see politeness as a set of norms to be followed, which see politeness as a mechanism to create an in-group and more significantly to oppress an out-group (Watts 1992, p. 47).

#### Power Differential

Yabuuchi's proposal is a universalist approach, an unpopular stance in 2006, as he himself acknowledges, but his claim is that by augmenting Brown and Levinson's model with hierarchy politeness, the model may account for all systems of politeness. Simplifying a little, Yabuuchi's model can be represented as follows:

1. fellowship politeness = positive politeness
2. autonomy politeness = negative politeness
3. hierarchy politeness

Yabuuchi claims that hierarchy politeness corresponds, in part, to a sincerity parameter (p. 331). In other words, surplus politeness (see Section 5.1.2) does not become impolite, it becomes ingratiation and/or flattery, which is obviously insincere, unlike positive politeness. Essentially, Yabuuchi argues that power differentials motivate both positive or negative politeness that is insincere and thus in excess of what one would provide to one's peers, or in other words, people "ingratiate upward" (p. 339).

Power differentials play off differently in collectivist/hierarchical societies (e.g., Japan) and individualist/solidarity-oriented societies (Western societies): "Upward deference tends to be exaggerated (therefore insincere) in collectivistic societies and minimized in individualistic societies" (Yabuuchi, 2006, p. 344). Hence, according to Yabuuchi, deference, that is, ingratiation of the superior, ends up being the distinctive feature of Japanese society, in opposition to the United States, for example.

## 5.2 Conclusion

Overall we can assess the discussion as having undergone three phases: a first theoretical phase in which the Brown and Levinson face-based model emerged as the most widely accepted theory. A second critical phase followed in which the scope of politeness theory was broadened both to impoliteness and to relational work. This phase is distinguished by a general reluctance to theorize. Furthermore, criticisms of cultural bias pushed away from the universalist stance of the classical models and led to the inclusion of other perspectives, primarily drawn from Asian cultures, such as *wakimae*, ingratiation, deference. These theories have been labeled discursive or postmodern (Eelen, Mills, Watts, Locher). A third phase, itself critical of the postmodern and discursive theories, and particularly of their refusal to even have a theory of (im)politeness, accepts the broadening of the coverage of politeness to include impoliteness and relational work, but at the same time stresses the need for theories (Haugh, Terkourafi) and applies insights from corpus linguistics and frame theory.

## 5.3 Politeness and SLA

Similar to speech acts, the investigation of politeness and particularly Brown and Levinson's concepts of face and levels of directness have been well represented in the SLA literature. There is also, of course, a clear overlap here between the two areas. For example, a request form that is "bald on record" may be perceived by an interlocutor as very impolite if they were expecting the use of a more indirect linguistic strategy.

From the outset, however, there have been many questions regarding the cross-cultural validity of some of these concepts and how this is managed by L2 learners from very different cultures. Matsumoto (1988), for example, states that "the Japanese concepts of face are qualitatively different from those defined as universals by Brown and Levinson" (p. 405). She proposes that the concept of negative face (i.e., the desire not to have one's time or attention impinged upon) is not as salient in cultures in which each member of the society is seen not as an individual but primarily as a member of a group who stands in a particular relation to other members of the group. As an example, she considers a standard expression of deference in Japanese that in the Brown and Levinson model would be a way of addressing negative face (i.e., minimizing imposition on the hearer). Roughly equivalent in function to nice to meet you, the expression *doozo yorosiku onegaisimasu* translates as *I ask you to please treat me well/take care of me*, a direct request that would seem to imply a high level of imposition. Within Japanese society however, Matsumoto argues that this acknowledges the interdependence between the interlocutors and thus the "seeming contradiction between deference and imposition" vanishes (p. 410). Gu (1990) similarly argues for a redefinition of negative face in the Chinese context. He notes that activities that are classed as FTAs in the model as they impose on the hearer (e.g., insistent offering or inviting a hearer to do something) are, in fact, considered to be polite and important evidence of a speaker's sincerity. He instead argues for his own Politeness Principle that prioritizes "denigration of self and elevation of the other" (p. 248). These examples clearly show that despite the best will in the world to be perceived as polite, L2 learners may come to even the most basic interactions with much different ideas of what, in fact, constitutes politeness.

There is a robust area of literature that attempts to disentangle some of these differences by labeling cultures as either primarily oriented toward positive politeness or, conversely, negative politeness, that is, as preferring one aspect of face over the other. Scollon and Scollon (1995, p. 37) refer to these as a preference for involvement strategies (positive politeness) or independence strategies (negative politeness). Involvement strategies highlight group membership (e.g., *all of us here...or I know just how you feel*), while independence strategies highlight the independence of the individual (e.g., *I'm sorry to trouble you but ...* or *I'm sure you're very busy but...*). Table (5.1) lists some of the generalizations that have been made in the literature (Ogiermann, 2009; Palivdou, 1994; Scollon & Scollon, 1981, 1995; Sifianou, 1992)

**Table 5.1** Cultural orientation toward negative or positive politeness

| Country | Prefers... |
|---|---|
| Britain | Independence strategies |
| German | Independence strategies |
| Chinese | Involvement strategies |
| Greece | Involvement strategies |
| Japan | Involvement strategies |
| Russia | Involvement strategies |

These can be used as a very rough guide to understanding why some linguistic formulas may be more likely to be used by native speakers than others. For example, as we saw, Polish has a high use of involvement strategies (Wierzbicka, 1985); thus, it is acceptable when talking to intimates to use a bare imperative to request something, for example, a husband might say to his wife *Get me the pan.* In English, which has a higher use of independence strategies, this lack of mitigation would probably be considered rude, and a spouse may say *Can you get me the pan (please)*? In the case of Polish, over-politeness, in fact, may be viewed as a face threat in the sense that it may be seen as mockery or as insincere (see Chapter 2 also).

Pickering, who is from the United Kingdom, a culture that has been recognized as having high use of independence strategies, has always responded badly to direct "pre-invitations" such as *Are you doing anything on Saturday?* In this case, the threat lies in the fact that the hearer does not know what they are about to be asked, that is, how high is the level of imposition going to be? A more direct approach is far more preferable, for example, *I'm about to ask you a huge favor and that's fine if it's not possible, but on Saturday I was wondering if....* Of course, these are broad generalizations; however, Scollon and Scollon (1981) suggest that "the patterns we are describing hold true in a general way and are the patterns on which people have developed ethnic stereotypes" (p. 13).

SLA research in politeness has also typically followed the division between pragmalinguistic and sociopragmatic development. As we noted in Chapter 3, pragmalinguistic development goes hand in hand to some extent with increased grammatical competence. It goes without saying that the more forms you are familiar with, the more language you have to work with and the fewer routines and formulas you may transfer from the L1 to meet a contextual or situational need. In a foundational article on pragmatic development, Thomas (1983) describes an example of pragmalinguistic transfer from Russian to English. The word *konesno* (of course) in Russian means enthusiastic agreement (e.g., are you coming to my party? Of course!). L2 learners may transfer this formula into English in cases where it is not appropriate and could sound insulting:

(67) A: Is it a good restaurant?
B: Of course! [Gloss for Russian speaker: Yes, indeed it is. Gloss for English hearer: What a stupid question!] (p. 102)

In contrast to pragmalinguistic development, sociopragmatic development requires increased knowledge of the sociocultural norms of a given speech community (e.g., social distance, rights vs. obligations, etc.). In this case, Thomas uses an example that highlights different perceptions of the size of an imposition between societies. She uses Goffman's (1967) difference between "free" or "non-free goods"; that is, in a given society, access to things that are perceived as "free" requires the least elaborate politeness strategies, whereas access to those that are seen as costly (non-free) requires more elaborate facework. At the time, Thomas lived in Russia where cigarettes were extremely cheap and could be asked for without fanfare (e.g., give me a cigarette!). Coincidentally, Pickering also lived in the Eastern Bloc, in Hungary, and can attest to the same situation. However, Hungarians who moved to the United Kingdom at that time would have been considered extremely rude if they transferred this notion as cigarettes were certainly seen in Britain as more costly and thus as "non-free goods."

A more recent study, Nguyen (2008), examined the way in which Vietnamese EFL learners gave criticism to each other as compared to native speakers of Australian English. All participants performed a writing task and then received peer feedback from each other. They also took part in retrospective interviews with the researcher. From a pragmalinguistic perspective, the Vietnamese learners produced less mitigated linguistic disagreement strategies than their Australian counterparts. For example, *I don't agree* (Vietnamese learner) vs. *I wouldn't necessarily agree with you* (Australian English speaker). Turning to sociopragmatics, Nguyen notes that there was a substantial difference between the two groups in using advice-giving strategies that the learners considered as a polite way of giving criticism but which were generally not used by the native speakers. In the retrospective interviews, the majority of the L2 speakers noted that this was a common approach in their society: "Vietnamese people usually advise one another, seniors advise juniors, people of the same age advise one another. This is a good way which is accepted by the society. It is soft" (p. 63).

Ogiermann (2009) further notes that in some cultures, rather than being associated with rudeness, directness is associated positively with honesty and openness. Conversely, heavy use of indirectness is associated negatively with deliberate obfuscation or potential deviousness. This is nicely demonstrated in a study by Savic (2016) who interviewed novice EFL teachers in Serbia about their perceptions of differences in politeness between Serbia and America. One of her interviewees who had participated in a five-month study abroad program in the United States stated that they felt that Americans are *too* polite:

> I would say that generally they are more polite than here; but sometimes you don't know what they're thinking; which I don't like. Sometimes they are so polite that it seems hypocritical.
>
> *(pp. 221–222)*

### 5.3.1 Politeness in the TESOL Materials

As with other areas of pragmatics in the classroom that we have seen, the prevailing view is that there has been a dearth of classroom materials with which to teach the pragmalinguistic and sociopragmatic aspects of politeness, particularly for EFL students (LoCastro, 1997). There are several consistently recognized critiques. First, that there is a lack of contextualization in the presentation of materials that makes it almost impossible to decide on the correct approach. As we have noted throughout, asymmetrical power relations, social distance, and perceived weight of imposition are all critical considerations in a speaker's choice of linguistic strategy. Materials designed for English for General Purposes (as opposed to materials for English for Specific Purposes) frequently underspecify these contextual variables and leave students with few choices. Nguyen (2008), for example, notes that many of his Vietnamese learners reported that they had learned only one way to express (dis)agreement regardless of context: "From the beginning I learned the verbs 'agree' and 'disagree', so when I want to express my agreement and disagreement I just say 'I agree' or 'I disagree'" (p. 62).

Second, that there is a focus on formulae and routines addressing pragmalinguistic issues but comparatively little information given with regard to sociopragmatic concerns. Limberg (2016) examines a number of textbooks used to teach English to German secondary students and finds that while there are plenty of examples of routine phrases and expressions to indicate politeness in English, there are few examples of context-based considerations and "the focus lies on formal aspects and learners are not asked to reflect upon language choices based on social constraints" (p. 285).

Finally, a lack of authentic and audio-visual materials has led to a primary focus on morpho-syntactic concerns and significantly downplays the role of prosodic features such as intonation and stress and nonverbal cues such as smiling and gestures. In a related anecdote, Pickering usually discourages Attardo from making requests to American waitstaff as they are almost always put off by his lack of smiling and eye contact despite his utterly correct grammar.

Before we close, it is interesting to consider how and whether impoliteness should be addressed as a classroom topic. As we noted in Chapter 2, troublesome areas of language such as taboo topics or swearing have typically been left out of language learning syllabi. However, Mugford (2007) proposes that this creates a "Pollyanna EFL world" (p. 375) and suggests that a discussion of impoliteness has an important place in the classroom. In order to conduct a kind of needs analysis for this kind of information, he interviewed both L2 learners and teachers in Mexico to ask if they had experienced impolite behavior in their L2. His participants had experienced multiple examples of flagrantly impolite FTAs ranging from impolite requests from strangers (e.g., *Move, move* to an L2 user in the way when walking along the pavement) to statements of blatant racism (e.g., *I don't want my son eating tortillas and beans*). As a result, Mugford proposes that both teachers and students need help in "extending their functional competence in order to deal with L2 impoliteness" (p. 382) and offers some thoughts on how such materials might be developed.

### 5.3.2 Sample Teaching Materials

Both these lesson plans come from the following website: https://americanenglish.state.gov/resources/teaching-pragmatics, which has freely available materials for download and immediate use in the classroom. These come from an edited collection (Bardovi-Harlig & Mahan-Taylor, 2003).

**Lesson Plan 1: Howard (2003) "Politeness is more than 'please'"**

This comprises two one-hour lessons for Japanese Intermediate learners of English and follows the typical presentation to practice model.

1. Have students discuss the following kinds of questions and reflect on whether the responses by native English speakers would be the same: Why should we be polite? How should we be polite? When and to whom should we be polite?
2. Give the students business letters in Japanese and in English. Have them note the differences/similarities between how politeness is expressed in each language.

3. Have the students practice working on the difference between direct and indirect expressions:

   (a) Match a set of direct and indirect expressions.
   (b) Guess the situations and speakers in which each expression might be used in the target language.
   (c) Give the students direct expressions and a situation and have them write the indirect equivalent.

**Lesson Plan 2: Barsony (2003) "Actually, Steve, the deadline was Friday of last week, not this week..."**

This lesson focuses on polite ways in which a speaker can correct or contradict their interlocutor. It is a 50 minute lesson designed for intermediate or advanced students.

1. Take a resource such as the following dialogues and present them first without softeners (e.g. actually) and then with softeners; have the students reflect on the difference in overall impression:

   Do you mind if I smoke?
   I'd rather you didn't

   Do you mind if I smoke
   Well actually I'd rather you didn't

   Where in the States do you come from?
   We're not Americans; we are Canadian.

   Where in the States do you come from?
   Actually we're not Americans; we are Canadian.

2. Students practice with open-ended conversations.
3. Students may also compare strategies between their native language and English.

# 6

# Functional Sentence Perspective

This chapter deals with the way information is presented in a sentence and a paragraph. This is known as functional sentence perspective (FSP). The main idea behind this distinction is that within a sentence there is new information (roughly, what the sentence tells us that we did not know already) and old information (roughly, what the new information is about). So, to use a very simple example, in

(68) Mary is asleep.

Mary is assumed known information (in other words, we know who this person is; she is part of the shared context). Indeed, we could replace "Mary" with the pronoun "she," which refers to Mary. Obviously, if we use the sentence, like we just did, out of context, we would not know who Mary is referring to, but in real life, for example, if Mary is the daughter of a couple who's been trying to put her to sleep for the past hour, *She's asleep* is perfectly contextualized. The couple would know who's the "she." Conversely, "asleep" is the new information, something that we did not know about Mary. We will call these two components, theme and rheme, respectively. So, "Mary" is the theme of the sentence and "asleep" is the rheme. Needless to say, all these concepts, "new," "known," "aboutness," and so on, need to be further specified and the rest of the chapter will attempt to do so.

## 6.1 Theoretical Background

### 6.1.1 Functionalism

Our discussion must start with a discussion of the term "functional." We can characterize a functional approach to language as holding two core tenets:

1. The main function of language is communication; there may be other functions, such as phatic communion, but they are secondary and derivative. Phatic communion is essentially making sure that the channel is working and the signal is coming through – a good example is back channeling; see Section 6.1.1.
2. Language is not a self-contained modular entity as a whole; it is determined by a number of factors including:

*Pragmatics and Its Applications to TESOL and SLA*, First Edition. Salvatore Attardo and Lucy Pickering.

- cognitive, for example, the preference of speakers for minimal effort;
- social, for example, the desire of speakers to index language use to social groups (see Chapter 7);
- physical, for example, mechanical facts such as the breathing patterns of humans or the physical limitations of the vocal apparatus; and
- historical, for example, language change.

The first point is central and functionalism in general gets its name from the emphasis on this aspect of linguistic communication. The second is more reactive and serves to distinguish functionalism from other approaches to language that privilege formal, syntactic aspects. It should be noted that not all functionalist approaches adhere to the rejection of a modular view of language (see Section 1.1.5).

**The Six Functions of Language**

Bühler (1934) introduced the idea of linguistic signs having three functions which correspond to the orientation toward a specific aspect of the communicative situation.

- the expressive function (expression of emotions), oriented toward the feelings of the speaker.
- the referential function (the connection between the sign and its referent; see Section 1.1.2), oriented toward the context the sign refers to.
- the conative function (addresses the hearer directly: e.g., orders), oriented toward the addressee.

Jakobson (1960) expanded the model to six functions. He introduced the following three functions:

- metalingual (metalinguistic) function, oriented on the code (language in our case)
- the poetic function, oriented toward the text itself (i.e., the message), and lastly,
- the phatic function, oriented on the contact (see below, for a short discussion).

This leaves us with the set of functions mentioned in Table 6.1.

**Table 6.1** The functions of language.

| Bühler | Jakobson | orientation |
|---|---|---|
| Referential | Referential | Context |
| Expressive | Emotive | Addresser |
| Conative | Conative | Addressee |
| n/a | Phatic | Contact |
| n/a | Metalingual | Code |
| n/a | Poetic | Message |

Jakobson's formulation has enjoyed widespread acceptance and the functions have become widely used. In particular, the metalinguistic function is crucial to the idea of metapragmatics (see Chapter 10). Jakobson's model can be represented as in Figure 6.1.

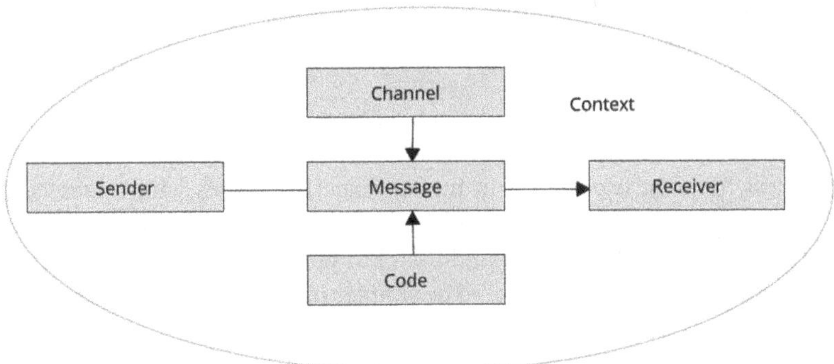


**Figure 6.1** Jakobson's model.

**Phatic Communion**

Phatic communion is concerned with keeping the channel of communication open. Pragmatically, beyond back channeling, such as saying "uh-huh" while listening, it takes the form of small-talk among strangers or intimates that has no telic (goal-oriented) purpose other than ensuring that the interactants feel acknowledged. Discussing an argument devoid of any major significance,[1] such as the weather, or sports, is a typical example of phatic communion. The term comes from Malinowsky (1923).

## 6.1.2 Markedness

What is markedness? What does it mean that some linguistic feature is marked or unmarked? In simple terms, a marked feature is a special case, which is somehow different from the normal form. Ice cream is probably the best example to grasp intuitively the concept of markedness: everyone knows that vanilla is the default ice cream, at least in the United States. If one asks for ice cream without further specification, one will get a scoop of vanilla. All other flavors (chocolate, strawberry, etc.) are marked, that is, not the default. They need to be especially requested.

Consider now a linguistic example, greetings. The unmarked, normal form is that a greeting is reciprocated, as in

(69) A: Good morning!
B: How are you today?

this is an expected response, so much so that if the dialogue had gone differently, as in (70)

(70) A: Good morning!
B: Uh...
A: Is something wrong?

A's reaction to the lack of response would appear entirely justified.

1 Except in unusual circumstances such as the approach of a bad storm.

So, clearly markedness has to do with lack of normalcy and unexpectedness. We can be more precise, however. Moravcsik and Wirth (1986) provide an excellent definition:

> There is [...] a three-way correlation [...] among *familiarity, variability*, and *complexity*. Closer familiarity tends to be paired with simpler structure and greater variability; less frequent occurrence in human experience goes with increased structural complexity and diminished variability. People tend to see familiar objects simpler in structure and more varied in kind than less familiar objects; and they tend to make things that are in common use to be simpler in structure and more variegated than those in less common use.
>
> (*p. 2; our emphasis, SA/LP*)

Linguistically speaking, this is clear in the fact that in most languages the singular form is morphologically simpler than the plural. The singular is also more frequent than the plural (think of *I* and *we* in English). The singular has more differentiation than the plural: consider the English pronouns, which are highly differentiated in the singular *he/she/it* and not at all in the plural *they*. So, in conclusion we would say that the singular is unmarked and the plural is marked, in English at least. In this chapter, we can make use of a fairly intuitive use of the term, whereby if we compare the following two sentences:

(71) a) Mary went to the store.
 b) To the store is where Mary went.

(71.a) is unmarked and (71.b) is marked. The reader can easily verify that (71.a) is simpler, more frequent, and more familiar than (71.b).

### 6.1.3 Word Order

Consider again example (68). We discussed how differences in choice of the full name or the pronoun, or in prominence may affect the way we interpret the sentence. We now consider how the order in which the words are arranged may also affect our interpretation. However one may object that

(72) *is asleep Mary.

is just ungrammatical (as indeed the * indicates). This is true, as far as English goes, but in other languages this is not the case. For example, in Italian both (73.a) and (73.b) are possible,

(73) a. Maria dorme.
 b. Dorme Maria.

although admittedly (73.b) is restricted to literary contexts. Be that as it may, in Latin both (74.a) and (74.b) are equally possible.

(74) a. Puella dormit.
 b. Dormit puella.

The technical term for this cross-linguistic difference is that English is a fixed word order language, whereas Latin has a freer word order. Italian would be somewhere in between. However, even languages such as Latin that have relatively free word order still have a preference for a certain order. Moreover, marked constructions, such as emphatic fronting, for example, may alter the preferred word order (e.g., *The bread, you ate!*). Traditionally, languages such as English are described as SVO, whereas Latin is an SOV language. The majority of the world's languages fit this pattern, but there are languages in any word order combination, even the rarest, which is OSV (e.g., Xavante, a language spoken in the Amazon basin, in South America).[2] So, *Paul eats bread* would appear as follows:

| Subject | Verb | Object |
|---|---|---|
| Paul | eats | bread |

whereas in Latin it would be:

| Subject | Object | Verb |
|---|---|---|
| Paulus | panem | edit |

There are even languages that have free word order, that is, in which any position is grammatically acceptable, albeit with different frequencies and pragmatic functions (on which more below). The best-known example is Warlpiri, an Australian aboriginal language. So, one may wonder how do speakers of Latin or Warlpiri distinguish between two sentences such as

(75) a. Mary kissed Paul
b. Paul kissed Mary

After all, in the example of Paul eating bread, there is no problem understanding because the semantics helps us out: it is unlikely that we mean that the bread is eating Paul. Conversely, in (75) either person could be the agent or the patient, the kisser or the kissee. The answer is morphology. Languages such as Warlpiri and Latin have relatively rich morphologies that most importantly indicate the case[3] of the nouns involved. In order to see this, we need to consider again the Latin example, using interlinear translation. This notation explicates and translates a sentence morpheme by morpheme. In what follows we give a significantly simplified version.

| | **Paulus** | | **panem** | | **edit** |
|---|---|---|---|---|---|
| (76) | Paul- | -us | pan- | -em | ed-it |
| | Paul | Nom + sing. | bread | DO + sing. | eat +3rdp. sing. |
| | *Paul eats bread* | | | | |

2 This is why when the makers of Star Wars wanted an "exotic" word order they made Yoda speak an OSV language. Linguists' humor.

3 Simplifying significantly, case is the grammatical/semantic role played by an argument in a sentence. Case grammar (Fillmore, 1968) is the fundamental reference on case.

As you can see from the interlinear glosses, the morpheme *-us* indicates that Paul is the subject (Nominative case) and singular, bread is the Direct Object (Accusative case), and the verb is in third person singular, matching its subject, as required in Latin. This is why word order is freer in Latin: you don't need to rely on the position of the words in the sentence (i.e., syntax) in order to reconstruct the case structure of the sentence. The morphology conveniently does the job for you, which then affords much more freedom of moving things around for effect. In fact, Latin would allow also any permutation of the order of the words. As we will see, languages use this freedom to express pragmatic meaning. Even English, with its fixed word order, does this. We will consider how in Section 6.3.3.

### 6.1.4 Prominence

We turn now to the last topic that needs to be introduced to be able to understand FSP. So far, all that we have said applies to both written and spoken language. However, in spoken language we have the additional resource of intonation, and specifically, prominence. Unlike written language, speech is not divided into sentences but into tone units (also often called "thought groups" or "sense groups" in the TESOL literature). These are units that we recognize as having an equivalent function to that of sentences in writing, and units are created by the speaker based on their perception of one idea or piece of information, for example, *I'm going to Florida*. Each unit is indicated by double vertical bars, as in example (80):

(80) // I'm going to Florida//

Within each unit, not every word is given equal weight. The speaker will typically assume that pronouns and prepositions, for example, are understood by the hearer (e.g., we wouldn't say *at Florida*) so these don't receive any intonational prominence. But Florida is definitely new information (e.g., *where are you going? I'm going to FLOrida*), and going may also be new (e.g., *what are you doing? I'm GOing to FLOrida*) thus these words receive intonational prominence on the lexically stressed syllable (indicated by the CAPS). Hearers "follow" the prominences to understand the important, or new, information that each spoken unit contains. The more important information a given unit contains, the more intonational prominences it will contain. Typically, in English, units comprise three to seven words and contain one or two prominences. Some examples are shown below from an Introduction to Psychology lecture from the MICASE corpus:

(77) //so if you WANna talk about evolutionary THEory// you HAVE to start with Charles DARwin//...//DARwin set off to COLLege// and INItially// his PLAN was to become a medical phySIcian// but he didn't STICK with that very LONG// (LEL500JU034)

## 6.2 Aspects of FSP

We are now in a position to explain how the information structure of the sentence (a.k.a. FSP) works. As we will see, FSP is a complex phenomenon that is the outcome of the interplay of the factors we just introduced: intonation, word order, the context in which the sentence is uttered, the communicative function of language, and obviously the semantics of the words used in the utterance.

### 6.2.1 Newness

The starting point of communication is that the speaker wants to convey some idea to the hearer. They must thus assume that the hearer does not already know this, that is, this is new information. For example, it would be very odd for Attardo to call Pickering on the phone to inform her that her name is Pickering, because as we all know, one is usually aware of one's name, barring special situations such as massive amnesia. However, speakers do not assume that the hearer knows nothing. Chafe puts this remarkably clearly:

> At any moment in a discourse, however, the speaker cannot be ignorant of the fact that the addressee already has certain other things in his[/her] consciousness. The speaker knows he[/she] is not introducing material from his[/her] own consciousness into an empty vessel, but that his[/her] task is to introduce new things into a consciousness (the addressee's) which already has some content. The trick is to arrange the new material so that it will be readily assimilated within the material the addressee's consciousness already contains. The speaker must make assumptions as to what the addressee is conscious of, and transmit his[/her] own material accordingly. Virtually every sentence a speaker utters is a mixture of what [...] the speaker assumes is already in the addressee's consciousness, and NEW material, which he[/she] assumes is not.
>
> *(Chafe, 1974, p. 112; capitalization in the original, SA/LP)*

Chafe further elaborated the newness dimension in three levels of consciousness (i.e., the degree of the speaker's awareness of a given idea or thought):

1. Focal: Active information, that is, present to consciousness. Active knowledge is in short-term memory (which was famously measured by Miller (1956) in $7 \pm 2$ units). An example of this would be information that the speakers are actually attending to in the speech act.
2. Peripheral: Semiactive; intermediate knowledge, while not in focus, is easily retrievable and easily activated. The immediate context of an utterance is in semiactive state. For example, when two people are talking, the environment in which they do so is generally not that relevant and is thus ignored, unless something in the context (say, a crying baby) becomes more salient (and thus draws the speakers' attention to itself).
3. Unconscious: Inactive; inactive information is stored in long-term memory, below the threshold of consciousness; it takes a long time to activate. Examples would be the names of your friends in elementary school, a recipe you have not cooked in years, or the definition of logarithm from high school (assuming you learned it!).

Chafe maintains that it is "impossible to understand the distinction between given and new information without taking consciousness into account" (1994, p. 72). Thus, for example, in Hamlet's soliloquy, Ophelia is not focal at the beginning, while he ponders whether "to be or not to be," but she is definitely semiactive (peripheral) because the two interacted a few scenes before and Hamlet is in love with her. Should the text mention the Spanish inquisition next, the effect would be jarring (and humorous) because it is not part of the context (since no one expects the Spanish inquisition). However, when Ophelia interrupts Hamlet's monologue, her presence is obviously not a newly introduced idea, since it was part of the context, but it is nonetheless "new" in the sense that it is not part of the active focal consciousness.

The next step is to realize that because of the tripartite structure of consciousness, there are "activation costs" to be borne, when moving information from long-term memory to focal status, to the point that there may be a perceivable lag in the processing of the text.

Returning to the activation costs Chafe notes that "Language works best when the expression of activation costs is listener-oriented" (p. 75) or in other words, that the speaker has to take into account what the hearer's situation activation-wise is, or risk not being understood. Chafe notes that both new and accessible information are expressed with "accented full noun phrases," whereas given information is "expressed in a more attenuated way," that is, often a weakly accented pronoun or in languages such Italian, where the pronoun can be omitted, by omitting it entirely (p. 75).

### 6.2.2 Known-ness

We have considered a generic sense of retrievability, along the lines of how easy is it to find the information. However, a more specific distinction has been made between information that, while shared by the interlocutors, is not retrievable from context and shared information that is retrievable.

Context can be divided into two parts: the context at large, basically the situation in which the exchange takes place (for a more detailed discussion, see Section 8.3), and the co-text, which is the rest of the discourse in which a given utterance occurs.

#### Prior Mention in Discourse

Consider the Sherlock Holmes story *The Sign of Four*. In a passage in the novel, Holmes has left and, as Watson and Jones (another character in the story) are in Holmes' study, a noise is heard on the stairs:

(78) A heavy step was heard ascending the stair, with a great wheezing and rattling as from a man who was sorely put to it for breath. Once or twice he stopped, as though the climb were too much for him, but at last he made his way to our door and entered. His appearance corresponded to the sounds which we had heard. He was an aged man, clad in seafaring garb, with an old pea-jacket buttoned up to his throat. His back was bowed, his knees were shaky, and his breathing was painfully asthmatic. (...) He came across sullenly enough, and seated himself with his face resting on his hands. *Jones* and I resumed our cigars and our talk. Suddenly, however, Holmes's voice broke in upon us. "I think that you might offer me a cigar too," he said. We both started in our chairs. There was Holmes sitting close to us with an air of quiet amusement. "Holmes!" I exclaimed. "You here! But where is the old man?" "Here is the old man," said he, holding out a heap of white hair. "Here he is, – wig, whiskers, eyebrows, and all. I thought my disguise was pretty good, but I hardly expected that it would stand that test." "Ah, You rogue!" cried *Jones*, highly delighted. (chapter IX)

Obviously, Holmes has been introduced in the story before this scene, and moreover he is the main character of the novel, so he is clearly part of the context and fully retrievable, however, as far as the text goes, when the old man wearing sailor clothing appears, that this is Holmes is *not* retrievable from the immediate context (the scene in the book) and thus completely new. Conversely, that the speaker uttering *ah, you rogue* is Jones is also new (insofar as it informs us of who said those words), but the presence of Jones is fully retrievable from co-text (we have italicized the two occurrences of his name, to facilitate recognition).

How long does an item mentioned in the text "last" in the active buffer (short term memory)? Firbas notes that the permanence of a co-textual element is about seven clauses (1992, p. 23); however, he also notes that the "retrievability span" can become less distinct and almost obliterated due to the length of a text and the constant influx of new referents. (p. 30). Speakers ensure that an extended text/conversation holds together on one topic, mostly by using repetition. Repetition can take several forms such as:

1. Repetitions of names, cf. (78) above, in which "Holmes" and "Jones" are both repeated.
2. Anaphoric (pronominal) chains, as in example (78) and *the aged man* is referred to by "his" and "he" repeatedly. These sequences are called anaphoric chains, because all the items in the chain refer to the same referent. Chains can be extensive and use pronouns, hyperonyms, synonyms, and other substitutions, provided the referent is identifiable. Halliday (1967, p. 296) points out that, after the first mention, thematic information tends to be referred to through anaphoric chains (though he does not use the term).
3. Ellipsis, which does not actually mention the item, but evokes it syntactically, as in *Mary went to the store and [...] to the gym* where the [...] marks the ellipsed element ("went").
4. Synonyms, which repeat many of the semantic content of the referent: for example, in (78) the *aged man* becomes *the old man.*

These are are all means of ensuring retrievability, essentially by keeping the referent in the retrievability span. An apt metaphor would be juggling balls: in order to keep the balls in the air, from time to time one has to grab each one and throw it back up. This aspect of textuality is usually called cohesion (Halliday and Hasan, 1976)

### 6.2.3 Definiteness

#### The Definite/Indefinite Article Opposition

The distinction between indefinite and definite article signals the degree of retrievability of the referent and thus correlates with thematicity and rhematicity. The definite article tends to signal known and hence thematic information, whereas the indefinite article tends to signal new, unknown information. Consider the following example,

(79) **A** boy walked in the room. **He** was wearing a red jacket. **The** boy stood by the window.

Note how the text switches from the indefinite article, indicating that we are not previously acquainted with the boy, to a pronoun ("he"), which co-refers to the NP, and then repeats the NP but with a definite article indicating that this is the boy we are familiar with, who was introduced in the first sentence.

In a naturally occurring conversation, we can see the same pattern, albeit in a more complex context:

(80) B.115 utt3: do you go see a lot of musicals? /
A.116 utt1: Just, + just ever so often –
B.117 utt1: Yeah. /
A.118 utt1: – D you know, **a** real, + **a** real good one like that one /
A.118 utt2: and, -/
B.119 utt1: That, + that would be, + that would be nice <laughter>. /
A.120 utt1: I went and saw, uh, I think it was, uh, SUGAR BABIES, /
A.120 utt2: that was good, /
A.120 utt3: that had good music in it. /
B.121 utt1: Was it? /
B.121 utt2: How, + how, - /
B.121 utt3: I can't, + I don't know what that's about. /
A.122 utt1: Uh, that was **the** one with Mickey Rooney /(Switchboard corpus: file sw_1201_2131)

Here we see speaker A introducing the generic idea of a good musical, which they then exemplify with the *Sugar Babies* example (a Broadway show that ran between 1979 and 1985). Note that when the musical becomes a specific one, that has been previously identified it is referred to as *the one.*

Obviously, there are plenty of contexts in which we can use a definite article even though the referent is not part of the immediate context and has not been mentioned before. This is the case when the referent is unique, within the boundaries of the relevant context, thus we speak of *the president.* Other examples are when the referent is uniquely famous: so we speak of the White House, the Cliffs of Dover, the Coliseum, the Acropolis, and the Great Wall. Another instance of definite article for a previously unmentioned item, is exemplified in (79) above: note that we have *the window* which has not been mentioned, and we would have expected *a window* along the same lines of *a red jacket* in the previous sentence. The reason we get *the window* is that windows are part of the stereotypical frame for rooms, so we expect to have windows, or light fixtures, or walls, for that matter. Note that if we had said *The boy stood by the cannon* the sentence would be odd or anomalous, as cannons are usually not found in rooms.[4] Finally, another situation when a new referent is introduced directly with a definite article is when it is present to consciousness.

(81) Context: the Speaker and Hearer live next door to a family with a boy, who has gone missing. Both of them are aware of this fact.
Speaker answers the phone, and then addresses the hearer: *The boy has been found.*

4 The room is introduced by "the," in the first sentence, so we must assume it is somehow known in context.

## 6.3 Applications of FSP

### 6.3.1 FSP Reflects the Organization of Ideas in the Mind

The fundamental idea underlying FSP is that the order of the words in the sentence corresponds to the order of ideas in the mind. In a sense, this is a pretty simple concept: after all, when we say something (say, *dog*) we must think about a dog. This is intuitively obvious and has been confirmed indirectly through eye tracking, which has shown that the eye gaze (i.e., where you look) matches attention. Obviously, this should not be interpreted in a strict one-to-one correspondence. It is clear that one can say something and think about something else, much like one can be staring at something and be lost in thought (the technical term for this is "mind wandering") and in fact not pay attention to what one is looking at. However, the duality of focus (external and internal) is marked and costly, in terms of mental load. So, we expect that the unmarked, ordinary word order will reflect to a large extent the order of the ideas in the mind of the speakers.

As we saw in Section 6.2.1, we also logically need to go from known information to unknown information, from old to new. We have to have new information, because otherwise, why bother telling it to our interlocutor. However, we have to relate it to what the other participants in the conversation already know, or they will be unable to integrate it into their knowledge. Consider the following example, which is the opening sentence of Haruki Murakami's novel *Kafka on the Shore*

(82) "So, you're all set for the money, then?" the boy named Crow asks in his typical sluggish voice. The kind of voice like when you've just woken up and your mouth still feels heavy and dull. But he's just pretending. He's totally awake. As always.

Chances are, you found it confusing and puzzling. Now, the first sentence of a novel is generally pretty de-contextualized, since the author has not had much of a chance to build a context for what is happening, but here Murakami is definitely going for an effect of disorientation and bafflement. What money? Who is the boy, beside being named *Crow*? Why is he pretending? Why is he *always* pretending? For that matter, who is the narrator? In other words, Murakami is doing exactly what a "thoughtful" writer should not do (confuse the reader), albeit obviously for esthetic purposes.

The point of all this is that the speakers must calibrate the introduction of new information in discourse to make sure that they don't get too far ahead of their audience. If they fail to anchor properly what they say, they run the risk of losing their audience or, as in the Murakami example, of hooking them in the story.

This is presumably a universal tendency cross-linguistically. Gundel (1988) considers a large sample of languages and identifies two principles governing the distribution of information. These principles are independent and thus may occasionally clash.

- *Given Before New Principle*: The given/topic/thematic should precede the new/comment/rhematic information.
- *First Things First Principle*: Important information should come first. (Gundel, 1988, p. 229)

### 6.3.2 Paragraph and Textual Organization

Much of the discussion on FSP concerns sentence or tone unit level organization; however, similar arguments can be made for structures larger than the sentence such as the paragraph, or the spoken language equivalent, the paratone, or indeed, the text at large. Although we will not devote time here to critiquing Kaplan's (1966) somewhat contentious[5] work on "contrastive rhetorics," we note that he argues that the organization of a paragraph comprises a topic statement and evidence supporting that topic. Kaplan's crucial idea was that in English, this topic sentence (often called the "thesis") occurs at the beginning of the paragraph and the evidence follows it, whereas in other languages this may not be the case. With regard to spoken discourse, we find similar units called "paratones" (or sometimes pitch sequences or phonological paragraphs), which rely primarily on pitch for their boundaries. Typically, they begin with a high pitch onset often with an accelerated rate and high volume, and close with a low pitch accompanied by a drop in volume and a narrowing of the pitch range. An example is shown in Figure 6.2.

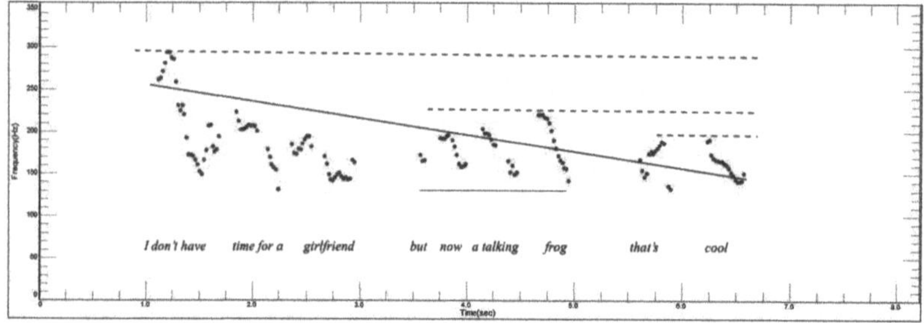


**Figure 6.2** A paratone, displaying the typical declination (solid line) and resets (dashed lines).

### 6.3.3 Marked Constructions

In this section we deal with constructions that are marked, that is, they indicate a special arrangement, either at a prosodic or at a syntactic level.

#### Marked Syntax

Prince's (1985) "fancy syntax" are precisely marked syntactic constructions. She examines two constructions, emblematic of two classes of constructions: left dislocation and topicalization.

#### Topicalization

An example of topicalization is

5 We cannot discuss Kaplan's work on "contrastive rhetorics" (1966) in any detail, let alone its evolution in "intercultural rhetorics" (Connor, 1996, 2004, 2011; Ene et al. 2019) and beyond (Belcher & Nelson, 2013; "translanguaging," Canagarajah, 2011; 2015; Lee & Canagarajah, 2018). However, we can mention that the choice of terminology ("rhetorics"), ignoring genre differences (academic writing is very different in terms of paragraphing from, say, journalism), and the rooting of the discussion in the controversial Sapir-Whorf hypothesis have obscured Kaplan's insight that paragraph organization is language-specific, much like FSP.

(83) I have a recurring dream in which... I can't remember what I say. I usually wake up crying. *This dream* I've had maybe three, four times. (Prince, 1985, p. 71)

This construction marks and thus emphasizes "shared knowledge": the audience knows what dream it is. Note that under normal unmarked circumstances the given/old/thematic information would be de-emphasized.

This is true of a set of marked focalizing constructions, such as

- There sentences: *There is something I need to tell you* vs. *I need to tell you something.*
- Clefts: *It's Mary who was elected president* vs. *Mary was elected president.*
- It extraction: *It's well known that Mary is famous* vs. *That Mary is famous is well known.*
- Fronting object or complement: for example, *Murder was the case that they gave me* vs. *they gave me murder as the case.* This construction foregrounds the expressive meaning of utterance;
- Fronting predicator: *publicize it they did* vs. *They publicized it.* This construction is the most marked of all thematic choices in English.

**Left Dislocation**

Left dislocation requires a pause after the NP, and a different prosodic pattern (*This dream, I've had....*). Gundel (1975) already had examined left-dislocation, a syntactic construction which moves a constituent to the front of the sentence (hence "left"), such as

(84) This pragmatics stuff, it's hard to learn it.

Compare to the fronted but non-left-dislocated version, noting in particular the absence of the "it" pronouns:

(85) This pragmatics stuff is hard to learn.

Prince claims that topicalization marks a referent as within the scope of consciousness, whereas left dislocation does not.

**The Passive**

So in the sentence

(86) **David** gave Lisa a picture

the bolded part is old (given) information, whereas *gave Lisa a picture* is new (Chafe, 1970, p. 218). Contrast now a passive:

(87) **The picture** was given to Lisa by David

where again the bolded part is old/given information. Thus Chafe concludes that "the passive (...) provides a useful device for assigning *new* to an agent (...)" (p. 221), which otherwise would always be relegated to old information status, as in (86).

This can go so far as "disappearing" the agent altogether, as in the infamous Ronald Reagan quote

(88) "we did not achieve what we wished, and serious *mistakes were made* in trying to do so" (http://www.presidency.ucsb.edu/ws/index.php?pid=34430#axzz1VhfZHQ00)

Hence the large use of the passive in scientific writing. In scientific writing agents are deemphasized. We don't need to know who specifically ran the statistics. All we need to know is that

(89) Among US adults, higher consumption of dietary cholesterol or eggs *was significantly associated* with higher risk of incident CVD and all-cause mortality in a dose-response manner. (emphasis added, LP/SA; Zhong et al., 2019; (https://jamanetwork.com/journals/jama/fullarticle/2728487)

Obviously, one of the authors, or perhaps a few of them worked as a group.

**Sentences Without Old Information**

Chafe points out that there can be sentences in which all the units are new, such as

(90) David emptied the box.

as the answer to *what happened next?* (and assuming we did not know that David had done something; Chafe, 1970, p. 222). Negative and emphatic positive statements are also marked: the latter must convey new information (*Lucy does like eating liver*).

**Marked Stress or Prominence**

Turning again to spoken discourse, the importance of prominence patterns such as the ones we looked at in Section 6.1.4 cannot be overemphasized as a way in which speakers signal marked constructions. Most TESOL teachers will recognize some variant of the following exercise as a way to demonstrate how changes in prominence placement can change meaning:

(91) Mary walked to the neighbor to borrow EGGS. [We did not know it was eggs she was looking for.]
Mary walked to the neighbor to BORROW eggs. [She did not go there to purchase eggs.]
Mary walked to the NEIGHBOR to borrow eggs. [She did not go somewhere else, the store, for example.]
Mary WALKED to the neighbor to borrow eggs. [Mary did not drive to the neighbor.]
MARY walked to the neighbor to borrow eggs. [It was Mary, not John.]

Prominence is a particularly important marker to show contrastive intonation, that is, a marked intonation pattern in English in which two items in an utterance are contrasted against each other. In the following example, speaker B corrects speaker A by using a contrastive stress pattern on staff and director:

(92) A: //Don't we have a staff meeting today?//
B: //No, it's not a STAFF meeting// it's a diRECTor's meeting//

Finally, it has an important role in highlighting new and old information. In the following example (Pickering, 2018, p. 36), prominence shifts from money to much as informational value changes:

(93) A: //I need to borrow some MOney// (money is the new information)
B: //How MUCH money// (prominence shifts to much because money is now old information)

## 6.4 History and Terminology

In this section, we outline, necessarily very briefly and without any hope at completeness, the various approaches to functionalism, with an emphasis on trying to elucidate the terminological problem which has plagued the field.

### 6.4.1 The Prague School

Functionalism in modern linguistics can be traced back to the Prague school. This was a circle of linguists and literary critics that gathered in Prague, roughly in the decade between 1928 and 1939. Mathesius was the founder and director of the circle. Jakobson, who had moved to Prague in 1920, was also a major influence, and brought in an influence from the Moscow school (Trubezkoy) and of course Saussure.

A full discussion of Mathesius's work goes beyond an introductory treatment, so we will briefly list the main points that most clearly influenced the discussion of FSP, using as our reference Mathesius (1975), which is based on work Mathesius had done in 1929. Among the ideas that resonated the most we find, first, the term "functional point of view" from which FSP comes; second, the awareness that, seen from a functional perspective, a sentence must "reckon with the hearer" (p. 79); third, the recognition that a basic simple declarative sentence contains "an element about which the statement is made" and the statement itself (p. 81); fourth, the terms theme and rheme to describe them; and, finally, fifth, the important of the order of the words in the sentence. On these points, Mathesius acknowledges the debt to Weil (1844), who had already divided the sentence in starting point (*"point de départ"*; p. 25) and goal of discourse (*"but du discours"*; p. 26) or enunciation (*"énonciation"*; p. 25) and who underscored the significance of the order of words, which according to Weil matches the order of ideas: "the order of words must reproduce the order of ideas" (1844, p. 12).

Figure 6.3 is meant to help the reader orient themselves in the field of functionalism and to capture some common points clustering around four approaches: Functional Grammar (FG), Systemic Functional Grammar (SFG), Generative Functionalism (GF), and West Coast Functionalism (WCF). The figure is not meant to be exhaustive; for one it is limited to works in English (and hence excludes Martinet, despite the obvious merit of his work). Even in the English language research, not all functional approaches are considered (e.g.,

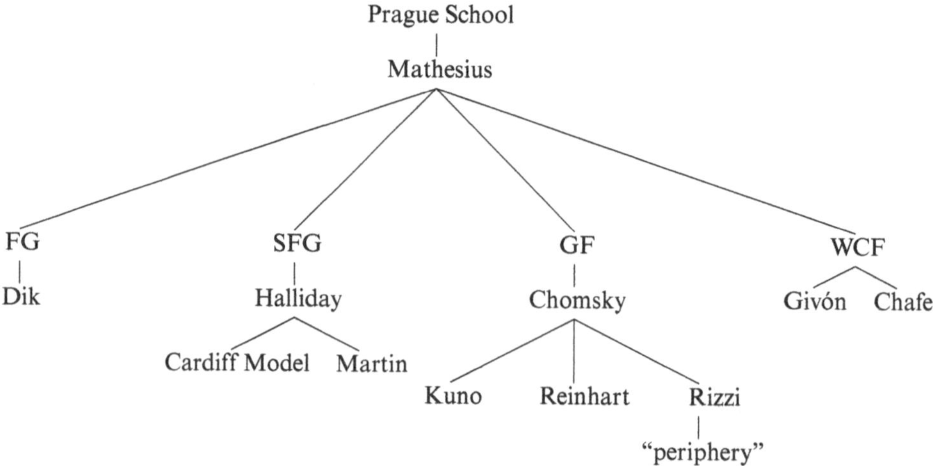


**Figure 6.3** The "schools" of functionalism.

Lexical-Functional Grammar, or Role and Reference Grammar are not included). We could have listed many more authors. The names are merely representative. Furthermore, the classifications are (necessarily) arbitrary to some extent. Finally, the labels are likewise more or less arbitrary.

The ideas of functionalism and markedness originate with the Prague school. Functionalism in the general sense was introduced in mainstream linguistics by Karl Bühler (1879–1963) and Roman Jakobson (1896–1982). The theory of markedness also comes into linguistics via the Prague School, as it was introduced by Jakobson (1932/1971) and Trubezkoy. Andrews (1990, p. 13) places the earliest formulation by Jakobson in 1921 and Trubezkoy in 1931.

Through the influence of Mathesius and Jakobson, these ideas took root in the Prague school. The Prague School's ideas were taken up by many linguists including Firbas, who developed the theory of communicative dynamism, which introduces the idea of a gradual increase of rhematicity, Vachek, Sgall, Daneš, and Hymes, who introduced some of their ideas to American anthropology and linguistic as early as 1962 (see Hymes, 1982, for a discussion of the connections between Hymes's work and the Prague School). The arrival of Jakobson to the United States in 1941, fleeing the Nazi occupation of Czechoslovakia, brought the ideas of Prague school functionalism in contact with American linguistics. Later, Vachek wrote a book on the Prague school (1966) and curated a collection of writings by Prague school authors (1964). The influence of the Prague school functionalism on American and British linguistics was significant, including beyond Hymes, Chafe, Bolinger, Givòn, Halliday, Dik, and even Chomsky.

### 6.4.2 European Functionalism

Independently, functionalist ideas arrived in England, where M. A. K. Halliday was working, and the Netherlands. In the Netherlands, Simon C. Dik (1940–1995) developed, an approach to functionalism called "Functional Grammar" (Dik, 1978, 1989, 1991, 1997).

After his death, the approach evolved into Functional Discourse Grammar, which accounts, as the name indicates, also for discourse level structures (Mackenzie, 2016a).

In England, Halliday developed SFG. SFG showed a direct interest in pedagogy, from early on, and has since developed even more in that direction. Later, Halliday moved to Australia, which is why his approach is sometimes referred to as the Sydney model. The most salient name in the Sydney model nowadays is Martin. The British "side" of SFG is known as the Cardiff model (see Figure 6.3)

Halliday's work (1967, 1985; Halliday & Mathiessen, 2014) was explicitly influenced by the Prague school. Halliday (1967) uses the terms "theme" and "rheme" as done in the Prague school. However, there is a significant difference: whereas Mathesius had considered the theme/rheme opposition the interplay of two aspects, the novelty of the information *and* the starting point of the predication, Halliday distinguishes between focality and thematicity/rhematicity (Halliday, 1967, p. 205).

### 6.4.3 Generative Functionalism

As Butler (2003, p. 27) points out, functionalist approaches tend, logically, to place pragmatic considerations center stage, differing radically in this from formalist approaches, which tend to relegate pragmatic issues to the margins of the discipline. In the 1970s, in North America, syntacticians took a perhaps unexpected interest in functionalism. In particular, the focus was on considering particular syntactic constructions and their functions. Prince (1985, p. 67) presents an impressive list of analyses of constructions with their functional correlates, such as clefting, the passive, existential there, and so on. We have provided examples and discussion of these and more in Section 6.3.3.

We can probably speculate that much of the interest in these constructions was sparked by Chomsky's (1971) analysis of sentences such as:

(94) It was John that was here.

Here the focus is on *John* which is taken to be new information (focus), and the proposition *John was here* is old information, labeled "presupposition" in a different use of the term seen in Section 1.1.2, with which it should not be confused. However, one should bear in mind that Hockett (1963) already argued for the universality of a topic/comment subdivision of the sentence. Conversely, if we look at some of the more recent developments of syntax with the attention to the left and right periphery of the sentence (i.e., the beginning and the end of the sentence, where thematic and rhematic positions are located), we can see that while interest may have shifted to more formal syntactic formulations, it has never really moved away from these topics. In any case, regardless of its origin we can definitely say that American discussion of the topic/comment or theme/rheme articulation has been more formally/syntactically oriented than elsewhere

Kuno's work on FSP was directly inspired by Firbas and the Prague school. Kuno examines Japanese and highlights the fact, which will be quoted repeatedly in the literature thereafter, that in Japanese theme and rheme are marked using two particles: *wa* and *ga*, respectively.

(95) a. John wa dokusin desu. = John is single.
b. John ga dokusin desu. = It's John who is single.

In (95.a), John is already part of the discourse and the speaker is informing the hearer that John is not married. In (95.b), the new information is that John is the only person who fits the "single" description. It is what Kuno calls an "exhaustive listing" (1972, p. 272). The interest of this finding, from our perspective, lies in that the marking of thematicity/rhematicity is done differently than using the position of the component or intonation, as seen in other languages, while confirming the universality of the functional arrangement in old/new information.

Prince (1981) presents a taxonomy of given/new information. Surprisingly, she only mentions Anglo-Saxon authors and makes no mention of the openly acknowledged influences of the Prague school on those very authors (Chafe, Bolinger, Clark, Chomsky, etc.). Prince identifies three types of givenness:

- Predictability/recoverability: As the name says, if the element is recoverable from prior context then it is old, and if not recoverable, new (Kuno, 1972).
- Saliency: Whether something is likely to be in the focus of consciousness (Prince, 1981, p. 228); see Chafe's work (Section 6.2.1).
- Shared knowledge: What speakers and hearers share in mutual knowledge/common ground; see Clark (Section 6.4.4).

Significantly she concludes that the three are not independent (1981, p. 231). Prince then proceeds to propose a new classification of shared knowledge. First, she changes the label to "assumed familiarity" to avoid confusion with the previous definitions. She then distinguishes three kinds of familiarity: new, inferrable, and evoked. The differences among them are as follows:

- *New*: New referents may be either unused (previously known but not in use, i.e., in consciousness) or brand new. Brand new referents may be anchored or unanchored: the former are linked anaphorically with another nominal entity in discourse; unnachored new referents are simply not connected to any referential chain (e.g., in *A student called me* uttered discourse initially "student" is unanchored.)
- *Inferrable*: A referent is inferrable if it is inferred situationally; for example, the referent of "grade" in a student question to their teacher at the end of a class: *How did I do?*
- *Evoked*: A referent is evoked by the text if some element of the text directs the hearer to look for the referent: for example, pronouns, as in *pardon, would* **you** *have change of a quarter* (Prince, 1981, p. 233). This corresponds to Chafe's "given." (Chafe, 1994, p. 177)

Other important researchers in the generative functionalism approach are Gundel (whose work we mentioned above) and Reinhart, who defines the topic as what the sentence is about. Usually this can be found by asking what question the sentence is an answer to. Thus for example (68) we would ask:

(96) What is Mary doing? She is asleep.

Reinhart proposes another syntactic test for aboutness: the construction HE SAID ABOUT [TOPIC] THAT... which yields

(97) He said about her/Mary that *she is asleep.*

where the original example (68) is italicized.

### 6.4.4 West Coast Functionalism

Under this label, used for example in Noonan (1999) and in Mackenzie (2016b), we are grouping a rather diverse group of scholars who are connected geographically (on the West Coast of the United States, precisely) who also share an interest in functionalism and to different degrees into "usage-based" theories (e.g., Bybee, 1999), such as construction grammar (e.g., Goldberg, 2006) and cognitive linguistics (Langacker, 1987). Another term that has been proposed is "functional-cognitive space" (Butler & Gonzálvez-García, 2014). We have already discussed Chafe's model above in Section 6.2.1. Givón's work on marked and focus constructions (Givón, 1990) is also worth mentioning, as well as Clark's psycholinguistic work (Clark & Haviland, 1974; Haviland & Clark, 1974), which is related to the idea of common ground (Clark, 1996; see Section 8.3).

## 6.5 Conclusion

This concludes our presentation of the development of functionalism. Its point was to show the wide reach of the functionalist ideas which originated with Mathesius and Jakobson and how they can be useful to linguists. The historical overview also concludes our overall presentation of FSP. We discussed the central constellation of ideas that underlie functionalism: markedness, word order, prominence, newness and known-ness, and we showed how they can interact with word order, syntactic constructions, and textual organization to reflect the subjective perspective of the speaker on their words. We now turn to the applications of functionalism to SLA and teaching.

## 6.6 FSP in SLA and the TESOL Classroom

### 6.6.1 FSP in SLA

Applications of FSP to SLA have flourished, particularly in the area of Halliday's SFG. Traditionally, metalanguage has been identified as language about language (see Section 10.1) in a narrow "grammatical" sense. However, in the systemic functional grammar approach, a functional metalanguage "includes terminology for connecting both structural and functional units of language systematically to their meaning-making potential" (Humphrey and Macnaught, 2016, p. 3). Thus, for example, being able to identify the thesis of an article *and label it as such* would be a functional metalanguage skill, which would not have been considered metalinguistic, in the narrow sense, but rather rhetorical. Further scaffolding is achieved by using "bridging terms," that is, age-/learner-appropriate terminology (e.g., metaphors, such as *opening and closing a door (to an argument)* to denote a concessive parenthetical).

Carroll and Lambert (2006) consider the way that advanced speakers of L2 arrange information in narrative texts. "Because information structure and the choices speakers make are multidimensional and thus highly complex, second language learners tend to maintain the basic selection patterns of their source language [...];" (Carroll and Lambert, 2006, p. 71) This applies to temporal shift, agent selection, zero anaphora, aspect marking, and more. The idea is that even near-native L2 speakers are still having some problems with matching the English system, because "this level of information organization may be the most difficult to reorganize" (p. 70). This echoes a similar conclusion reached by Gumperz (see Section 8.5).

### 6.6.2 FSP in TESOL

SFG has also been applied to TESOL. For example, Humphrey and Macnaught (2016) report successful use of metalinguistic scaffolding in a high school Australian ESL setting (English for Academic Purposes). Macken-Horarik (2005) documents the use of metalinguistic constructs such as genre and register for literacy development in TESOL classes, also in Australia.

Intercultural rhetoric has also undergone many changes since Kaplan's early work on contrastive rhetoric (e.g., Simpson, 2000) and has played an important role in assessing the differences between L1 and L2 writing. One of our students, Alotaibi (2013) used a model created by Swales (2004) to investigate the differences between the introductions of research articles in Arabic and in English and found considerable differences between their structure, particularly in terms of establishing a research space which was considered less important in the Arabic papers. In another example of the work of one of our students, Hsiung (2014) created a corpus of 120 articles in similar disciplines in American English and Mandarin in order to compare paragraph structure. Six hundred paragraphs were analyzed to identify where the thesis statements were typically found. There were striking differences:

- 97% of English paragraphs had the thesis the first sentence, as opposed to 56% of Chinese paragraphs.
- 1% of English paragraphs had the thesis in the last sentence, as compared to 25% of Chinese paragraphs.

Thus, in general, while English paragraphs overwhelmingly had the thesis in the first sentence, there was a great deal more variation in the Chinese paragraphs.

Work on L2 spoken discourse has also expanded, particularly in terms of the cohesive devices that "hold together" texts such as the paratone structure we described in Section 6.3.2. Pickering (2004) compared the structure and function of intonational paragraphs in native and nonnative instructional discourse. Analysis of the American English data showed instructors systematically using pitch height to distinguish information structure. For example, using a lower pitch register to distinguish subsidiary content (e.g., short glosses or asides) from the main, informative content of the lectures. In addition, paratone structure matched topic structure and additional cues to the organization of the information such as boardwork and other extralinguistic devices. In contrast, paratone structure was difficult to assess in the discourse of the Chinese learners of English. It was hampered by a compression in overall pitch range that made it difficult to assess salient differences in pitch height. In addition, the internal structure of the spoken paragraphs was disrupted by pause patterns, and phonological cues often did not match cues at other levels of the discourse so could not be reliably used by hearers as an organizational cue.

### 6.6.3 Sample Teaching Materials

#### Lesson Plan 1: Contrasting Intercultural Writing Patterns

There are countless materials available to teachers and students on academic writing for nonnative speakers and they most often begin by describing the expected organization of specific kinds of texts (e.g., the five-paragraph essay or the research paper). However, this can of itself be a source of confusion for adult learners who are not starting with a blank slate but are trying to work out the ways in which their L1 writing genres are constructed differently. This can be addressed in activities similar to the ones given below.

**Step 1:** The teacher has chosen a specific written genre (it may be as large as a work report or as small as a paragraph depending on the class goals) and asked students to bring in L1 samples of the genre.

**Step 2:** The teacher outlines the structure of the specific genre in question following a process similar to that described above in Section 6.3.2 with paragraph or research paper structure.

**Step 3:** Taking their L1 samples, depending on the L1s and proficiency levels comprising the class, the students work alone, in pairs or small groups describing any differences between the structure of their L1 samples and the structure of the L2 samples to discuss as a class.

**Step 4:** As part of the class discussion, the teacher should ensure that they emphasize the need for the L2 writers to take their potential readers' expectations regarding structure into consideration as part of their writing process.

#### Lesson Plan 2: The Role of Repetition in Cohesion

**Step 1:** The teacher presents students with the following two dialogues and discusses why the repetition in the first one does not work (repeated information that is already understood) but the repetition in the second one does (B echoes sentiments of A to increase social convergence).

Dialogue 1
A: When does the train leave?
B: The train leaves at 7 o'clock
A: Can you give me a ride to the station?
B: Yes, I can give you a ride to the station

Dialogue 2
A: It seemed weird to me
B: Oh yeah – totally weird
A: Do you think he's crazy?
B: Maybe, I'm not entirely sure what crazy looks like... definitely weird...

### Step 2

The students discuss the features of effective repetition that builds cohesion and social convergence.

### Step 3

Samples of either spoken or written discourse can then be used for student to discuss the effects of repetition:

### Spoken Sample

Pickering: Hi Sal!
Attardo: Hi! What's that box in the truck?
P: I bought us a chainsaw
A: A chainsaw?
P: Yes, it was on sale!
A: On sale, really?
P: Yes, really. 20% off.
A: I cannot believe you bought a chainsaw
P: Why not?
A: Let me tell you why not: this is the third chainsaw you bought in as many months!
P: I did not buy three chainsaws!
A: You didn't? The Echo, the Husqvarna, and this one, too...
P: The Echo was to replace the old one that broke!
A: So what? You bought three chainsaws in three months!
P: We needed the Echo.
A: Fine, but what about the other two?
P: We needed a bigger one!!

A: We did not need a bigger one! The Echo was big enough!
P: It was not!
A: I still cannot believe you bought another chainsaw!
P: We needed a bigger chainsaw!
A: We needed a bigger chainsaw? A bigger chainsaw?
P: Is there an echo in here?
Alexa: Ordering an Echo chainsaw
P and A, together: Alexa, stay out of this!

### Written Samples

These written discourse sentences examine the stylistic functions of repetition in writing (examples come from https://literarydevices.net/repetition/)

1. If you think you can do it, you can do it.
2. The boy was a good footballer, because his father was a footballer, and his grandfather was a footballer.
3. The bird said, "I don't sing because I am happy, I am happy because I sing."
4. The politician declared, "We will fight come what may, we will fight on all fronts, we will fight for a thousand years."
5. The judge commanded, stamping his mallet on the table, "Order in the court, order in the court."
6. The refugees were crossing into the neighboring country when they saw blood all around – blood on the passageways, blood on the fields, blood on the soles of their feet.
7. When they came out of the cinema hall they all agreed, the film was a waste of money, it was a waste of time and energy.
8. The boy was terrified when he was taken to the hospital; he shuddered at the least sound, and he shuddered at the least breath of air into the room.
9. The president said, "Work, work, and work," are the keys to success.
10. The orator said, "Good morning to the old, good morning to the young, good morning to each and every one present."

# 7

# Stance, Deixis, and Pragmatic Markers

When speakers say or write something, they are, at a very basic level, expressing a "thought." They may also, in the process of expressing that "thought," express their attitude toward what they are saying, how they are saying it, and any aspects of the context (situation) in which they are uttering the thought. This attitude is called stance, modality, deixis, attitude, markers, and many more terms, which are part of the field of metapragmatics.

The relationship between deixis, stance, pragmatic markers, broadly conceived, and metapragmatics is complex, as their scopes seem to overlap. In fact, any division of the field is largely arbitrary. The reader may wonder then why we have two separate chapters dealing with metapragmatics (Chapters 7 and 10). The reason is primarily one of size: in order to avoid having an overlong chapter we decided to split the topic in half. Roughly speaking then in this chapter we focus on pragmatic and metapragmatic topics that are closer to grammaticalization (e.g., modality) or lexicalization (e.g., discourse markers), whereas in chapter 10 we focus on topics more distant from linguistic form (indexicality, reflexivity (i.e., the awareness of one's linguistic choices), pragmatic appropriateness, for example, politeness – in short more pragmatic phenomena). Nonetheless, the reader should expect significant overlaps and repeated cross-references between the two chapters.

At a very schematic level, we can consider that stance, pragmatic markers, indexicality, and metapragmatics all share a distinction between the facts expressed by the utterance (propositional meaning) and an attitude or evaluation of either the propositional content or the circumstances of the utterance. The reader will recall from Section 3.1 that we can distinguish between a proposition and the illocutionary force of the speech act, so that the difference between

(98) Dinner is ready. = $\vdash$ (p)

and

(99) Get dinner ready = ! (p)

where *p* is the proposition corresponding to the English sentence *Dinner is ready*, which does not change. Likewise, we can have, given p = *John loves Mary*:

*Pragmatics and Its Applications to TESOL and SLA*, First Edition. Salvatore Attardo and Lucy Pickering.

(100) I think John loves Mary = p + lack certainty

(101) I am afraid John loves Mary = p + lack certainty + negative evaluation of p

(102) Hopefully John loves Mary = p + lack of certainty + positive evaluation of p

(103) John may love Mary = p + possibility

(104) John might love Mary = p + lesser possibility

Thus, metapragmatics is concerned with the evaluation of the proposition (including its illocutionary force) *and/or* of the context in which it occurs. The speaker may convey an attitude toward the utterance itself, toward the force (illocution) of the utterance, and toward the circumstances of the utterance (the context), and possibly about all three of them at the same time.

## 7.1 Modality

It is quite clear that metapragmatic phenomena, even at this initial stage of conceptualization, have a lot to do with modality. It will be useful to review quickly some aspects of English modality. Modality is expressed grammatically in most Indo-European languages, of which English is one, through moods (which take their name from Medieval "modes" of signification), such as the subjunctive and the conditional. The primary semantic fields expressed by modality in English are as follows:

- The realis/irrealis continuum: Is this fact part of reality or is it imagined, or hypothetical, or made up? Compare: *I am sixteen. I run fast.* vs. *Were I sixteen, I'd run a lot faster.* (= I am not sixteen and I don't run fast.)
- Intentionality versus factuality: *I will exercise every day* (= I intend to do so, but I am not currently doing so) versus *I exercise every day.*
- Certainty/uncertainty: *I will go* versus *I may go.*
- Possibility versus actuality: *I may go* versus *I am going.*
- Capacity versus incapacity: *You can lift the weight* versus *you cannot lift the weight.*
- Obligation versus lack of obligation: *You must eat the cake* or *you ought to eat the cake,* versus *you eat cake.*

English has a conditional, mostly used in "if …" sentences (*If you get up now, there may still be some breakfast left*) and there was a subjunctive, but it is at this point a relic, found only in stock expressions such as *If I were you*; *God save the queen*; or *Let it be.*

### 7.1.1 Modal Verbs

In English, modality is primarily expressed through "modal verbs," of which there are three kinds. They are charted in Table 7.1. As we saw, modality expresses intentionality, capacity, obligation, necessity, optionality, volition, and reality. An interesting issue is

**Table 7.1** Classification of English modals; central modals are in order of frequency

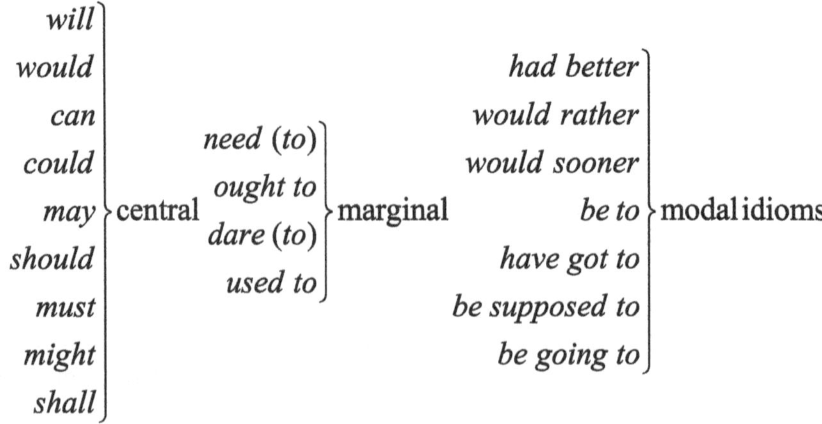


that some central modals appear to be paired according to a present/past opposition, along the lines of

| | |
|---|---|
| may | might |
| can | could |
| shall | should |
| will | would |

However, careful consideration of their meanings will show that this is clearly not the case, except perhaps for some meanings of the *can/could* pair. It seems more likely that the pairs differ by a feature of [realis/irrealis]. The difference is that the "past" forms are really distal forms, that is, they express a distance from the propositional content and this distance is interpreted as the difference between referring to reality or to an imagined state of affairs, so that if one says

(105) I may clean the gutters

there is a real possibility of so doing, whereas if one says

(106) I might clean the gutters

one is merely contemplating the theoretical possibility of doing so. This comes in stark focus with the "will/would" pair.

(107) I will clean the gutters → I have the intention to do so
I would clean the gutters → Either I do not have the intention to clean the gutters or something prevents me from doing so

The distance is also mapped on politeness:

(108) Can you do me a favor? versus Could you do me a favor?

where tense is completely irrelevant (I am obviously not asking for a favor in the past), and the remote form is interpreted as more polite. Finally, let us note that the use of *could, should, would*, and *might* as markers of reported speech has nothing to do with tense,

(109) John: "I may go home."
Mary: "John said he might go home."

but iconically matches the one-degree-removed nature of reported speech.

### 7.1.2 Epistemic and Deontic Modality

Modal verbs have an epistemic (a.k.a. extrinsic) or deontic (a.k.a. intrinsic) interpretation, meaning that they can refer to theoretical, knowledge-based issues, or to empirical, real-world issues, respectively. Consider *may*: its deontic meaning is that someone is allowed to do something (*You may leave now*); its epistemic meaning is that of possibility (*It may rain tomorrow*).

However, stance is not limited to modality. Consider the following examples:

(110) Pickering (2018) demonstrates that ...
Pickering (2018) concludes that ...
Pickering (2018) shows that ...
Pickering (2018) states that ...
Pickering (2018) claims that ...
Pickering (2018) alleges that ...
Pickering (2018) would have us believe that ...

arranged on a rough scale of "believing/agreeing with" the ideas expressed in Pickering (2018). So, the attitude or evaluation of the propositional content is not limited to modality or modal-like attitudes, but extends broadly to any form of evaluation and attitude. Evidentiality is a good example of non-modal stance. Evidentiality is a separate category, which encodes grammatically whether the speaker witnessed directly an event, visually or sensorily, whether they heard about it (hearsay), or whether they are drawing an inference (Aikhenvald, 2006). Whorf (1956) gives an example of the differences between English and Hopi in evidentiality: in Hopi one has to distinguish between seeing with one's own eyes (*tïwạ' -q*) and hearsay (*kị̣r*) (p. 121), whereas in English the distinction can be ignored: "Mary arrived" is non-committal in terms of evidentiality: I may have witnessed it or someone may have told me, or I may have figured it out by some other clue. The second major area of stance to be covered is its indexical nature and for this we will consider the notion of deixis more broadly.

## 7.2 Deixis

Deictics are "pointers." The etymology of the word makes it remarkably clear as it goes back to the Greek *deiknumi* ("to point, to show") which is related to the Proto-IE root *deik, with the same meaning and is related to Latin *digitus* meaning "finger," that is, the pointer by default. Our discussion of deixis is based largely on Fillmore (1971/1997), which is the classical text on deixis.

The reader will recall from Section 1.1.2 that signs such as "cat" or "house" refer to entities in the real world via a semiotic process which involves a reference to a sign, stored in the mind of the speakers. Deictics refer to something in the real world in a slightly different way: they directly point to the real-world entities they refer to. So, when Pickering is choosing chainsaws at the local hardware store she may say

(111) I'll take this one.

pointing at a given chainsaw. So, a word like *this* literally can be used along with a pointing gesture to select an entity in the real world as the topic of one's utterance. Obviously, more abstract uses are derived from this original physical sense. Consider the following example, which occurs in adjacent turns from the same speaker and recall that they come from a corpus of phone conversations, in which obviously the speakers cannot see what the speaker would be pointing to.

(112) A.8 utt1: (...) I can't understand why anyone would abandon this dog, though.
A.8 utt2: She's, I mean she's (...) this young
(Switchboard corpus; sw_0175_2729)

While the first instance of "this" can be explained as discourse deictic (i.e., the speaker is "pointing" to the prior reference to the dog) and so, while metalinguistically doing so, we can argue that it points to a concrete entity, the second "this" (utterance 2) is clearly pointing at an abstract concept ("youth") and so obviously "this" must modify "young," so that the speaker means "as young as the dog is" which is clearly a non-concrete referent.

Deictic words like *here, now, tomorrow, I, you,* and so on, are obviously fully semantically determined only by knowing who the speaker is, where they are located, and the time of speaking. In other words, they are indexed to the act of speaking: *I* is the speaker, *you* is the hearer, *he/she* is a third party not currently addressed by the speaker, *here* is the place where the speaking is taking place, and *now* is the time of speaking. So if Pickering is explaining to Attardo why he is wrong, Pickering would say "I told you X" and in that situation "I" means Pickering, "you" means Attardo and the past form of "tell" indicates that at the time of speaking Pickering is referring to a prior time in which the event of telling took place. The referral to a time prior to that of speaking is usually called the "past tense." Tenses are thus deictic as well. Obviously, when someone else speaks, the roles of speaker and hearer will be taken over by the new speaker/hearer and the time of speaking will be the time of that speaking. Other interesting deictics are the pairs *here/there, come/go, bring/*

*take* which encode the proximal/distal opposition (one comes toward the speaker, who is "here," and brings to the speaker, whereas one goes away from the speaker, and takes something *there*).

Deixis, the branch of linguistics that deals with deictics, is usually divided into person, time, and place deixis, followed by discourse and social deixis. Time and place deixis are more "basic" while discourse and social deixis are derived from the first two.

### 7.2.1 Place and Time Deixis

Let us examine place and time deixis and the idea of "deictic center." Deixis, in Indo-European languages at least, is egocentric. The speaker's location and the time of the utterance serve as the center of the deictic space (see Figure 7.1).

Likewise, the speaker is the center of the proximal space and the distal space develops away from them, note that the proximal/distal space opposition can be articulated as a binary feature (near/far; close/distant) or as a tripartite one: "here/there/yonder." Some languages have even more complex systems.

Temporal deixis is based, in Western cultures, on a metaphorical vector (geometrically, a line with a direction): the past is behind us and the future is ahead. However, in Aymara, the past is in front of us (since it is known) and the future is behind (since we don't know what will come) (Núñez & Sweetser, 2006).

Summing up, Western culture conceptualizes spatio-temporal deixis as two distinct axes, a temporal past–present–future vector, and a spatial proximal/distal opposition. At the intersection of these two axes lies the deictic center, the speaker, in the here and now.

### 7.2.2 Discourse Deixis

Discourse deixis is essentially a transference of spatio-temporal deixis onto speech and/or writing. Thus, we can refer to "this sentence" meaning the present one, or to "that sentence" meaning another one uttered at a prior time. Likewise, we can refer to the "previous" unit of discourse (sentence, paragraph, section, etc.) or the "next."

Some interesting further refinements are the pair "former/latter," used primarily in formal language, which indicate the first and second of two possible referents present in the

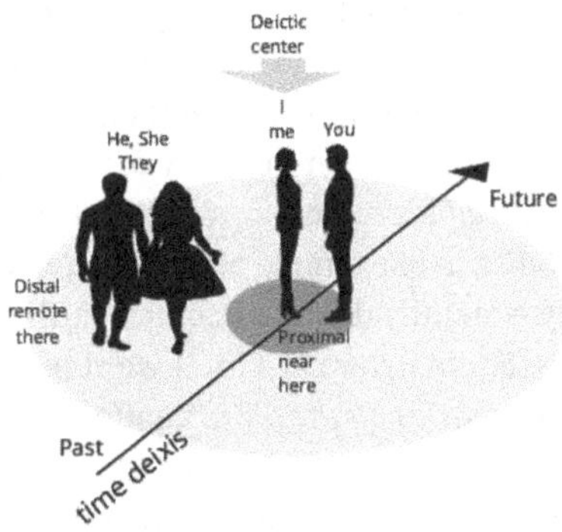


**Figure 7.1** The deictic space.

domain selected. “Respectively” is also an interesting deictic marker which indicates that two prior referents are pair-wise related to two new ones:

(113) The national tour of the Tony-nominated Peter Morgan play Frost/Nixon – co-starring Stacy Keach and Alan Cox as, respectively, disgraced former President Richard Nixon and TV talk-show host David Frost – kicks off Sept. 30 in Des Moines, IA. http://www.playbill.com/article/frost-nixon-tour-with-keach-and-cox-launches-sept-30-com-153761

Thus, Stacy Keach plays Nixon and Alan Cox plays David Frost.

### 7.2.3 Social Deixis

Social deixis is defined as the linguistic features that “reflect or establish or are determined” by the social situation in which the utterance occurs (Fillmore, 1971/1997, p. 112). This pellucid definition has the advantage of highlighting the dialectical relationship between social situation and language: social deixis is both reflected and determined by the social environment in which it occurs. In other words, the causality goes both ways.

Two topics in social deixis that have received a great deal of attention are T/V pronouns and honorifics. We already addressed these topics in Section 5.1.2.

## 7.3 Pragmatic Markers

A pragmatic marker is a deictic linguistic expression that provides primarily information relative to the pragmatic aspects of discourse. Consider *well*. As in,

(114) F: Oh, two they’re going to change.
D: *Well*, one they’re taking [off]
(Switchboard corpus, sw_0088_3073, A.15)

Even without knowing the F and D are discussing TV shows they like to tape, we know immediately that D’s response is going to be a disagreement or a correction. In this case, F is saying that two shows are going to change, whereas D corrects him/her, stating that only one show will be terminated (taken off the air). F then cuts D off, interrupting. The function of *well* here is to introduce and soften the blow of the disagreement. In this case, most of the information carried by *well* is pragmatic, and could be paraphrased along the lines of *sorry to disagree with you, but....* The example also showcases an important aspect of pragmatic markers, that is, they generally do not affect the truth conditions of the propositions expressed in the utterances. So, in example 114, if we remove the pragmatic marker *well*, the truth of *they are taking one series off the air* is unaffected.

Needless to say, *well* is merely one example of pragmatic marker. There are many more and a lively field of research has developed, beginning a roughly in the mid-1980s (Bazzanella,

1985, 1990; Schourup, 1999). In fact, the field has attracted so much attention that problems have arisen.

One of the areas of contention is terminological: we find pragmatic, discourse, linguistic, or text relation markers, discourse and conjunctive particles, connectors or connectives, indicators, pointers, operators, cue phrases, and more (see Bazzanella, 2006, p. 449; Fischer, 2006, p. 1; Fraser, 2009, p. 2; Schourup, 1999, pp. 228–230 for long lists of terms). Some authors differentiate between connectors and markers, for example, Pons Bordería (2001) argues that connectors are a hyponym (subset) of markers. Another topic that has been widely discussed is whether markers such as *so* or the above mentioned *well* have a fundamental core meaning from which all the different meanings they can acquire in context are derived, or whether they are polysemic, that is, have different meanings, that may or may not be ultimately related. Since the discussion is largely tied to the theoretical model adopted by the various proponents of the approaches, we will not concern ourselves with the distinction, while noting that most pragmatic markers indeed serve several functions at several different discourse levels.

In contrast to the lack of agreement on the terminological side, there are several points on which most researchers on pragmatic/discourse markers would agree. The first, as we saw, is that they do not affect the truth value of a proposition. Another area of agreement is that there are no grammatical restrictions on the markers; they do tend to be short, but they can be nouns, verbs, adjectives, and so on. Furthermore, due to high frequency of use, they tend to be semantically bleached, that is, they lose their original meaning, see for example the use of *say* to indicate a hypothetical example, as in (115)

(115) Right, well, well, also what I don't think is fair, either, is when you have like a, *say* a rapist, come in, and, and his attorney gets his sentences, sentencing reduced because he's gone to a lesser charge (...)
(Switchboard corpus, sw_0120_3113., B.33

where, of course, there is no actual "saying." (On *say* as a pragmatic marker, see Brinton, 2008; Goossens, 1982; Lee, 2003; Stavan, 2006; Van Olmen, 2013). This semantic bleaching eventually leads to grammaticalization, through a diachronic process. This is another important aspect of the research on pragmatic markers.

### 7.3.1 Schiffrin's Discourse Markers

Schiffrin's (1987) book on **discourse markers**, while not the first study on the matter,[1] is rightly considered one of the foundational works in this area of linguistics and is one of the most cited works on the subject, albeit not always without criticism, for example, Redecker (1991); Schiffrin blends discourse analysis with quantitative methods, in an exceptionally broad theoretical framework informed by the work of Sacks, Gumperz, and Hymes, and a microscopic attention to linguistic phenomena that are often ignored or

1 Pons Bordería (2001, 2005) points out that a European tradition of the study of connectives, in a syntactic sense (Halliday & Hasan, 1976), in a semantic sense (Van Dijk, 1977), or in an argumentative sense (Anscombre & Ducrot, 1976, 1983) preexists the American models.

brushed under the carpet, because they do not fit any traditional grammatical category and are not truth-functional.

A discourse marker is defined as a linguistic device that gives "contextual coordinates for ongoing talk" (p. 41). More specifically, speakers comment metalinguistically on the status of the information they receive or present, or on the shifting nature of the conversational common ground that develops.

Let us consider a couple of the discourse markers analyzed by Schiffrin: *Oh* is used to acknowledge a change in the status of information. When two or more speakers talk, they assume a shared common ground (also called "conversational scoreboard"; see Section 3.1.6). At a minimum, the common ground will include the context in which the interaction is taking place and what the speakers know about each other. Each utterance will introduce either new material (e.g., someone may introduce someone else, hence making their name part of the common ground) or will focalize previously shared material: for example, in this short exchange, the speakers are talking about a street they both know:

(116) Debby: (...) the street is noisy. (...)
Zelda: **Oh**, yeh. Right. (Schiffrin, 1987, p. 95)

Since both speakers share knowledge of the street it is in the common ground, but the fact that it is noisy may not have been particularly salient, so Debby, by topicalizing it, brings it to the forefront of Zelda's awareness, who acknowledges the shift with the *Oh* and then assents (*Yeh. Right.*). In this case, Zelda is essentially backchannelling, because Debby continues her turn (not shown in the example) but in other cases, the *Oh*, may be at the beginning of a turn in which the speaker claims the floor.

Another example is *well*. Schiffrin finds that *well* is used to reassert the coherence of the discourse when "the upcoming contribution is not fully consonant with prior coherence options" (1985, p. 103). This analysis is not novel per se, for example, both Lakoff (1973) and Pomerantz (1984) had noted that *well* introduces insufficient or dispreferred answers. To put it more simply, if you ask the teacher how you did on a test and the teacher starts their answer with *well*.... it is not a good thing! Schiffrin's contribution is to frame the discussion in the context of discourse coherence. So both *oh* and *well* can be seen as operating within discourse coherence maintenance, *well* operates at the interactional level, essentially smoothing over "bumps" in the overall coherence, whereas *oh* operates at the cognitive level, marking readjustments of the common ground (p. 127).

Schiffrin points out that discourse markers have different functions at different levels in discourse. For example, besides the informational functions we have discussed earlier, they have a deictic function, insofar as *oh* points backward to prior information, whereas *well* points both backward and forward since it relates to both what was said before and what is about to be said. *Now*, conversely, "displays what is coming next in the discourse" (1987, p. 237). Another function that most markers have is a semantic (or "ideational") function, that is, they carry some linguistic meaning (such as for example the difference between *and* and *or*).

Which of these functions is attended to by the speakers is determined in context (i.e., pragmatically) and is therefore governed by the inferential capacities of the principle of cooperation or of relevance. Relevance theory (RT) has made much of this aspect of the issue (e.g., Blakemore, 2002).

### 7.3.2 Procedural Information Markers

RT's position is that discourse markers encode "procedural information" which is used to interpret the relationships between propositions. For RT then discourse markers constrain and direct the inferential process governed by the principle of relevance.[2] Procedural elements are non-truth functional: this may appear counter-intuitive, but it is a common argument in logic. For example, both in Gricean semantics and in the RT approach to meaning, the following sentences have *the same meaning* but different implicatures or procedural meanings.

(117) Mary played well but Bob did too.

and

(118) Mary played well and Bob did too.

The idea is that the meaning of both sentences is the sum of the first and the second parts (propositions) of the sentence (i.e., Mary played well + Bob played well) and the connector *and/but* merely tells us what the relationship between the two propositions is: in (117) the relationship is one of opposition, whereas in (118) the relationship is an addition. Along the same lines, then, the connector *so* in the following example

(119) She is very smart, so I expect more from her.

is considered to be semantically empty, unlike the two propositions *p*1, "she is very smart", and *p*2 "I expect more from her".[3] Instead *so* encodes procedural information, roughly to treat *p*2 as a consequence of *p*1.

### 7.3.3 Connectors

Connectors are a subset of discourse markers that provide coherence, primarily at the intra-sentential level, that is, they tend to connect two sentences, as in

(120) Actually, uh, they just recently started a policy of testing drugs, which was kind of interesting,
*because* w-, when I went to work for them, uh, they didn't do that, (Switchboard Corpus, sw_0002_4330.B2)

---

2 Pons Bordería (2008) points out that RT has a more restrictive definition of discourse markers than other approaches, including, we may add, the approach used in this volume. The reader should be aware of possible confusions and refer to the relevant sources when necessary.

3 Needless to say, logicians would object to unresolved deictics in a proposition. This is irrelevant in this context.

in which *because* connects the first utterance about the new policy of drug testing to the second one which explains that when the speaker started working for the company, they did not use to do that. So, the speaker is connecting the two utterances by several links (e.g., the pronominal anaphors), building an argument but also justifying the tellability (i.e., the worthiness, the intrinsic interest of the point)

Modality, deixis, and pragmatic markers thus anchor utterances relative to their context, either in the beliefs of the speaker relative to their utterances (i.e., whether they believe their utterance to be factual or not, necessary, required, etc.) or in the circumstances of the utterance (its context, including the social context), or in the pragmatic and discursive context in which they occur. However, the opinion and attitudes that speakers have in relation to what they say may vary even more broadly.

## 7.4 Stance

Consider the following example,

(121) A.37 # these people # beating the heck out of this guy. Um, /
B.38 Unfortunately that kind of thing is not limited to <lipsmack> a big city like Los Angeles. /
B.38 You're going to have it just about anywhere. /
(Switchboard Corpus, sw 0029 4152.)

Clearly, speaker B in her first utterance expresses a negative attitude toward the fact that she is about to state (i.e., that beatings are not limited to big cities). This is a pretty obvious case, in which the negative stance is explicitly marked. However, in many cases, the stance of the speaker is less obviously visible, while being nonetheless there. A few lines below, speaker B utters the following:

(122) That's *almost* when you *kind of wish* that there *were* standardized sentences.
(Switchboard Corpus, sw 0029 4152., B.56)

which shows B's desire to "soften" her claim (probably for fear of being seen as naive) that there should be mandatory sentencing for criminals. Note the hedges highlighted in italics in the example. *Almost* and *kind of* are clearly hedging devices meant to reduce the force of a statement. *Wish* and the subjunctive *were* indicate the irrealis mood, which indicates the fact that the speaker is not referring to a factual state of affairs but only a wished for one. The expression of attitudes toward what is being said is called stance (Biber & Finegan, 1989; Du Bois, 2007).

Stance is the positioning of the speaker vis-à-vis what they say or imply by what they say. This implies that stance is a contextual phenomenon: while there may be aspect of stance that can be abstracted away from the circumstances of the utterance, for example, lexical choice, most of the work in stancetaking will take place contextually. The position of the speaker is chosen within a system of values, which are both defined by and affect the social context of the utterance. In its simplest form a value system is articulated as good versus bad. So, in a first pass at a definition, we could say that *unfortunately* expressed a [+ negative] stance toward *people beating guys* and by implication toward *big cities*, since bad things happen in them. Conversely, we would say that the utterance by B.56 expresses a [+ positive] stance toward *standardized sentences*. Utterances such as *Water freezes at zero degrees Celsius* have a neutral stance [- negative, - positive]. Generally, this is defined as evaluation (Hunston & Thompson, 200), affect, attitude, appraisal (Martin & White, 2005), or assessment. Another form of stance is agreement/disagreement: consider the following example

(123) B.7 utt3: And I think that it's not my responsibility to police myself and pay Pennsylvania what they believe they are owed even though, you know, the revenue stream went to another state.
B.7 utt4: I don't, I don't think that that's my responsibility as a, as a conscientious consumer.
A.8 utt1: <Lipsmack> I, *I'll agree* it, it's not your responsibility
A.8 utt2: but, b-, is it also legal,
B.9 utt1: [rustling noise]
A.10 utt1: for you to do that?
(Switchboard Corpus sw 0035 4372.)

in which the speakers are discussing the practicality and legality of paying state taxes when purchasing something by mail. In utterance A.8 speaker A aligns themselves to what speaker B had stated earlier, namely that they did not feel they had a responsibility to pay taxes to the state they lived in. However, speaker A does it in a hedged manner *I'll agree*, rather than *I agree*, as reinforced by the immediate challenge as to the legal status of such a position. DuBois refers to this intersubjective aspect of stancetaking as the *dialogic* aspect of stance.

Note also that in example (121) the speaker is expressing an emotional, personal attitude toward the violence, whereas in example (123) in turn B.7 utt4, the speaker is expressing their evaluation of the degree of certainty they credit the utterance with, in this case merely an opinion (*I think*) as opposed to fact (*I know*, or *It has been proven that....*). The former is called affective and the latter is usually known as epistemic stance (see Section 7.1.2). These are the two main types of stance (Gray & Biber, 2015, p. 219). There are other types of stance, and much more fine-grained taxonomies have been proposed, to be sure. We will review some of them in the rest of this section.

Du Bois (2007) situates his discussion of stance within intersubjectivity. You can think of a continuum from objective facts to subjective facts (i.e., how the self feels about the facts and about themselves, relative to the fact) and intersubjective facts (i.e., how all the participants to the exchange feel about the facts *and each other*. So, as Dubois has it, intersubjectivity is the "relation between one actor's subjectivity and another's" (DuBois, 2007, p. 140). Practically speaking, what this means is that speakers express a stance toward the matter at hand, possibly unwittingly, and "the very act of taking a stance becomes fair game to serve as a target for the next speakers' stance" (DuBois, 2007, p. 141). We saw a reflection of this recursive nature of stance in the reluctance expressed by repeated hedging (*almost, kind of wish*), with which the speaker in example (122) takes a stance about mandatory sentencing.

The dialogic intersubjective agreement/disagreement is often highlighted by syntactic parallelism among (parts of) the utterances. DuBois introduced a tool to highlight this aspect of conversation, the diagraph. Example (124) below displays a diagraph for example (123) earlier.

| (124) | | | | | |
|---|---|---|---|---|---|
| | B.7 | utt4: | that's | | my | responsibility |
| | A.8 | utt1: | it's | not | your | responsibility |

The vertical alignment of the components of the utterances highlights the parallelism. Note that the *not* in A.8 turn echoes the *I don't think* in B.7.

Summing up Du Bois's model is a triangle, as represented in Figure 7.2, involving the two subjects (interlocutors) and the object of the stance. Each interlocutor orients to (evaluates) the object and in turn is positioned vis-à-vis the object by doing so; furthermore, both interlocutors align with each other.

Du Bois and Kärkkäinen (2012) specifically address the emotional (affective) aspect of stance. Generally speaking, affective stance is merely part of how the participants position themselves in relation to the exchange. However, affective stance is clearly not a matter of binary choices (recall the [+/− positive] feature we introduced in our first pass at a definition) but rather affective evaluations range on a set of continua (happy-sad, love-hate, grateful-resentful, funny-serious, etc.). In relation to affect, alignment (the intersubjective interaction in the stance triangle) thus becomes not merely negotiated, as we saw in conversation and discourse analysis speakers negotiate the common understanding of a situation, but

> Alignment becomes a subtly nuanced domain of social action, in which speakers negotiate along a continuous scale the precise nature of the relation between their presently realized stance and a prior stance, whether overtly expressed or left implicit by another. Participants deploy subtle and often elusive signals to articulate the complex and highly variable mapping of the stance-alignment relation.
>
> *(Du Bois & Kärkkäinen, 2012, p. 440)*

In particular, Du Bois and Kärkkäinen (2012, p. 440) stress the "strategic ambiguity" carefully orchestrated by speakers, if they want to keep their options open as to how they want

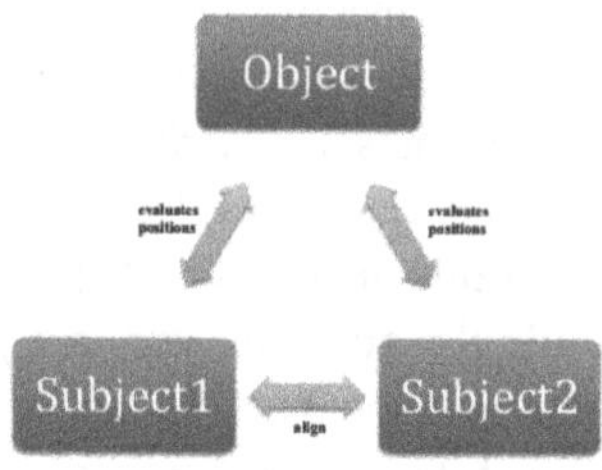


**Figure 7.2** The stance triangle (adapted from Du Bois, 2007).

to position themselves. Consider again example (123) earlier. What is exactly A's stance vis-à-vis B's refusal to pay taxes they admit to owing? A agrees but questions the legal status of the choice. How very strategically ambiguous of them!

Needless to say, participants do not always nicely cooperate. Often they disagree on how the exchange should go and stance and particularly affective elements are front and center in such exchanges. Goodwin (2007) analyzes an exchange between a father and daughter, in which the father is trying to show to his daughter how to do some math homework, whereas, in a nutshell, the daughter wants him to just tell her the right answers. Goodwin stresses the interplay of the cooperative, moral, and affective stances. During the interaction, after the daughter has refused to perform activities related to the homework, she flat out asks the father to tell her the answers. The father responds: "I can't just tell you. (...) you have to be nice to me okay. Don't talk to me in that tone of voice" (p. 65) which clearly mixes moral and affective stances. Interestingly, later in the conversation, after the participants have literally rearranged themselves and their props (textbook, scrap paper, pencil, etc.), the daughter finally cooperates and the tone changes radically, with both participants eventually laughing.

## 7.5 Corpus-Assisted Work

A final important way in which pragmatic markers have been investigated and classified is through corpus linguistics and particularly through the work of Doug Biber, Randi Reppen, and their colleagues. One of the most compelling findings from this work is that there are significant differences in the frequency of occurrence of various words and parts of speech depending on the different genres and styles of the texts. This has direct consequences for language teaching: different kinds of text will require different emphases on words, parts of speech, and syntactic constructions, not to mention that in ESP it is necessary to expose students to the right kind of text for them to be able to absorb the stylistic and generic requirements of the text. Exposing business students to literary texts, while meritorious, is not likely to be as beneficial as exposure to business texts.

### 7.5.1 Stance Markers

Biber and Finegan (1989) present an analysis of stance markers in various styles of English. The markers they examine are as follows:

1. Affect markers
2. Certainty markers
3. Doubt markers
4. Hedges
5. Emphatics
6. Modals (possibility, necessity, predictive)

They use a four-way classification of stance, summarized in Table 7.2.

**Table 7.2** Biber and Finegan's (1989) four-way classification of stance

| Affect | | Evidentiality | |
|---|---|---|---|
| *Positive* | *Negative* | *Certainty* | *Doubt* |
| luckily | unfortunately | surely | allegedly |
| amazing | sad | obvious | dubious |

Biber and Finegan proceed to cluster their texts based on the frequency of the stance markers in them. Thus, for example, personal letters display a lot of affect markers whereas face-to-face conversations do so much less. One can speculate, although Biber and Finegan do not do so, that writers compensate for the lack of interpersonal feedback available in face-to-face conversation by overtly expressing affect. Another cluster is labeled "faceless stance" and as mentioned earlier, it includes written expository material, including fiction, academic prose, radio broadcasts, and prepared speeches. In fact, even a third of face-to-face conversations belong to the faceless cluster. This leads Biber and Finegan to conclude that the use of affective and evidential stance is "marked" in English, that is, the normal choice is *not* to mark affective and evidential stance (Biber & Finegan, 1989, p. 108). A cluster labeled "interactional evidentiality" is well exemplified by example (122). This kind of text is usually conversational, and makes frequent use of evidentials. There are other clusters, but they are less clearly delineated; the interested reader should consult the work by Biber and Finegan.

Biber's work on registers shows that academic writing marks stance significantly less than spoken registers or written registers that are more personal, such as news, or fiction. In other words, academic writing is impersonal ("faceless" Biber & Finegan, 1989, p. 108) and "objective." This is true even within academic discourse: spoken academic discourse has more expressions of stance than the written kind (Gray & Biber, 2015). Additional notable work on the differences between spoken and written registers and the use of pragmatic markers has been conducted with workplace corpora. Vine (2016) explored the use of *eh*, *you know* and *I think* in New Zealand workplaces collected as part of the Language in the Workplace Project that has been ongoing since 1996 (retrieved from http://www.victoria.ac.nz/lwp). As anticipated, *eh* was used least in formal contexts and most commonly in informal conversations. Similar patterns were shown for *you know* although frequencies were much closer across contexts for this marker. However, there was no clear correlation between *I think* and the formality of the context in which it appeared. Vine suggests that this is in part because the marker is shifting from its traditional role as a speaker-oriented marker to one that primarily indexes informality.

Lastly, we examine the work completed in this area using the Augmentative and Alternative Communication (AAC) and Non-AAC Workplace Corpus (ANAWC) (Pickering & Bruce, 2009). This corpus was built to compare the typical language patterns of both AAC users and comparable non-AAC users in the workplace. AAC devices are usually portable speech-generating technologies that can be housed in laptops or smartphones and accessed using a keyboard or head or eye tracking technology. They are used by people who have some form of speech impairment due to disorders such as ALS or motor neuron disease. There is a common misperception that these devices enable users to contribute to conversations in ways that closely match natural speech; in fact, they are quite limited in terms of providing quick access to context-specific language and AAC users have expressed their frustration as to how long it can take to produce the language necessary to join in the conversations around them. One user states: "Of course, the speed is not like normal speech. So, often a moment passes before one can type a comment. And I find it necessary to edit my comments, and therefore my thoughts are sometimes oversimplified" (McNaughton et al., 2001, p. 187).

This has very particular ramifications for the use of pragmatic markers. When the corpus was divided into two sub-corpora of AAC and non-AAC speakers, AAC user discourse lacked all the typical pragmatic markers that appeared in the language of the non-AAC speakers (e.g., *you know, I mean, and so on*). This is the result of the "trade-off" that AAC users report they often have to make when faced with communicating in real time. It simply is not possible to generate the typical interactional features of conversation and stay relevant in the "time stream" of the conversation. Two examples adapted from the corpus are shown below. In the first example, AAC-user Ron uses only the nouns *city* and *address* to communicate with one of his co-workers (bolded). In contrast, in the second example between two non-AAC users, we see the more typical kinds of stance and pragmatic markers (bolded) that would normally appear:

(125) AAC-Ron: **City**
Co-worker: He wants me to do the epic route power out tomorrow morning. They've got a big swim meet he wants me to get up at three and check if it's snowing go in at four coz the rest of the crew comes in at six on Saturday so I'm gonna get a jump on it
AAC-Ron: **Address**
Co-worker: But it's a good thing you asked. I'm listening where is this going in? On the side? On the bottom? You got these upside down sir
AAC-Ron: **Right address**

(126) Marissa: **Alrighty**, January or March?
Charly: You go because I am so glad you got your stuff in order because my stuff is so scrambled up
Marissa: **Well** I got all the minutes **right here** that I know have been written if we need to put copies in the other book
Charly: I was working on it then somehow
Marissa: but I kept it here so we got it
Charly: **Thank you**
Marissa: **You're welcome**

## 7.6 Conclusion

In conclusion, the expression of the speakers' attitude or stance vis-à-vis what they are saying is now a mature field of research in pragmatics. Particularly such areas as deixis, modality, pragmatic markers, and stance have reached a significant level of research and sophisticated models have been proposed. The research on the applications of this area of metapragmatics to SLA and TESOL has been heavily influenced and boosted by corpus-assisted studies, to which it lends itself, even as it has not quite fully developed yet. Possibly because speakers tend not to be aware of their use of metapragmatic markers, a consistent result is that overall language proficiency parallels the acquisition of pragmatic markers. The full effect of the explicit teaching of pragmatic markers has not yet been considered in detail.

## 7.7 Pragmatic Markers in SLA and TESOL

### 7.7.1 Contrastive and Intercultural Studies in SLA and TESOL

Different languages have different pragmatics markers, indeed even different varieties (dialects) of the same language often have different markers (cf. Foolen, 2011, p. 220). Even when there is a formal equivalence, as in Italian *allora* and French *alors*, which are obviously very close, even phonologically, there are subtle differences (Bazzanella et al., 2007). If we compare *allora* with English *then*, which is (one of) the translations of *allora*, the differences are even greater. To name one case, *allora* (which corresponds to both *alright* and *then*) can be used along the lines of *alright!* sentence initially to wrap up a previous topic and start a new one, while this use is definitely not allowed with *then*.

Contrastive studies and translation studies concur on the problematic aspects of transferring pragmatic markers use across language. Contrastive studies such as Romero-Trillo (1997, 2007; English–Spanish), Cuenca (2003, Cuenca & Bach, 2007; English–Spanish–Catalan), Bazzanella et al. (2007; Italian–French), confirm that not only do different languages have different repertoires of pragmatic markers, but they use them differently. For example, Romero-Trillo (1997, 2007) shows that English and Spanish have different pattern of markers for discourse management, for example, English uses more *you see* and *you know* whereas *entiendes* is only used in interrogatives in Spanish. House (2009) finds that ELF speakers use *you know* differently than L1 speakers.

Translation of pragmatic markers is notoriously difficult. Bazzanella (2006) notes that "translating them into other languages (...) is an extremely delicate task, much more so than with respect to other parts of discourse" (p. 452) 'also because "the conditions of use of the interjections are not the same" (Cuenca, forthcoming). For more discussion of translation of pragmatic markers, especially with the use of parallel corpora, see Foolen (2011, pp. 227–228). Parallel corpora are corpora made up of a text, say *War and Peace*, and its translations, preferably more than one.

Despite their semantic agnosticism, we know that pragmatic markers are important in L1 comprehension, particularly in discourse genres that are very informationally "heavy" such as classroom lectures. Flowerdew and Tauroza (1995) showed, for example, that lectures from which discourse markers had been removed were significantly harder to understand than those with the discourse markers left in.

This has significant consequences for L2 learners who are in high stakes positions in EAP (English for Academic Purposes) environments such as the International Teaching Assistants (ITA) that we mentioned in Chapter 6. In general, research has found that NNSs use fewer discourse markers in L2. NNSs have a smaller repertoire of discourse markers (Fuller, 2003; Müller, 2005; Sankoff et al., 1997); moreover, those they use are used in limited functions (Fung & Carter, 2007; Hong Kong L2 speakers–British English). Conversely, Sankoff et al. (1997), Hellermann and Vergun (2007), and Liao (2019) report that L2 learners' integration and acculturation correlate with increased native-like use of markers. Wei (2011) also finds a positive correlation between the English proficiency of Chinese learners and the use of discourse markers. The finding is not limited to English: for example, Tsai and Chu (2017) find the same pattern for L1 Chinese speakers and L2 Chinese learners. Studies have also looked at the acquisition of specific markers such as *you know, well,* and *yeah.* Fuller (2003) reports overuse of *you know* by proficient NNS, which she interprets as formulaic learning of easy to acquire targets. Huang (2019) shows that Chinese intermediate learners significantly underuse *well,* whereas Swedish ones overuse it. Liao (2009) considers Chinese ITAs and finds significant differences of usage between NS and NNS, including overuse of some discourse markers, such as *yeah,* and different functions.

As with other topics in pragmatics, studies have also addressed classroom instruction. Pragmatic markers seem to be below the threshold of consciousness, insofar as their pragmatic function is concerned; so, the question arises, can they be taught explicitly? Fordyce (2013) tested this question using epistemic stance in English with Japanese learners (e.g., modal verbs and adverbs and evidential verbs). His results show a significant positive difference for explicit instruction (pp. 15–16). In the opposite context of English learners of Japanese, Narita (2012) investigated whether the inclusion of conscious-raising activities increased the development of hearsay evidential markers (i.e., pragmatic markers used by the speaker to indicate that they heard something from a third party such as *I heard that*). She found that following a focus on hearsay reports in their L1 and then L2, a treatment group performed significantly better than the control group on both knowledge and production of these markers and that this was maintained in a delayed post-test.

Salsbury and Bardovi-Harlig (2000) showed that epistemic stance marker acquisition parallels L2 proficiency development. Gablasova et al. (2017) show that variation in the use of epistemic stance markers exists at the level of different tasks (academic presentation vs. conversation, for example) and even of the individual speaker. Explicit instruction in pragmatic markers has been found to be beneficial in EFL classrooms for both writing performance and improved listening comprehension (Sadeghi & Heidaryan, 2012; Vahid Dastjerdi & Shirzad, 2010). Pickering and Byrd (2008) also note the importance of L2 learners being able to make connections between what they read for class and what they hear in class. They worked with two corpora – the Academic Word List corpus of written English (AWL) and the Michigan corpus of academic spoken English (MICASE). They compared typical stance marking between the two. In the AWL, stance marking typically appeared as impersonal markers such as *is likely to be, should be able to, it may be that.* Conversely, in MICASE these were usually personal markers such as *I don't know, I think it was, you don't have to.* In their view, it seems clear that students will require help in transferring written forms to their spoken counterparts and thus specific textual realization, for example, spoken or written, should be clearly modeled.

There seems to be a fair consensus that stance markers align with pragmatic markers more generally in that L1 speakers differ from L2 speakers in their use and that increased proficiency comes closer to NS models. Stance markers can be taught explicitly, but there is a lot of variation both in how individual speakers use them and of the generic constraints imposed by various situations. From a teaching materials standpoint, there is an agreement that pragmatic markers have typically either been ignored (e.g., Sankoff et al., 1997: "a feature that is not explicitly taught in school" p. 191) or systematically under-taught. In addition, Römer (2006) concludes that actual usage is not well represented in textbooks: "researchers found considerable mismatches between naturally-occurring English and the English that is put forward as a model in pedagogical descriptions." (p. 126). The development of teaching materials based on natural language usage as collected in large corpora (e.g., the Collins COBUILD series and the *Longman Grammar of Spoken and Written English*) go some way toward alleviating the problem (see Römer, 2006, 2011 for excellent reviews); however, given the complexity of the subject, the lack of agreement in the field, and the general difficulty of teaching polyfunctional items, we note the need for further work on teaching pragmatic and discourse markers.

### 7.7.2 Sample Teaching Materials

**Lesson Plan 1: Using COCA to Investigate Language Function**

**Step 1: Collecting Corpus Data**
The corpus of contemporary American English (COCA) is a corpus of over 500 million words collected between 1990–2015 which is freely available online. It is possible to search for any of the kinds of pragmatic markers that we have discussed in this chapter. This lesson focuses on the functional uses of *well*.

Either the students or teacher can collect multiple examples of the form. The example in Figure 7.3 displays the first 10 instances of the use of *well* in the corpus.

**Step 2: Students Discuss the Different Kinds of Uses They Find**
For example:

1. *Well* as a pragmatic marker, for example, *well, when we initiated the show....*
2. *Well* as an adverb, for example, *Wen was not sleeping well*
3. *Well* as a conjunction, for example, *as well as new residential towers*

**Step 3: Collecting Examples**
Students focus on collecting examples of the pragmatic marker *well* specifically and describe typical contexts of use, for example, different discourse genres such as conversation, academic talk, etc. This will give them an idea of how widely the function is used in natural language.

**Lesson Plan 2: Recognizing and Practicing Stance Marking in EAP Writing**
This lesson is based on Coxhead and Byrd (2007) who note that "academic prose [is made up of] particular kinds of nouns combined with particular kinds of verbs and used with a range of other grammatical features expected by members of that discourse community" (p. 134).

| | | | | | | | |
|---|---|---|---|---|---|---|---|
| 1 | 2019 | SPOK | NBC Today | A | B | C | Fenway Park, the ballpark that his famous grandfather called home for twenty-three years. **Well**, Mike also got the chance to play left field in the same spot his |
| 2 | 2018 | SPOK | CBS Morning | A | B | C | true, to denigrate these women, to eviscerate these women certainly could not sit **well** with certain of these jurors. It did not sit well with the public. |
| 3 | 2018 | SPOK | NPR Sunday | A | B | C | that people may not be familiar with. GARCIA-NAVARRO: Like what? 1CHARLES2: **Well**, when we initially started the show, we didn't do gender f-word, |
| 4 | 2018 | FIC | NewEnglandRev | A | B | C | risk. Building was always a risk. # By fall Wen was not sleeping **well**. He would lie awake and think of the men sitting there at the site |
| 5 | 2018 | MAG | TechCrunch | A | B | C | president of automotive. Guillen will oversee all automotive operations and program management, as **well** as coordinate Tesla's supply chain. Guillen previously headed up Tesla's truck program |
| 6 | 2018 | NEWS | Washington Post | A | B | C | 's other Trump-branded towers in the cities of Pune, Mumbai and Kolkata, as **well** as new residential towers just a few miles away from the planned IREO office tower |
| 7 | 2017 | SPOK | CNN: CNN Newsroom | A | B | C | secret communications attacking when and where they could. ISIS' -changing-cir# All right. **Well** let's turn our attention now to those four U.S. soldiers killed in Niger. |
| 8 | 2017 | SPOK | Fox: Media Buzz | A | B | C | of the media don't like Trump pushing these NFL protest. it's worked **well** for him. It's controversial, but a lot of his supporters like it |
| 9 | 2017 | SPOK | NBC: Today Show | A | B | C | quite movie that broken to the -- KATHIE-LEE-GIFFORD# -- I love to see those do **well**. TIM-STACK# Yeah. It's really supposed to be great and that broken to |
| 10 | 2017 | MAG | The Verge | A | B | C | teams, the White Walkers and the wights pick up +60 each for city-sacking as **well**. Bran gets +50 for warging to the Wall to see all this happen ( |

**Figure 7.3** Instances of *well* in COCA.

**Step 1** The teacher selects texts for analysis and study: Preferably, these would be tailored to the students' academic disciplines.

**Step 2** The teacher analyzes the texts to prepare them for student use: Key lexicogrammatical features that indicate stance are marked. Further examples are drawn from authentic data (or corpus-based materials such as the COBUILD materials).

**Step 3** Students work with the texts to identify and discuss the ways in which stance is conveyed.

**Step 4** The teacher sets a writing task that requires students to practice using the most common examples of stance marking with discipline appropriate nouns. These can cover multiple disciplines (e.g., the Academic Wordlist) or a single discipline (e.g., Smith et al., 2007).

# 8

# Interactional Sociolinguistics

In this chapter, we introduce interactional sociolinguistics, an influential component of pragmatics. We focus primarily on the work of John Gumperz, and particularly on the idea of contextualization, which as we will see, is now a central idea in pragmatics. To do so, we reconstruct the intellectual environment in which his approach developed, particularly the work of Hymes, Garfinkel, and Goffman. We then explore how interactionism has been applied to teaching English and to SLA generally.

## 8.1 The California Milieu

Our discussion starts from an interesting confluence of scholars with related ideas in a relatively small geographical area. When we talked about ordinary language theory as a predecessor of speech act theory, we argued that the ideas of ordinary language philosophy were "in the air" so to speak, in post-war England (Oxford and Cambridge). Likewise, in Chapter 6 we talked about the Prague school, located in what was at the time Czechoslovakia. With the birth of the interactionalist approach to socio-pragmatics we witness a similar phenomenon with a group of like-minded scholars that happened to all be in Berkeley, Los Angeles, and Stanford or nearby, roughly in the decade 1960–1970.

Indeed, even a cursory glance at the faculty at Berkeley and UCLA during that period shows a remarkable group of scholars who influenced each other in different ways. John Gumperz joined UC Berkeley in 1956 and stayed on until his retirement in 1990, when he left for UC Santa Barbara where he worked until his death, in 2013. Dell Hymes, the founder with Gumperz of the ethnography of communication approach, was at Berkeley between 1960 and 1965, when he left for the University of Pennsylvania. Together they co-edited the foundational book: *The Ethnography of Communication* (1964). At the same time, still at Berkeley, were philosophers John Searle (at Berkeley 1959–present) and Paul Grice (at Berkeley from 1967 until 1988, the year of his death). Slightly later, the Lakoffs arrive at Berkeley as well: Robin Lakoff (at Berkeley 1972–present) and George Lakoff (at Berkeley 1972–2016, when he retired). Both Stephen Levinson and Deborah Tannen were students of Gumperz at Berkeley: Levinson from 1970 to 1977, when he graduated with his PhD and Tannen, from 1976 to 1979, when she also earned her PhD.

*Pragmatics and Its Applications to TESOL and SLA*, First Edition. Salvatore Attardo and Lucy Pickering.

If we turn to sociology, we find that Erving Goffman, who influenced Gumperz and sociolinguistics at large, was at Berkeley between 1958 and 1968. Harvey Sachs and Emanuel Schegloff both completed their PhDs at Berkeley, in 1966 and 1967, respectively, while Gail Jefferson completed hers at UC Irvine, in 1972. If we look only slightly south of Berkeley we find Harold Garfinkel, also a sociologist, who joined UCLA in 1954 and spent his entire career there, until his retirement in 1987 and then became emeritus until his death in 2011. Gregory Bateson, an anthropologist who influenced Goffman and Gumperz, was active in Palo Alto in the early 1950s and joined UC Santa Cruz in 1972, where he held a visiting appointment. He died in 1980. We have barely scratched the surface. As Bauman and Sherzer (1975, p. 99) note, for example ten out of fourteen authors contributing to the special issue of *American Anthropologist*, co-edited by Gumperz and Hymes in 1964, were at that time either at Berkeley or at Stanford. The "Berkeley milieu" is briefly described in Levinson (2015). The sociology department at Berkeley in the 1960s is described in Fine and Manning (2003).

### 8.1.1 The Sociological/Phenomenological Approach

Gumperz, Hymes, conversation analysis (CA), and discourse analysis have all been clearly influenced by a sociological application of phenomenology that goes under the label of social constructivism, that is, the social construction of the self/experience. This was mediated by the work of two influential sociologists: Harold Garfinkel and Erving Goffman. We will briefly explain the significance of their work as fundamental influences on Gumperz's thinking and interactionism.

Garfinkel, the founder of ethnomethodology was a sociologist, but he was influenced by phenomenology (Alfred Schütz's attention to everyday life, in particular). He introduced the term "ethnomethodology," coined as a compound of *ethno-* (as in ethnobiology, that is, the beliefs and knowledge a given society has about biology) and *methodology*. By "methodology" Garfinkel referred originally to the "work" that jury members, in one of his studies, did in order to establish what counted as evidence, factuality versus hearsay, and other such methodological issues. So, ethnomethodology is the sense-making activities that a given social group engages in to establish its "rules and procedures." He also introduced the "breaching experiments" in which one deliberately goes against social expectations in order to highlight the unspoken expectations of the participants. For example, when playing tic-tac-toe one participant deliberately placed a circle so as to overlap with a line, rather than fitting in a square, eliciting the remark: "What is this, a joke?" which reveals that participants in a game engage in it seriously and with the expectation that all participants will follow certain commonsensical practices (placing the circles and crosses in the correct location, in the correct order, etc.).

Goffman's work is well known and he is widely considered one of the most important sociologists of the 20th century. We already saw the significant influence he had on politeness theory with the idea of "face." We can only consider in any detail one other aspect of his work here, namely frame analysis, but it bears keeping in mind that frames and face are only two aspects of Goffman's overarching interest in the social construction of personality and social life.

The principal exposition of Goffman's work on framing is in the classic *Frame Analysis: An Essay on the Organization of Experience* (1974). Frames, in a different but not entirely unrelated sense than the one we have seen in semantics (see Section 1.1.2), are the social structures that organize experience. In other words, they are the ways that we make sense of the world and of experiences. For example, imagine that several employees of a company walk roughly at the same time into a room and most of them sit at a table. That does not constitute a meeting. In order for a meeting to count as such, someone must have called the meeting and the participants must have agreed previously to meet; there must be some agenda, that is, a reason to meet, the participants must be at least two, and so on. In other words, the behavior (being into a room together, sitting at a table, etc., must be framed as a meeting for it to be one). However, suppose that the same employees happen to be in the lunch room eating their lunches. Mary starts discussing a problem and the others join in, suggesting solutions, volunteering to help, and so on. One of the employees might remark: "Are we having a meeting?" Samantha, Mary's boss, who is also having her lunch, might say "We are now!" Note that Samantha must have the authority to re-frame to situation as an extemporaneous meeting, which is why we made her the boss. Imagine now that, absent Samantha, Mary asks John to do some research that will help fix the problem. John might reply, "Hey, this is not a meeting, I am eating my lunch." John is here refusing to re-frame the situation as a meeting, essentially arguing that one cannot be given work assignments while one is on lunch break.

Goffman argues that there are primary frames, along the lines of the meeting example above. They are "seen as rendering what would otherwise be a meaningless aspect of the scene into something that is meaningful" (1974, p. 21). A random assembly of people in a room becomes a meeting only if the meeting frame is activated. Primary frames may be natural or social. Natural primary frames are things like the weather. If it rains, it rains regardless of our intention. Social frames, on the contrary, "incorporate the will, aim, and controlling effort of an intelligence, a live agency, the chief one being the human being" (p. 22). Weather forecasting, for example, is a social frame as is the use of paper money, as we saw earlier (see Section 1.1.1). Consider now the following situation:

(127) Two men walk toward one another; when they come into contact they throw their arms around each other, and slap each other's backs, while emitting loud vocalizations.

and contrast it with the following

(128) Two friends who have not seen each other for a long time greet each other.

Clearly, (127) is closer to a natural frame, whereas (128) is a social frame. The presence of intentionality and control should be fairly easy to spot in the description of the two men as "friends" (which obviously requires human intelligence and emotional awareness; two rocks cannot be friends, except metaphorically or figuratively), and the "explanation" for their extreme greeting (they have not seen each other in a long time) which again presupposes human agency and emotions: a rock cannot miss another rock, or, say, the rain. Only humans (or highly evolved animals) can experience the feeling of loss and the proprioception of the passing of time required to miss someone.

There exists a second layer of framing, called "keying." Goffman starts his discussion of keying by referencing Bateson's work on play. Bateson's example is easy to understand. In a 1955 essay titled *A Theory of Play and Fantasy*, Bateson asks the question of how monkeys that are playing can distinguish between reality and play, that is, a real bite and a playful one. The answer is that play carries the metamessage "this is play" and thus "frames" the situation as playful. More specifically, if the bite were real, it would hurt the monkey and perhaps draw blood. By acting as if they were about to bite each other seriously but then delivering only a "nip," the monkeys convey to each other that this is not a real fight, but a pretend fight, a playful one.

This idea can be extended to framing/keying more generally. Goffman extends Bateson's idea by identifying several keys: make-believe, contests, ceremonial, technical redoings, and regroundings. Of course, the absence of a key is in a sense, another key. We can think of it as the ordinary, real, actual, untransformed activity (Goffman, 1974, pp. 46–47). Goffman notes that when opposed to play (make-believe) the primary frame is labeled "serious" (Goffman, 1974, p. 46). Keys are thus secondary frames. Let us briefly consider the five keyings described by Goffman:

- Make-believe: Make-believe is the overall category for fiction, theatrical, film, and television performance, play, and humor, including hoaxes. Essentially all "pretend" play.
- Contests: In this category fall all sports and competitions. Goffman notes that "the rules of the sport supply restrictions" (1974, p. 56), for example, in American Football, one can do all sorts of aggressive things such as shoving, literally running into another player, or violently tackling them to the ground, but one cannot grab the face mask or the helmet of another player. In running, shortcuts are not allowed, despite the fact that the ostensible goal of a race (i.e., getting as fast as possible from point a to point b) would seem to allow for, or even encourage them.
- Ceremonials: Ceremonials include weddings, funerals, ribbon cuttings, launching of ships, and so on. Goffman notes that unlike in make-believe performances, such as acting, one is usually oneself during ceremonials (p. 58) or one is a representative of an entity (the state, the university, etc.). Hitting a ship with a bottle during a ceremony is radically different from doing so in real life (the latter may get you arrested for vandalism).
- Technical redoings: Under this category fall all types of practice, including simulations and demonstrations. For example, a father taking his daughter to practice driving in an empty parking lot or an orchestra performing the same piece over and over are all examples of technical redoings. Note how it is perfectly normal for the director of the orchestra to stop the rehearsal performance to comment on it or to correct errors, but this would be unacceptable during a real-life performance. Likewise a simulation may be paused, unlike real life. A demonstration (or demo for short) is a redoing for the purpose of showing off aspects of a device or activity. Demonstrations typically are limited in time and costs incurred. Cinematic previews (trailers) can be thought of as demonstrations. It would not make sense to have a trailer as long as the movie itself or that costs as much as the movie itself to produce. Conversely, the trailer must present enough affinity

to the movie that patrons will not feel deceived if they decide to view the movie after seeing the trailer.

- Regroundings: Regroundings are situations in which an activity is shifted into a different one, for example, in charity work, someone who is not a professional carpenter (such as former president Jimmy Carter) builds or renovates houses for a charity, such as Habitat for Humanity. Models who become spokespersons for animal rights organizations play a similar role. Goffman lists apprenticeships, in which labor is rekeyed as a learning opportunity, as another example. The essential idea behind regroundings is that an activity that has already a primary frame, say home building, is rekeyed as charity work. In all these situations, the person doing the work agrees not to be compensated, or to be compensated much less than usual, for the sake of charity, to support a cause, or to gain experience. For example, Bill Buford, a New Yorker writer, worked as an apprentice in Mario Batali's kitchen, for a period, for no wages, but then went on to author the successful nonfiction book *Heat*, in which he describes his culinary adventures.

### 8.1.2 Conversation Analysis

CA was founded by Harvey Sacks, Emanuel (Manny) Schegloff, and Gail Jefferson. CA is arguably one of the most influential approaches to interactional pragmatics. Garfinkel met Harvey Sacks in 1959 and eventually brought him to Los Angeles in 1963. Sacks lectured at UCLA and UC Irvine from 1964 until his death in an accident in 1975. Garfinkel and Sacks collaborated closely and co-authored a paper. Schegloff was at UCLA from 1972 until 2010, when he became emeritus. He worked closely with Sacks and co-authored several papers with him, as did Jefferson. Jefferson, originally a student of Sacks, went on to shape the whole transcription process of CA, which has a very significant role in the CA process.

We can see a very clear influence of phenomenology on CA, in the focus on ecologically valid data and interpretations, that is, interpretations have to make sense to the participants in the social fact and on the emphasis on bracketing, that is, suspending preconceived ideas about the phenomena to be observed. The transcription system grew increasingly sophisticated and complex and plays a major role in bracketing expectations about how conversations work. Most of the examples of conversations in this book, for example, are transcribed using variants of Jefferson's transcription system.

CA emphasizes the social construction of the order in dialogue. For example, what makes an answer an answer? A typical linguistic approach would look for a given set of features, for example a special intonation, or a given connection with the prior turn such that there is an information gap in the prior turn and the answer fills that gap. A phenomenological approach looks at properties that are emergent from the social situation. Thus if the speakers involved in the conversation orient (react) to the turn as if it were an answer, then the turn is an answer. On this basis, CA identifies sequences and other organizational patterns. Thus an adjacency pair is a sequence of turns that are required to be one after the other (adjacent). Question and Answer or Greeting – Greeting are adjacency pairs. Note how if you say hello to someone and they do not reciprocate the hello you will immediately perceive this as an insult or as a problem (perhaps they did not hear you).

## 8.2 Communicative Competence

One of the major influences of Gumperz's work comes from Hymes' ethnography of communication (Gumperz, 2015, p. 309). The very significant term "communicative competence" comes from Hymes (1972). In a nutshell, the communicative competence of a speaker is all the knowledge one needs to be able to function as a speaker in a community, which includes grammatical competence, obviously, but also includes when it is appropriate to utter a sentence and to whom one can address a given utterance. More specifically, communicative competence (see Figure 8.1) includes the following:

- Grammatical competence: In the Chomskian sense, it is the capacity to put together sentences and derive their meaning.
- Sociocultural competence: This is the knowledge of the social aspects of communication, such as to whom can you speak, when is it appropriate to speak to them, what sounds friendly, what sounds ironical, and so on. Social status, taboos, appropriateness, politeness, and impoliteness are all subsumed by this competence.
- Strategic competence: This is the capacity to communicate successfully, especially in situations in which the communication may be problematic (e.g., speakers of different languages, or of different cultures). It may include paraphrasing, slowing down, repeating, and even increased use of gestures, such as miming an action[1], but also more high-level strategies such as omitting information, ignoring errors, and simplifying.
- Actional competence: This is capacity to choose the right speech acts to convey a given illocutionary force, such as apologizing, requesting, or complaining, but also showing interest and expressing emotions; and, in writing, the choice of the right moves (Swales, 1990), for example, supporting a thesis with evidence, or the organization of news reports.
- Discourse competence: This is the capacity to organize sentences/utterances in larger units such as conversations, lectures, poems, contracts, emails, shopping lists, joke telling, and encyclopedias. The rules and organization of each genre vary significantly, for example, oral genres are very different from written texts. This competency also subsumes cohesion, coherence, the given/new organization of discourse, paragraph organization, and so on.

Summing up, there is a lot more to being a competent speaker than being able to construct a sentence. Yet, despite the significant breadth of the definition of communicative competence, it is "restricted" to communication. Context is of course part of communicative, competence but it is an even broader construct.

1 For example, the thumb and index finger are arranged in a C shape and the other three fingers lined up with the forefinger and the hand is raised to the mouth. This gesture mimics "drinking" and is also the ASL sign for "drink."

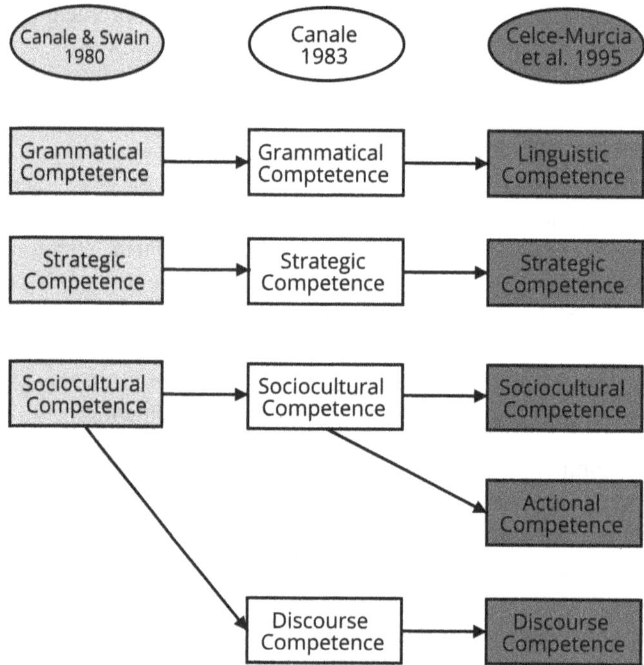


**Figure 8.1** The evolution of the communicative competence model (adapted from Celce-Murcia et al., 1995).

## 8.3 The Definition of Context

### 8.3.1 Context

With interactional sociolinguistics, the concept of context, which has been more or less overtly present in all of pragmatics, really comes to the foreground. So, it is necessary to look into its definition, which is far from self-evident. First, we need to start from the paradoxical point that in the late 1960s the world of linguistics was captivated by context-free grammars, championed by Noam Chomsky. The idea was literally that the syntax of a sentence (i.e., its grammaticality) could be generated (calculated, predicted) purely by formal rules of grammar that need not reference the context at all (context-free). Thus the stance of Gumperz and Hymes was that while grammatical competence may possibly have been context-free, communicative competence was certainly not, as we saw in Section 8.1.

There is agreement that the full meaning of a linguistic expression can be grasped only within the situation in which the linguistic expression is uttered, that is, the context of the utterance.

Consider now a simple example and let us reconstruct as best we can the context for it: Pickering says to Attardo: "You have to stop eating donuts." Attardo replies: "Over my dead body." These will be our two utterances. Obviously, we have our participants, Speaker 1

(Pickering) and Speaker 2 (Attardo). Also obviously, we have a situation in which the two speakers are present. In this case, they could be sitting in their car driving to the donut shop outside the university (let's call this situation 1). Alternatively, they could be in a hospital room, with Attardo in the bed, where he is recovering from bariatric surgery (situation 2). It is clear that depending on the situation, the overall meaning of the utterances changes radically: while in situation 1 Pickering's remark is a gentle tease couched as an imperative and Attardo's retort is an idiom here used in its standard meaning of emphatic denial, in situation 2, Pickering's remark is either epistemic (given the evidence of the bariatric surgery I conclude that you should stop eating donuts) or an expression of concern (facial expressions would disambiguate, for example, if she had a concerned look on her face), whereas Attardo's remark takes a completely different turn by literalizing the idiom (i.e., he may be willing to die in order to continue eating donuts). Furthermore, we would need to know what both speakers think about weight-loss surgery, eating habits, Attardo's will to live without donuts, Pickering's feelings toward Attardo (and vice versa, naturally), their attitudes toward food, eating habits, surgery, and so on. Furthermore, we would need to know about their mutual history of joking together.

In short, the list of potentially relevant factors is long and indeterminate, that is, we could keep adding more factors, for example, are there other people who may be hearing the exchange? Are they strangers or intimates? How well do they know Pickering and Attardo? As Attardo (2016) put it, there is some agreement that

> certain factors within the situation are particularly significant, including gestures and facial expressions of the participants, their social roles, the setting of the exchange, the objects surrounding the participants, the linguistic, cultural and educational backgrounds of the participants, their beliefs, including those concerning the situation, the social procedures and conventions that regulate the situation.

We cannot go into the detail of each of these factors, and moreover some of them are rather obvious: if one utters a sentence with exaggerated facial expressions or gestures, one is likely to be altering the overall meaning of the utterance; likewise, the cultural beliefs of the participants will affect whether one receives the utterance "You have put on some weight" as a compliment or an insult (many societies do not share the American obsession with thinness). One may question other factors that are seemingly less prone to affect the understanding of a sentence. For example, one may wonder how the setting of an exchange may affect the meaning of an utterance such as "I left the book at home." However, if the exchange takes place in a classroom between a student and their teacher, in a library, or at a coffee house where friends are meeting for their book club discussion, the import of the sentence will be inevitably quite different.

Thus, the rather extensive list of contextual factors affecting the interpretation of utterances can be shown to be necessary. And, there's more! Most researchers agree that context is a psychological construct, that is, it is not a given in the world, which we can observe objectively, but it is a mental representation of the world. In other words, the speakers have a representation of the context in their minds (not necessarily above the threshold of consciousness, that is, the speakers may not be aware of it). For example, Gumperz (1982, p. 101) describes the establishment of context as "*informed guessing* based on what we know about the physical setting, the participants and their backgrounds, and how they relate to the situation at hand to other known activities" (Our emphasis, SA/LP). This representation is not static: the speakers build it and update it on the fly, that is, it is dynamic and not limited to linguistics actions: again, according to Gumperz (1982, p. 101), the "initial hypotheses [=the informed guessing discussed earlier] are subject to *constant modification* by our perception of information signalled in both the form and content of speech" (our emphasis, SA/LP). Finally, the representation is reflexive; the speakers are mutually aware of their beliefs. This becomes very important when we consider theory of mind phenomena, in which how we behave is predicated on how to what we think our interlocutor's mental representation of the context is.

Several theories of pragmatics have introduced ways of accounting for the reflexive representation of context in the speakers' minds. Clark's (1996) "common ground," relevance theory's "mutual knowledge or manifestness," and the "contexts" in so-called dynamic theories of interpretation (see Roberts, 2012 for a summary) are all examples of how this can be handled. The basic idea is that both speakers keep a "score board" (the metaphor comes from Lewis, 1979, one of the first to address the issue) of entities and referents known to both speakers. The idea extends to multiple speakers naturally.

So, interactional sociolinguistics is based on communicative competence and on a strongly contextual view of language. However, there is more to the approach.

### 8.3.2 Communicative Practices

Gumperz's starting point is that all human communication occurs within a communicative practice, that is, a social environment distinct from the social factors external to communication (say, social status) and likewise distinct from the purely linguistic factors of, say, grammar. Communicative practices are goal-oriented, that is, the speakers engage in them for a purpose, albeit not necessarily a practical one (e.g., buying fish for dinner). In other words, speakers may engage in a conversation for entertainment, or to reinforce social bonds (phatic communion, see Section 6.1.1).

However, Garfinkel (1967) had shown that talk is based on "practical reasoning" to convey what speakers really intend, since language inevitably underdetermines the reality it refers to. Consider the following example, which is one of Garfinkel's famous breaching experiments, in which conventions of social behavior are deliberately violated to reveal their nature:

(129) Case 3: On Friday night my husband and I were watching television. My husband remarked that he was tired. I asked, "How are you tired? Physically, mentally, or just bored?"

S: I don't know, I guess physically, mainly.

E: You mean that your muscles ache or your bones?

S: I guess so. Don't be so technical. (After more watching)

S: All these old movies have the same kind of old iron bedstead in them.

E: What do you mean? Do you mean all old movies, or some of them, or just the ones you have seen?

S: What's the matter with you? You know what I mean.

E: I wish you would be more specific.

S: You know what I mean! Drop dead! (Garfinkel, 1964, p. 230)

The repeated *You know what I mean* is very revealing because it addresses directly the indeterminacy of language. We all know what someone means when they say they are tired at the end of a workday, but linguistically the expression "I am tired" can mean all sorts of things. Furthermore, when one says "I am tired" one expects or is trying to elicit sympathy, thus an expected response would be "Let me pour you a glass of wine, dear," or similar expressions of sympathy.

Thus on the one hand we have the fact that speakers do not, as Garfinkel notes, and cannot in principle, say everything that they need to say for communication, and on the other hand the obvious fact that speakers do fill in the unsaid background and inferential practical reasoning needed of the smooth functioning of social exchanges. Gumperz's point is that the gap is filled by Grice's theory of conversational implicatures (Grice, 1975, 1989). Note also that the husband in example (129), like many others in the examples reported by Garfinkel (1964), loses his temper. This is easily explained if we consider that the interlocutors are violating a very basic rule of conversation, that is, being cooperative. The shock of realizing that the speaker is not being cooperative is akin to the realization of having been deceived (indeed, deception is one of the cases of non-cooperation). So the contribution of the communicative practices is both linguistic and social, as we would expect from its intermediate place between sociological phenomena and linguistic phenomena.

### 8.3.3 Conversational Inferences

As we saw earlier, Gumperz sees Gricean implicatures and cooperation as bridging the gap between linguistic and social facts, thus providing the unstated and assumed extra meaning identified by Garfinkel. Gumperz sums up his view that Grice "lays the foundations for a truly social perspective on speaking" (Gumperz, 2015, p. 310). In what follows we briefly examine the specifics of Gumperz's conception.

Gumperz starts out his argument with a broad Gricean argument: "situated understanding is to a large extent a matter of contextual indirect inferences" (Gumperz, 1977a, p. 191, 1996, p. 374, 1999, p. 131) with an emphasis on the importance of context: "the significance of what happens at any one point can only be understood in relation to what precedes and what is expected to follow" (p. 375), but he soon focuses on a subset of Gricean implicatures, those that require deliberate, conscious, or at least not purely automatic following of the maxims and the CP:

> Although, as Grice has argued (1989), all understanding presupposes conversational co-operation, this collaborative activity must be *actively initiated and maintained*, for the most part through talk (Gumperz, 1996, p. 375; our emphasis, SA/LP).

Gumperz notes that engaging in a conversational interaction requires cooperation, regardless of the nature of the exchange, that is, even if the speakers are "actively disputing" (p. 378). For example, "topical and thematic continuity has to be maintained" (p. 378), so if one of the speakers changes the subject this will be noted. Likewise, turn taking must be regulated, even if people are fighting. Interruptions are of course parasitic on there being an expectation of turn taking, if two people are talking at once, because for example they are not talking to each other, they are not interrupting each other. Consider for example, two audience members exchanging comments while the speaker is talking. In other words, even if people are actively trying to interrupt each other, for example by shouting over each other, they still assume in the background a regulated one-speaker-at-a-time model of turn taking. They just want to commandeer the floor, they have not given up on there being a floor.

Gumperz both acknowledges and goes beyond CA by noting that "positioning alone is not enough" (p. 379): "propositional content can only be assessed [...] with reference to shared frames and common ground." (p. 379). So, Gumperz concludes, "we must assume that participants rely on additional signs produced as part of the talk" (p. 379). The additional signs include (but are not limited to) contextualization cues. Contextualization cues are defined as "one of a cluster of indexical signs [...] produced in the act of speaking that jointly index, that is invoke, a frame of interpretation for the rest of the linguistic content of the utterance" (p. 379). We deal with contextualization cues more in detail in the following section. It should be noted that Gumperz quotes explicitly Silverstein's work on enregisterment (see Section 10.2.3).

### 8.3.4 Contextualization

Gumperz notes that contextualization starts with establishing a broad "general perspective or interpretive frame" (1978, p. 395) explicitly quoting Bateson and Goffman (see Section 8.1.1). It is important to understand that the interpretive frame is essential to establishing what is going on and changes the force of speech acts, the implicatures drawn by assuming or flouting the principle of cooperation, and more generally the rules of the game. Consider for example classroom discourse. Once we have established the interpretive frame of "classroom" the frame tells us that there is going to be at least one "teacher" and an unspecified number of students. The frame also pre-determines that the ultimate goal of the students is to learn a subject matter (as well as other factors, which we can ignore in this context) and the goal of the teacher is for the students to do so. Consider now the following question, uttered by the teacher, followed by a sampling of responses.

(130) What part of speech is "yesterday"?
   a. An adverb.
   b. Beats me!
   c. I am surprised they let you graduate if you don't know such a simple thing about grammar!

In (130.a), the student is fully in the frame "classroom" and answers correctly. In (130.b) the response is already pragmatically inappropriate because the informal style and the attitude of indifference conveyed by the expression "beats me" are not what is expected in class (a student answering this way would have ended up in the principal's office in our time). Students are expected, per the interpretive frame, to want to know the answer and expressing indifference about not knowing constitutes a (mild) rejection of the frame. Response (130.c) is instead openly outside the frame. It presupposes a different frame, such as a debate between two peers, with the respondent having strong opinions about grammatical knowledge. Furthermore, it negates the pedagogical nature of the question, assumed in interpretations (130.a)–(130.b), that is, that the speaker knows the answer and is checking if the addressee also knows it. Note how the felicity conditions of the speech act "asking a question" (namely, the person asking the question does not know the answer and wants to know the answer) are tacitly modified within the classroom discourse interpretive frame.

### Contextualization Cues

As we saw earlier, contextualization cues can be verbal and nonverbal (1996, p. 379); they are indexical, metalinguistic (Gumperz, 1977a, p. 192; on metalanguage and the metalinguistic nature of indexicality, see Chapter 10), and not limited to prosody and paralanguage. An important and complex question is "how do contextualization cues convey meaning?" Since they are not words, as in the case of "dog," for example, they don't have a lexical meaning. Gumperz clarifies that contextualization cues "foreground and set off segments of the stream of talk [...] from the surrounding strings. Co-participants who perceive and respond to the shift are then led to resort to their background knowledge, and (...) to retrieve contextual presuppositions in terms of which the signs can be understood." (Gumperz, 1996, pp. 379–380). In other words, they are "cues" to meaning, not meaning per se.

The following are all examples of contextualization cues, found in Gumperz's work or his close associates. The list should give an idea of the breadth of the phenomenon.

- Prosodic (intonation, stress, etc.). Recall the cafeteria workers example, discussed in Section 1.2, in which falling or rising tones acquired emotional connotations.
- Rhythm, tempo (speech rate).
- Shifts in pitch (lowering/raising).
- Pauses, hesitations, overlaps, latches, turn taking practices, and so on. For example, "overlap is a contextualization cue interpreted not in isolation but in the context of a focus on solidarity (the high involvement style) or power (the high considerateness style)" (Kiesling, 2015, p. 627).

In a high involvement style, an overlap will be mostly supportive, whereas in a high considerateness style, it would be interruptive (Tannen, 1984). An example involving pauses is the difference between restrictive and non-restrictive relative clauses, the latter of which are, as is well known, set aside by a parenthetical intonation, expressed orthographically by matching commas

(131) a. My sister who lives in New York is very nice
b. My sister, who lives in New York, is very nice
(Gumperz, 1982, p. 110)

Another example, also here reproduced using punctuation, rather than the tonal information in the original, is the following

(132) a. I said sit down
b. I said. sit. down.
(Gumperz, 1982, p. 110; example from Crystal, 1975)

(132.a) is the unmarked version, reporting the fact that the speaker said "sit down." Conversely, (132.b) indicates annoyance, or particular emphasis.

- Paralinguistic (smiling voice, laughter, etc.). For example, laughter is often used to signal the humorous intention of the speaker, by following one's humorous remark with laughter, thus effectively inviting matching laughter (Jefferson, 1979). Vocal fry (a.k.a., creaky voice) may be used to signal boredom and relaxed affect (Gobl & Chasaide, 2003; Laver, 1980). High volume is often associated with anger (e.g., Schröder et al., 2001).
- Selection among the items of a repertoire (Gumperz, 1996, p. 379)
- Code switching (Gumperz, 1982, p. 98): "In situational switching, where a code or speech style is regularly associated with a certain class of activities, it comes to signify or *connote them*, so that its very use can signal the enactment of these activities even in the absence of other clear contextual cues. (Our emphasis, SA&LP)" (see Section 8.3.4).
- Formulaic phrases (Gumperz, 1982, pp. 133–134) The following is an example of failed contextualization, in an intercultural setting, which occurred between Pickering and Attardo. Pickering texted Attardo a picture of a common friend, followed by the text "Guess who??" Attardo, apparently unaware of the formulaic nature of the expression, replied "What do you mean guess who?" Pickering who was contextualizing the exchange as the routine "pre-announcement" (Guess what/who/where, etc.) interpreted Attardo's failure to "play along" (e.g., by saying: "Oh, look who the cat dragged in!" or "fancy seeing you there!") as not recognizing the mutual friend, eliciting an indignant denial from Attardo. In this case, the contextualization cue does not work as intended precisely because Attardo does not recognize its formulaic nature (possibly because of the inversion of the "natural" order of the formula; "1) Guess who I ran into? 2) Name of the person." ) and thus he mis-contextualizes the utterance as a request for information, which is however obvious, and hence his further request for clarification (On Guess wh-? routines as pre-announcements, Schegloff, 2001, p. 236).

#### Learnability and intercultural issues

Experiences of communication lead to expectations. Essentially, we associate certain cues to certain types of actions: "cooccurrence expectations [...] are learned in the course of previous interactive experience and form part of our habitual and instinctive linguistic knowledge. Cooccurence expectations enable us to associate styles of speaking with contextual presuppositions" (Gumperz, 1977a, p. 199). It should be noted that in his 1982 discussion Gumperz qualifies these associations as "connotations." The term "connotation," in the sense meant by Gumperz, has not been used much in linguistics lately, but it used to be quite popular in pre-structuralist semantics (e.g., "associative meaning"; Leech, 1981, pp. 12–13). It has now been replaced, in part, by the idea of "enregisterment" (see Section 10.2.3).

Gumperz claims that "contextualization cues are not readily learned, and certainly not through direct instruction" (p. 383) due to their complex nature and "inherent ambiguity" (p. 383). Moreover, their relational nature, as seen earlier and in the following citation, "as carriers of meaning, dialect symbols function purely relationally. Their meaning is generated by juxtaposition of forms in relation to the interpretive presuppositions associated with the activity enacted" (1978, p. 408), will result in different groups/cultures having different contextualization cues, because presumably the correlations of forms and interpretations will be different. This of course may lead to intercultural problems (i.e., when two different cultures come into contact). See subsequent text for discussion.

We could ask why is it that some miscommunications, such as the "Guess who?" example, do not result in negative reactions, whereas the "gravy" example and many examples reported in Gumperz (1982) result in significant upset. The difference is that for run-of-the-mill implicatures that fail to trigger, the hearer is faced with a perplexing utterance that fails to mean anything. Conversely, with many or most contextualization cues, the cue has an alternative interpretation. In other words, it triggers a different, and possibly negatively marked, interpretation.

#### Code-switching

Code-switching is a complex and vast subject that could easily fill a book on its own. In this context, we will not attempt a balanced view of the field, or even an up-to-date one, as that would take us too far afield from our concerns in this volume. We will merely will present a few ideas about code-switching as a contextualization cue that originated with Gumperz and that fit in with his broad view on communicative competence. Gumperz studied code-switching in Norway and India. In Norway, he and Blom worked on the repertoire of the community of Hemnesberget, where all speakers are fluent in a local dialect (Ranmål) and standard Norwegian (Bokmål).

Gumperz noted that certain situations, for example, talk at home by local residents, took place in Ranmål, the local version, whereas official talk and talk by college students who had moved to the "big city" to study tended to use standard Bokmål. Therefore, he introduced the distinction between situational code switching, which is more or less dictated by the situation, and metaphorical code switching, which is a deliberate choice on the part of the speaker to convey a certain meaning associated with the use of the form. A well-known example of metaphorical code switching is Kennedy's quote *Ich bin ein Berliner.* ("I am from Berlin"),[2] which coming during a 1963 speech in Berlin, right around the time that the Soviets had started building the wall, clearly expressed full solidarity with the people of Berlin, much better than saying "I am one of you" could ever have.

Because of this indexical aspect, code switching can also be a contextualization cue, by signaling that a certain situation counts as another. For example, Gumperz remarks that teachers will lecture in standard Bokmål, but switch to Ranmål when they want to encourage student participation, clearly signaling a more informal, relaxed situation in the classroom. See Chapter 10 (esp. Section 10.2.3) for discussions of indexicality.

#### Repertoires

We have touched several times on the idea of repertoire. This is a central concept in interactional pragmatics. Let us consider briefly why this is so. The repertoire of a speaker is the set of choices that are available to them. Consider for example asking for a spoon. Any speaker of English knows several ways of doing so:

---

2 The urban legend that the expression actually means "I am a jelly donut" is, as they say today, fake news.

- May I have the spoon?
- Can I have the spoon?
- Could I have the spoon?
- Would you mind giving me the spoon?
- Could I borrow the spoon for a second?
- Would it be possible for me to have the spoon?

You can probably add to this list easily. The choices are here more or less intuitively ranked by degree of politeness. Needless to say, we could also add another series along the lines of

- I need the spoon
- Give me the spoon.
- The spoon!
- Spoon!

arranged by degree of impoliteness, this time. These options are part of the repertoire of a speaker, but do not exhaust it. Grabbing the spoon without saying anything is another option. Naturally, it is frowned upon in polite society and may get you punched on the nose, but it is one option. Yet other options include for multilingual individuals, doing so in other languages/varieties: Attardo, for example, could be asking in Italian, or in French, or in a few dialects of said languages which he can (tolerably) produce/imitate. Pickering's repertoire covers numerous varieties of English (both from Great Britain and worldwide) and French. In a bilingual/multilingual community, these choices would not be just a matter of accommodation (obviously when visiting relatives in Belgium, both Pickering and Attardo would ask in French) but would be weighted with sociocultural significance: for example, the wording of street signs in Belgium (divided in French and Flemish-speaking areas) was a significant matter of contention. Our point is simply this: choices may be significant, that is, they may be contextualization cues.

The significance of repertoire for interactional pragmatics is summarized well by the following quote: "The concept of linguistic repertoire is a fundamental departure from the traditional conception of one people-one homogeneous and unitary code" (Bauman and Sherzer, 1975, p. 104). By introducing the idea of variation in the core of the systematic choices by the individual speaker, the idea of repertoire opens the door to the investing of these choices with social significance. Wherever there are choices, there are meanings attached to these choices. In part, the choices become contextualization cues, and are thus endowed with associative meaning, and in part choices regularly associated with a given group or subgroup acquire indexical force and thus meaning. Again, we refer to Chapter 10 (esp. Section 10.2.3) for a more detailed discussion of indexicality.

Gumperz, quoting Bernstein (1964), describes linguistic interaction as a process of "decision making, in which speakers select from a range of possible expressions (...) reflecting contextual and social differences in speech" (Gumperz, 1964, p. 137). Nowadays, the concept is in flux. For example, Busch (2012, 2015) revises the definition of repertoire to include attention to power differentials (whose choices are directed to whom matters) and the disappearance of "stable" communities due to migrations.

### Speech Events

Hymes (1972) considers speech acts in the context of interactions, thus broadening the kind of analyses that Austin and Searle would consider (see Chapter 3). Speech acts occur as part of speech events which themselves are part of speech situations. The difference is primarily one of size ("magnitude," p. 56). The following quote is enlightening: "a party (speech situation), a conversation during the party (speech event), a joke within the conversation (speech act). [...] the same type of speech act may recur in different types of speech event [...] Thus a joke (speech act) may be embedded in a private conversation, a lecture, a formal introduction" (Hymes, 1972, p. 56).

Gumperz (1972, pp. 16–18) lists the following feature of speech acts:

- They are viewed by members of a society "as distinct wholes"
- They are considered "separate from other types of discourse"
- They are "characterized by special rules of speech and non-verbal behavior"
- They often have "recognizable opening and closing sequences"
- They often have a "special name" (p. 17)

### Activity Types

Activity types are similar to frames or scripts (Goffman, 1974; Gumperz and Tannen, 1979, p. 307), although the dynamic nature of the concept of activity type is emphasized whereas frames and scripts are considered more static. Let's also note that Hymes' speech events (Hymes, 1972) correspond to activity types. In short, the idea was part of the intellectual milieu we have described. The best known characterization of activity types is Levinson's.

Levinson (1979) starts from Wittgenstein's idea of language game (which we examined briefly in Section 3.1). Just as Wittgenstein noted that there are many language games, each with its own set of rules, Levinson notes that "the understanding of what is said depends on the understanding of the 'language game' in which it is embedded" (1979, p. 367). Consider a job interview. The stereotypical question *Where do you see yourself in five years?* has a completely different meaning than the same question asked in other activity types (say, in a conversation between newlyweds). In a job interview the question is intended as a chance for the candidate to expound on their intermediate career goals whereas the newlyweds are probably talking about having children (or getting a dog). Activity types constrain the behavior (verbal and not) of the speakers. Of course we mustn't forget that some activity types do not involve speech at all, for example, gestures used by monks having taken a vow of silence or by special operations soldiers who are infiltrating an enemy camp. So, in the job interview case, the applicant will ask a few questions, but the bulk of the questioning will be done by the hiring personnel. The language choices will be fairly formal (reflecting the professional nature of the encounter). It will be understood that the applicant will try to present themselves in the best light possible, but without actually falsifying the facts. So, for example, expressions that would be considered "bragging" under normal circumstances, will be perfectly acceptable in a job interview: *I am the best candidate for this job!* So, activity types both guide the way we "take" things and constrain what counts as an appropriate or acceptable contribution to the activity. If a candidate for a job were to say *I am not very good at leadership* in an un-ironical fashion we would be forced to interpret this statement as a sign that the candidate either is very bad (and naive at that!) or that they don't really want the job.

Activity types may be completely "pre-packaged" or "largely unscripted" (Levinson, 1979, p. 368), which can be exemplified by a graduation ceremony (which is almost completely scripted, the exception being asides and improvisations from the speakers, or students' antics on and off stage) and by a conversation among friends (almost completely improvised). Regardless all activity types will have some sort of "structure," that is, will be organized (even informal conversations are organized, this is one of the central findings of CA). Importantly, Levinson sees the structural and stylistic aspects of activity types as tied to the goals and purposes of the activity type (p. 369). So, in the job interview, the stylistic choice of formality and the question and answer sessions are all chosen with the goal of finding an applicant who is a good fit for the job.

## 8.4 Conclusion: Gumperz's Interactionism

Methodologically, Gumperzian interactionism is based on an ethnomethodological foundation: the ethnographic component is a significant step in the process of analysis, beginning with audio/video recording of interactions, detailed transcriptions and annotations according to the topics of interest (e.g., prosody, gestures, gaze, etc.). This allows for the micro-analysis of conversational features (i.e., the individual occurrences in a single conversation), also facilitated by post-recording interviews, which allow the researcher to find out, at least in part, how the speakers were orienting to and interpreting the interaction. The micro-analyses are then brought together to generalize on communicative and cultural patterns that hold at the level of the community, broadly or narrowly defined (e.g., we may consider as broad a context as "the English language speakers" or as narrow as family's conversational style). Finally, and this is an important characteristic of the Gumperzian approach, the cross-cultural implications of these communicative or cultural patterns are investigated (e.g., comparing British and Indian English speakers).

Communication is to be understood broadly, much more broadly than Chomskian or philosophical approaches (à la Austin/Searle/Grice) did. It is a thoroughly contextual and social fact. Communication is negotiated: speakers must agree to at least some extent on what they are doing in the exchange, that is, they have to cooperate in the Gricean sense but also beyond the Gricean focus on what is said and what is implied. The organization in turns of conversation and the very fact that two speakers are engaging in conversation need to be negotiated in an on-going cooperative effort. However, this does not mean that the playing field is level: Gumperz was very much aware of the social and power differences within a community and in intercultural encounters. His work was very much motivated by this awareness and by the desire to remedy unnecessary conflict and establish a fundamental decency in asymmetrical exchanges. The idea of the linguistic penalty (see section 8.5 below), for example, comes directly from this social awareness and from the recognition of the non-uniformity of the playing field.

Likewise, the fundamental idea of the indexicality of communication is at the root of one of the most developed areas of interactional socio-pragmatics, that is, identity presentation (e.g., gender).

Finally, an important aspect of Gumperz's view of linguistic communication needs to be underscored. One of the simplifying assumptions of structuralist linguistics was that language was a uniform system. In other words, one would try to describe the grammar of one speaker (usually, the linguist himself/herself). However, especially in urban societies the uniformity of the linguistic code cannot be assumed at all, in fact, the norm is the heterogeneity of the linguistic repertoire: speakers have at their disposal several (dialectal or diastratic, in the case of diglossia) varieties of the same language, or several languages altogether. Bilingualism, trilingualism, and multilingualism (polyglossia) are the norm in many societies. For example, in Nigeria, four hundred languages exist alongside English and Nigerian Pidgin. Three languages (Hausa, Igbo, and Yoruba) are widely used, including in the press and media, and English is spoken by about a third of the population. Other languages are regional (Igboanusi, 2008). So, for example, one may be a native speaker of Ebira, speak Hausa when in Lokoja (the state capital of the state of Kogi, where Ebira is spoken), interact with some Igbo immigrants to the state, write a letter to a friend in English and attend a standup comedy event in Pidgin.

Once multilingualism and the heterogeneity of linguistic systems are recognized as the norm, it follows that if speakers use different language conventions, and particularly different contextualization cues, misunderstandings and miscommunication may (or practically speaking, inevitably will) occur. However, the various linguistic choices are not neutral. Differences in social, political, ethnic, and economic terms will be reflected by the choices. For example, English in Nigeria is a language of prestige and so being able to use it is seen as a path to social betterment. So, the linguistic choices that speakers make in a multilingual situation reflect these socio-political realities and affect the status of the speakers. This has a significant impact on intercultural interactions and the pedagogy of SLA, which we will consider in the next section.

## 8.5 Sociocultural Interaction and SLA

As we established earlier, Gumperz proposes that speaker-hearers in any given speech community infer the discourse message through cueing systems that rely on conventionalized choices at all levels of the discourse structure (i.e., lexical, syntactic, prosodic, and nonverbal/paralinguistic). For the production and interpretation of these devices, speaker-hearers use institutionalized linguistic and cultural knowledge in combination with moment-by-moment inferences regarding the speaker's intent.

Over time, these cues have become tacit markers (i.e., largely unconscious choices) between members of the same speech community, and successful interaction relies on interactants' mutual understanding. This reliance on a shared linguistic and sociocultural background for interpretation of the discourse message has particular implications for cross-cultural communication. Experiences of communication lead to expectations which "form part of our habitual and instinctive linguistic knowledge" (Gumperz, 1977a, p. 199). In other words, the way in which participants orient themselves to the interaction and to each other depends on their on-going interpretation of conversational behaviors that they are largely unaware of and thus unable to compensate for. In fact, research in cross-cultural interaction tells us that those behaviors that differ across speech communities may not be immediately evident to interlocutors because interpretation rests on such deeply rooted, culturally based presuppositions which are not easily retrieved by speakers. As a result, discourse participants frequently implicitly assume they are working from a shared framework of production and interpretation.

The consequences of misinterpretation of these signals can range from the benign to the highly disruptive. The difference usually is that for run-of the-mill implicatures that fail to trigger, the hearer is faced with a confusing utterance (see Section 8.3.4) that simply fails to mean anything. The result of this in real-time interaction is often a "let it pass" approach (Firth, 1996) in which "the hearer lets the unknown or unclear action, word or utterance 'pass' on the (common-sense) assumption that it either become clear or redundant as talk progresses" (p. 243). Conversely, critical disruption may occur if the cue has an alternative interpretation. We have already discussed the very real-world situation that Gumperz encountered at Heathrow airport between male, British workers and female, East Indian workers in Chapter 1 that centered on different conventionalized uses of rising and falling pitch. As another example, consider the role of volume (i.e., loudness) in speech. In American English, increased volume is usually associated with anger or agitation on the part of the speaker. In a study of male Arabic learners of English, Abu-Al-Makarem and Petrosino (2007) found that "young Arab men speak generally louder than Euro-American men" (p. 579). This opens the door to a possible misconstrual of the prosodic cue in which a speaker operating within the conventions of American English may attribute a feeling of anger to a speaker operating within the Arabic conventions, without either speaker being at fault or even aware of each other's reaction.

Gumperz focused much of his research on the vulnerability of nonstandard and nonnative speakers in high-stakes situations; for example, workplace environments in which the consequences of failed interactions may be severe such as being passed over for salary increases or promotions. This has been termed the linguistic penalty (Roberts & Campbell, 2006), which may trigger when communicative styles differ:

> Different ethnic groups, whether they use English as their heritage language or not, may use culturally specific styles of communication which are different from local or standard English... Differences include a range of rhetorical and self-presentational features [including] a range of paralinguistic features such as intonation and rhythm.
>
> *(p. 24)*

In this part of the chapter, we will focus on sociocultural interactional research that has been conducted with a particular L2 learner group in the United States that often find themselves struggling with these issues: International Teaching Assistants (ITAs). There are currently thousands of international graduate students teaching mainly STEM classes to US undergraduates in higher education contexts. These are often in large state universities where departments rely on their ITAs to teach multiple laboratory sections in the basic sciences or problem-solving study sections in math or engineering. Although specific support structures vary widely from institution to institution, it is the case that many of these teachers walk into their classrooms with little or no training in the classroom context or in addressing the particular needs of US undergraduates. Researchers in this area unanimously agree that ITAs frequently lack not only linguistic training but also a critical understanding of cultural and pedagogical norms. Stevens (1989) notes that "we need to ask ourselves just where does the linguistic aspect of the ITA problem end and the cultural part begin? Obviously, there is no clear boundary. Speech is understood in terms of a cultural context" (p. 183).

This critical examination of the interaction between language and culture is well served by interactional sociolinguistics as the model prioritizes the established sociocultural use of the linguistic code and provides a means to examine these daily cross-cultural encounters.

An early program espousing Gumperz's approach was designed in the 1980s and 1990s by Andrea Tyler and her colleagues at the University of Florida.[3] In an investigation of recorded ITA presentations produced in this context, Tyler showed that ITA discourse frequently demonstrated "a lack or a misuse of most of the [contextualization] cues native speakers of American English use to lead listeners through their discourse" (1988, p. 102). Three early studies (1988, 1992a, 1992b) focused specifically on information structuring, that is, were the cues that NS listeners would use to make sense of the information as it comes in present in the ITA discourse? The analyses highlighted a range of discourse features that would violate NS expectations and potentially cause confusion and are described as having "a scrambling effect for the listener" (p. 109).

1. Prosodic miscues: Unexpected stress patterns and interference in thought group organization (e.g., multiple internal pauses)
2. Syntactic miscues: Overuse of coordinating conjunctions where subordinating conjunctions would be expected
3. Lexicalized discourse markers: Inappropriate use of markers such as BUT and SO when these do not match the actual relationship between the two pieces of information

This work continues, most recently with Tapper et al. (2018), who performed a replication of these early studies. The results were compatible with Tyler's overall findings in terms of the use of discourse management devices; however, native speaker opinions of the ITAs' overall comprehensibility was more promising.

Tyler (1995) focuses instead on miscommunication based primarily on the different schemas that the ITA and undergraduate student bring to their interaction and in which miscues accumulate until both participants complained that the other was uncooperative. In fact, by the end of the unproductive session, the student felt that the ITA was "playing games with her head" and the Korean ITA thought the student was "rude and disrespectful" (p. 144). In this instance, the student had come to the tutor for help with a computer programming assignment based on scoring bowling games. At the very beginning of the interaction the student asks the ITA *Well, do you know how to score the game?*

3 Davies & Tyler, 1994; Tyler, 1992a, 1992b, 1994a, 1994b; Tyler & Bro, 1992; Tyler et al., 1988".

and the ITA responds *Yeah approximately*. In a subsequent playback session, the tutor explains that this would be a typical response in Korean and in no way suggests a lack of knowledge, but rather the appropriate level of modesty as it would be "considered rude to baldly state that one is an expert in an area" (p. 136), particularly one that was recognized as part of the culture of the other interlocutor. When the student then responds that she doesn't know how to score either (*see I don't know how to score*), the tutor responds with surprise (*oh, you don't know how to score the bowling game?*). The tutor later remarked that he was surprised that she did not know this as she was American, but that as he was comfortable with the scoring, he did not want to make the student look foolish by pointing out her lack of knowledge any further. At this point, the student is no longer clear who has the requisite knowledge to solve the problem and thus the higher status, and the tutor does nothing further to reassure her. As the session deteriorates, the student becomes frustrated and at one point, slaps the paper directly in front of the tutor asking *Is this for this? Do I need to know this?* (p. 134). The same schema of the teacher–student relationship that leads the Korean tutor not to want to unnecessarily embarrass the student also requires the student to treat the teacher with absolute respect thus the tutor is also now dismayed and unclear where the exchange has gone wrong. This kind of moment by moment micro-analysis gives remarkable insights into why misunderstandings can be so pervasive in interethnic communication.

Building on the work of Tyler, Pickering has focused on prosodic contextualization cues. Prosodic contextualization cues (intonation and stress) are particularly vulnerable to misinterpretation in cross-cultural interaction as they are processed at such an unconscious level; they are often not perceived as linguistic choices at all, but as expressions of a speaker's attitude or personality:

> A speaker is said to be unfriendly, impertinent or rude, uncooperative or fail to understand... miscommunication of this type in other words is regarded as a social faux pas and leads to misjudgments of the speaker's intent... it is not likely to be identified as mere linguistic error.
>
> *(Gumperz, 1982, p. 139)*

To exemplify this, let's return to tone choice, this time in the context of the ITA classroom. Pickering (2001) compared the tone choices made by NS TAs and Chinese ITAs in laboratory presentations and math sections. There was a significant difference in the number of rising tone choices produced by each group (NS TAs: 30% rising tones; ITAs: 4–10% rising tones). An examination of ways in which rising tone choices were used by the NS TAs showed that the teachers systematically exploited tone choices to increase the accessibility of the lecture material and to establish rapport with their students. For example, rising tones were used to cue information that the TA assumed students would remember (e.g., //now of course you remember that potassium was ⇗ PURple//) and to encourage participation from the students (e.g., // any ⇗ suGGEStions//). In contrast, these uses were highly restricted in the ITA spoken discourse. Overall, while the NS TAs created a sense of community in the classroom (a participating we), the ITAs projected a lack of rapport-building and a sense of a speaking I (p. 237).

### 8.5.1 Interactional Sociolinguistics in the TESOL Classroom

Davies and Tyler (1994) developed a teaching approach oriented to pragmatics within the ITA framework discussed earlier that draws on both interactional sociolinguistics and Schmidt's concept of noticing (see Section 4.3.2). It relies on "strategically given feedback," that is, feedback that is situated, balanced, nonthreatening, and demystifying following videotaped interactions. Students engage in a role-play exchange between a teacher and student which includes conflicting goals (e.g., an instructor needs to leave a class immediately to take an exam and the student wants to talk to the instructor immediately as they have a conflict with the regularly scheduled office hours). The participants are then asked the following kinds of questions (pp. 204–205):

> What were you trying to communicate?
> Is that the message you got?
> Now that you know what your interlocutor was trying to communicate, how could they have said it in a way that would have been clear to you?
> Were there any moments when you felt uncomfortable or confused?
> Was there anything that you expected or wanted to hear from the other person that you did not?

This kind of approach elevates pragmatic feedback to the level we are used to seeing with other kinds of linguistic errors (e.g., phonological, syntactic or lexical). In this case, the "error" may be a misunderstanding of cultural schema or specific linguistic choices that cue something unexpected, and so on. Davies (2018) further expands on this technique by adding "reverse roleplays" (p. 16) in which the student and teacher play each other's roles and can experience each other's point of view.

### 8.5.2 Sample Teaching Materials

The first lesson plan is a pared-down version of one that appears in Tyler (1994). Possible examples of scenarios as well as transcriptions are given in Tyler (1994, pp. 126–133). The second lesson is based on Gorsuch et al. (2013), a textbook for ITAs, and focuses on using rising tone choices to answer questions.

#### Lesson 1: Role-plays with Pragmatic Feedback

**Stage 1: Analyzing the situation:** The role-play session begins with an introduction to a difficult exchange between an ITA and student. This could be a videotaped exchange or a detailed description of the circumstances and the result of the exchange. At this stage it is also important to focus on the goals and intentions of each of the speakers in the exchange. For example, does the student want to have their grade reconsidered? If so, why? Should the ITA consider addressing the issue in private rather than in front of the class?

**Stage 2: Enact the role-play:** It is best to have actual undergraduate students playing the roles of the undergraduate students rather than other L2 learners in the group. As we have seen, many of the contextualization cues that are typically in play are specific to the linguistic and cultural group in question and below the conscious level of manipulation by a speaker so cannot be easily mimicked.

**Stage 3: Review the enactment as a group:** Assess whether goals and intentions that were discussed in Stage 1 are met successfully. The group should give balanced feedback regarding all aspects of the enactment including behaviors (linguistic and otherwise) that successfully conveyed the discourse message.

**Stage 4: Continue practice:** Depending on the success of the resolution of the scenario, either re-enact the same role-play a second time or move onto a new one. Enactments can be recorded and played back for more specific one-to-one feedback regarding linguistic choices of grammar, lexical items and so on at a later time.

### Lesson 2: Using Intonation in Asking/Answering Questions in the Classroom

1. Remind your students (ITAs) that establishing a good rapport with plenty of interaction with their undergraduate student is both expected in lab contexts in the United States and is an excellent way of increasing learning and establishing where students may be having difficulty.
2. Practice listening for the use of leading questions with rising tone choices using a pre-recorded dialogue such as the one below, in (133):

(133)

| | |
|---|---|
| TA: | can anyone tell me what an ⇗ Ecosystem is |
| S: | uh // PLANTS that are in the same ⇗ Area |
| TA: | you're on the right ⇒ TRACK // here's a ⇘ HINT besides // ⇘ PLANTS // what ELSE do we find in this ⇗ Area |
| S: | ⇗ ANimals |
| TA: | ⇘ RIGHT // what ELSE something very very ⇗ TIny |
| S: | ⇗ microORganisms |
| TA: | ⇘ exACTly // now what's the reLAtionship between the PLANTS ANimals and ⇗ microORganisms |
| S: | they ⇗ reLATE to each other |
| TA: | ⇘ YES // they ⇘ interACT with each other // you ⇘ GOT it |

3. Have students practice the technique by asking each other a series of questions about their area of specialization (if they overlap) or US culture/language/history, for example, What four states border Mexico? What does it mean if your student says "That's dope!"
4. Have the students record a short mini-lecture (5 minutes) in which they define a family of two or three related terms and include guiding questions and give feedback.

# 9

# Data Collection and Research Design in Studies of L2 Pragmatics

Graduate pragmatics seminars often include a student research component such as a proposal for a new study or a replication study. This chapter focuses on the research designs that are typically used to investigate L2 (Lx) pragmatic phenomena. We re-examine areas of the field that we have previously addressed, but this time from the perspective of how these methodologies have developed in the fields of SLA and TESOL.

## 9.1 Discourse Completion Tasks

As we noted in Chapter 3, one of the most fruitful lines of research in interlanguage pragmatics has been the investigation of speech acts. Some routine formulae, for example, greeting sequences may be common in everyday speech and thus comparatively easy to collect as natural language data, albeit necessitating carrying a notebook or a recording device. Others (e.g. direct complaints or refusals) are more difficult to capture, particularly in high numbers and between different kinds of interlocutors (e.g., strangers vs. family members and so on). For this reason, the most common research technique is called a DCT or Discourse Completion Task. These can be either spoken or written and typically look like the examples below:

(134) I am going to read you some situations. Pretend you are the person in the situation. You must refuse all requests, offers and invitations. Respond as you would in actual conversation.

You are in your third year of college. You attend classes and you take really good notes. Your classmate often misses a class and asks for the lecture notes. On this occasion, your classmate says, "oh no! We have an exam tomorrow but I don't have the notes from last week. I am sorry to ask you this, but could you please lend me your notes once again?" Refusal situation.

*(Nelson et al., 2002, p. 185.)*

(135) Please read the following situations. After each situation you will be asked to write a response in the blank after "you."

You teach English at a university. It is just about the middle of the semester now. One of the students asks to speak to you.

Student: Ah, excuse me, some of the students were talking after class yesterday. We kind of feel that the class would be better if you could give us more practice in conversation and less on grammar.

You:___________

Student: Well, it was only a suggestion

Refusal situation. (Keshavarz et al., 2006, p. 399.)

Much has been written on the (dis)advantages of DCT data. Advantages include the ability to collect hundreds of responses to the same situations from multiple speakers. Nelson et al. (2002), for example, collected 298 American English refusals and 250 Egyptian Arabic refusals (p. 170). This allows for both quantitative and qualitative analyses of the kinds of responses given by native speakers and/or learners and provides a base from which to study development across proficiency levels or many other specified variables such as gender, age, or social status. However, there are clear disadvantages: most crucially, the simplified and hypothetical nature of the situations that are presented. As Nelson et al. note, "What people claim they would say in a hypothetical situation is not necessarily what they actually would say in a real situation" (p. 168). In fact, this problem is demonstrated in their own study. They created a number of refusal situations that their Egyptian and American informants said were plausible. However, when later discussing their responses to each situation in interviews, it seemed that with regard to at least two of the situations that required the Egyptians to refuse a person of a higher status, the methodology had forced a response that may have been contrived:

> Since Egyptians stated that they would not have refused in these situations, they may have had no intuitions on which to base their responses... The disparity between the DCT and interview data suggests that the DCT may not capture the sociopragmatic complexity of refusing in Egyptian Arabic... In effect, Egyptians refusing in these situations would be committing a sociopragmatic error in refusing at all.
>
> *(pp. 182–183)*

In other words, the pragmalinguistic response that was suggested may never in fact occur due to the sociopragmatic conditions. Kanik (2012) proposes that this issue can be allayed by using a reverse DCT (R-DCT) in which the language is given to the participants and they are then asked to create a situational context in which they feel that language would be appropriate. In this way, the R-DCT "can give researchers more direct access to L2 respondents' knowledge of sociopragmatic variables like power, distance and imposition" (p. 85). An example scenario is given here:

(136) Write a situation in which the statement below could be uttered. Also, provide information regarding setting, who the speaker is, who the listener is, and what is asked.

Speech act: I know you came from another city but to reach a final decision about you I need to see you again next week.

Situation: ____________

Setting: ____________

Speaker: ____________

Hearer: ____________

Request: ____________

(Kanik, 2012, p. 89)

These were requests previously collected by the author and the previous example was in fact a human resources manager requesting an applicant to come again the following week for a second interview. Most of the learners who participated correctly judged this as a situation in which there was a high power or distance differential between the speaker and hearer and guessed that this was an employer–employee interaction making comments such as: "you are requesting an employee [applicant] to come again next week to have a job interview" (p. 92). Also using DCT-based testing, Li (2012) and Li and Taguchi (2014) have focused on learners' processing of speech acts in addition to performance. Based on skill acquisition theory (see DeKeyser, 2007), the researchers used a "pragmatic listening judgment task" to investigate the speed at which learners could assess whether the form and function of a request matched the context provided. This is an experimental method that is relatively new to the field of pragmatics and shows promise for assessing practice-based gains.

Two alternative collection methods are field notes and natural conversational data. Yuan (2001) conducted a large-scale study on compliments in Mandarin and her field-note data revealed that compliments and compliment responses were often produced over a number of turns, something that is not usually evident from DCT data where responses are constrained. However, this method also had its drawbacks as with no recording of the data, Yuan had to rely on memory: "no matter how hard I tried to memorize what I had heard, when it came to writing, I always found it difficult to recall the exact wording of the verbal exchange that had just happened a minute before" (p. 287).

The collection of hundreds of hours of naturally occurring data to demonstrate L1 usage is usually not a feasible option; however, it might be possible to find these data in spoken corpora. Jucker (2009) suggests that a large corpus, such as the British National Corpus (BNC), can be mined for examples of speech acts by performing searches either for the actual action involved (e.g., examples of the verb "compliment") or for the kind of language that might appear as part of the speech act. An example of a compliment from the BNC is given here in (137):

(137) Erm, I would like to particularly compliment the Fire Service on the magnificent job they were doing there, in, in the most appalling conditions (British National Corpus J3s, 337) (Jucker, 2009, p. 1616).

Although deception-based research is not usually encouraged (and requires a very specific kind of human subjects protection board approval), it is also a way to simulate natural data collection. One of Pickering's students investigated the speech act of refusal across people representing different social distances using this technique. She sent out email requests to her colleagues, friends, and family inviting them to participate in a fabricated volunteer tree-planting on Arbor day. She deliberately only specified when it was to take place (very early in the morning) but did not specify where so that if people agreed to attend, she could let them know that the event was not actually occurring. As no one agreed to attend, it became a very productive way to investigate refusals!

Finally, depending on the purpose of the data collection, it may be enough to have approximations or representations of the kind of language that we would expect to appear in a given speech act. These might be based on what Jucker (2009) calls the "armchair method" of data collection in which the researcher or participants are asked about their intuitions regarding language choices or asked to perform a recall protocol in which they reflect back on their language use (Golato, 2003). They may even be examples taken from films or novels. Rose (2001) collected compliments from 40 contemporary American films and found that overall, they were comparable to natural conversation and reasonable models for teaching appropriate pragmalinguistic formulae to L2 learners.

## 9.2 Interactional Studies

Although speech act research lends itself to empirical methods, other areas of L2 pragmatic research that we have focused on fare less well. Interactional sociolinguistics (IS) (Chapter 8) relies on the micro-analysis of contextualization cues, many of which are below the threshold of consciousness and thus cannot be simulated well in researcher-created materials. As the concerns of cross-cultural research in IS typically also involve socioeconomic or sociopolitical concerns in high stakes situations (e.g., the reaction of in-group members to the discourse of out-group members), it is difficult to replicate outside of its natural context. Example situations investigated by Gumperz and subsequent researchers in this tradition include authentic conversations, job interviews, counseling interviews, committee proceedings, and classroom interaction among others. As ecological validity is so critical in IS, there is often discussion of the "observer's paradox"; that is, the possible effect of having an observer (using video or audio equipment) on the authenticity of the situation. This has been discussed at length in other fields such as anthropology where participant observation is crucial to the process. Duranti (1997) argues rightly in our view that "people usually do not invent social behavior, language included, out of the blue" (p. 118), and that given some initial time to get used to the new setting, participants will go about their normal business:

(138) I believe that most of the time people are too busy running their own lives to change them in substantial ways because of the presence of a new gadget or a new person. As shown by many researchers over and over again, even with a lens aiming at them, participants still manage to argue with one another, be overrun by emotions, reveal intimate aspects of their private lives, or engage in lengthy evaluations of the private lives of other people. (p. 119)

Pickering's own work in this area required setting up a camera at the back of university classrooms and laboratories and asking international teaching assistants to wear headset

**Figure 9.1** Recording of an ITA teaching in a chemistry laboratory, using a headset.

microphones in order to gain clear audio recordings for the analysis of their use of intonation and stress (see Figure 9.1). Both teaching assistants and students rapidly became used to the new circumstances as the researchers attended their classrooms regularly throughout the semester.

### 9.2.1 Follow-up Interviews

An important part of IS research in L2 pragmatics is the follow-up interviews conducted with the researcher in which the video is played back and the participants describe their reactions as they remember feeling them in real time. This is akin to other kinds of stimulated recall methodology (see Gass & Mackey, 2000). We discussed follow up interviews in some detail in Chapter 8 with reference to the Korean tutor and North American undergraduate discussed in Tyler (1995). This triangulation of data allows the researcher to discover what behaviors were salient to each of the participants and the ways in which they interpreted them.

Although authentic situations are the gold standard in this area of research, simulated interviews or role-plays have also consistently been used (e.g., Gumperz, 1982). Ideally, these simulations are based on situational contexts that have previously been investigated and thus can be approximated as closely as possible. We saw this in Davies and Tyler (1994), who developed a teaching approach for ITAs based on pragmatic feedback following role-plays. These scenarios carefully mimicked situations that had been routinely observed between teachers and students in this context. See also Louw et al. (2010) for the use of simulated job interviews with L2 prospective job candidates.

In contrast to interactional sociolinguistics, we have seen that other areas of L2 pragmatics conventionally use researcher-created materials. This is particularly true of the investigation of L2 learners' understanding of Gricean implicatures that we discussed in Chapter 4. Research in this area has focused on L2 comprehension and interpretation of implicatures rather than production and has been shaped by Bouton's early development of multiple-choice items (see Section 4.3.1). Later researchers have argued that re-using many of these test items makes sense as "there already existed a literature on their use, and the test items had been extensively trialed and validated" (Abdelhafez, 2016, p. 455). However, that may not be the case with all subsequent research populations. For example,

Kim (2012) used an instrument adapted from Bouton (1988) to test South Korean learners' understanding of implicatures and obtained one anomalous result for the relevance-based implicature shown below:

(139) Rachel and Helen are jogging together.
Rachel: Slow down Helen! I'm running out of breath.
Helen: ⋇ I'm glad I don't smoke.
(a) Helen does not want to slow down.
(b) Helen wants Rachel to jog as fast as her.
(c) Helen has never smoked and is glad that she hasn't.
(d) Helen is saying the reason Rachel is out of breath is because she smokes.
(pp. 75–76)

Kim found that 63% of the participants who answered the item correctly did not, in fact, understand the implicature (as compared to only 4% for the other relevance-based implicature). Learners typically went beyond the implicature to offer advice or admonitions. Kim suggests that this is because "the act of women smoking in public is generally frowned upon" in Korea, thus the example may have been inappropriate for this particular population. In this way, the methodological addition of asking learners to explain their choices can also identify potential problems with particular items.

## 9.3 Pseudolongitudinal

The research designs that we have examined thus far in the chapter are similar in that they are cross-sectional, that is, they focus on the comprehension and/or production of pragmatic phenomena by learners at one point in time. Single time designs may also be pseudolongitudinal; that is, multiple proficiency levels are tested at one time in order to simulate typical learner development over time. An example of this is Menjo's (2018) study of perception of English prosodic patterns by Japanese learners. Three groups of learners were tested – beginning learners who had lived only in Japan; intermediate learners who had been in the United States for no more than 4 years; and an advanced group who had been in the United States for no less than 10 years. The participants were tested on their ability to recognize whether a speaker liked or disliked an item based on the intonation contour they used. Menjo found that the advanced L2 learners performed no better than the beginners at recognizing this pragmatic function of prosody despite their time spent in the United States suggesting that this function may need to be taught directly to learners.

## 9.4 Longitudinal

Longitudinal research in which the development of a small group of learners or a single learner is tracked across time are the least common research designs due to the inherent difficulties of maintaining the researcher–participant relationship. Learners are usually only in temporary residence in language learning institutions and are then often difficult to locate.

One model for this kind of research is a diary study such as the one we discussed in Chapter 2 undertaken by Schmidt (1983) over a three-year period with one Japanese learner. At least two SLA researchers, Cohen (1997) and Hassall (2006), have also published diary studies examining their own pragmatic development in a second language. Schmidt's study is quite unique in that it spans 3 years which is far longer than most studies in this area. In a meta-analysis of longitudinal studies published by Taguchi (2010), recent studies ranged from 7 weeks to 14 months, with many lasting less than 4 months (or the length of one semester). Multiple study designs are used in the studies reported by Taguchi including conversations, judgement tests, multiple-choice tests, and observations.

### 9.4.1 Study Abroad

Another increasingly popular context in which to study longitudinal patterns in L2 pragmatic development is study abroad (SA) programs (Kinginger & Blattner, 2008; Kinginger & Farrell, 2004; Warga & Schölmberger, 2007). Aspects of both production and comprehension have been examined both in situ and at different points in time following the experience to assess long-term retention. Matsumura (2007), for example, investigated Japanese students' production of advice-giving following an 8-month stay in Canada. Over time, the students maintained appropriate pragmalinguistic choices for advice-giving to equal or lower status interlocutors; however, they became increasingly wary of their responses to interlocutors of a higher status, often taking the "opt-out" choice in the multiple-choice items. A follow-up group interview suggested that, in part, this was the result of a far more nuanced understanding of the ways in which relationships are perceived across cultures following the students' stay abroad as the following quote from one of them demonstrates:

> Before I left for Canada, I chose not to give advice in all items relating to a professor because I didn't know what to say. In Canada, I realized that unlike Japanese professors, Canadian professors were very friendly. They allowed me to address them on a first name basis. So, I felt it was OK to talk to them the way I did to my roommates. I know it would be impossible to do that with Japanese professors. If I talked to them without using polite expressions, they would probably feel uncomfortable.
>
> *(p. 179)*

Shively (2011) focused instead on changes that students made across the length of their stay. In her study, US students who went to Spain for one semester audio-recorded a number of their service encounters in shops, banks, and so on. Overall, at the end of the semester she reports that changes in their typical conversation openers and request patterns showed that they were becoming more familiar with appropriate pragmatic norms, and she suggests that both explicit socialization (e.g., corrections from host families) and implicit socialization (e.g., negative responses from interlocutors) were key in this development.

Taguchi (2011) is an example of an investigation of comprehension rather than production and focused on implicatures and possible gains from study abroad experience by L2 Japanese speakers. Compared to learners who had no study abroad experience, the SA group showed an increased ability to comprehend nonconventional implicatures (e.g., A: Did you like the movie? B: I was glad when it was over) and routine expressions (e.g., that's so sweet of you). As Taguchi observes "due to the situation-specific nature of the routines, experience in the target country, which potentially afforded access to many similar situations, served as a critical factor in comprehension" (p. 927). It is worth noting that overall, Taguchi's study showed a "complex interaction" between proficiency level, SA experience, and different types of pragmatic comprehension; thus it would be a mistake to think of SA as a panacea for pragmatic development.

## 9.5 Computer Mediated Communication

An alternative way in which communication has been increasingly facilitated between NSs and L2 learners is through computer-mediated communication (CMC). Much has been written in this area and for an excellent overview see Taguchi and Sykes (2013). CMC research designs in pragmatics have used multiple platforms from asynchronous channels such as blogging (e.g., Takamiya & Ishihara, 2013) to online synchronous immersive environments (see discussion of CARLA below) and have been shown to be equally as effective as face-to-face instruction in initial research findings (Eslami & Liu, 2013). They have also been used to investigate both written and spoken discourse. Wishnoff (2000), for example, looked at the development of hedging techniques in writing (e.g., *it seems highly likely that....*) in chatroom talk following a pedagogical intervention and found it to be an effective environment for students to practice the forms. Cunningham and Vyatkina (2012) used Web conferences to develop politeness behaviors in spoken discourse in a professional context for learners of German in the United States. A combination of teleconferences with German professionals and simultaneous classroom instruction resulted in learners' increased ability to manipulate modal verbs and to a lesser degree the use of the subjunctive to establish social distance. Sardegna and Molle (2010) used videoconferencing to develop Japanese EFL learners' appropriate conversational behaviors with regard to back channels (e.g., *hu-huh, mhm*) and reactive expressions (e.g., *really, sure*) and demonstrated some short-term improvement. In a series of studies, Belz and her colleagues have developed a technique of telecollaborative pedagogy based on a bilingual learner corpus. The "Telecollaborative learner corpus of English and German" (Telekorp) comprises CMC-based bilingual exchanges between NS peer keypals who are English learners of German and German learners of English (Vyatkina & Belz, 2006). All chat and emails are archived and thus can be used to show development over time. For example, Belz and Vyatkina (2008) traced the development of the use of conversational markers or modal particles (e.g., *ja, denn, doch*) in their L2 learners of German. Despite the frequent occurrence of these attitudinal markers by their German partners, these were not "noticed" (i.e., did not become intake) by the learners until an additional pedagogical intervention was incorporated.

A number of researchers have investigated forms of address using CMC as a way to expand the limited variation that occurs within the constraints of classroom discourse (Belz & Kinginger, 2002 in French and German; González-Lloret, 2008 in Spanish). Kim and Brown (2014) extended this to naturalistic language learning by conducting a case study of address term usage with four L2 learners of Korean who were using a number of

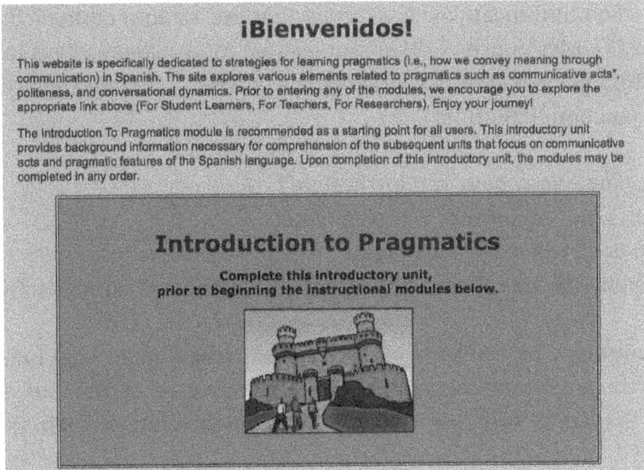


**Figure 9.2** A screenshot from CARLA.
Retrieved from http://www.carla.umn.edu/speechacts/sp_pragmatics/home.html

tools including Skype, Facebook, and Kakao Talk (a mobile phone messenger application popular in Korea). In all these cases, electronic transcripts are collected and analyzed, and in many cases retrospective interviews with participants are also conducted. We also note here the pioneering work that has been ongoing at the Center for Advanced Research on Language Acquisition (CARLA) at the University of Minnesota. Sykes and Cohen (2006), for example, report the development of an online "synthetic immersive environment," Dancing with Words, in which L2 learners of Spanish can access a range of modules supporting the development of pragmatic features (see Figure 9.2).

CARLA has also played a leading role in providing guides for both students and teachers on preparing students for the linguistic and cultural challenges of study abroad programs (Paige et al., 2002).

## 9.6 Action Research

Finally, we discuss the kinds of projects that teachers and students initiate or conduct themselves. Action research, or as it is also termed, teacher research is in a very general sense "classroom-oriented research conducted by classroom teachers" (Renandya & Richards, 2003, p. i). As Burns (2009, 2011) notes, it is usually locally based, often collaborative, reflective, and uses qualitative types of data collection such as observation or diary studies. Green (2003), for example, observed that her Japanese secondary students based in Singapore made frequent pragmatic errors in their expression of requests. She initiated an action research project in which she used a questionnaire to establish where the difficulties lay and based on her findings created a series of six lessons that addressed standard pragmalinguistic formulas for requests and sociopragmatic issues such as level of imposition and relationships between interlocutors. In her final reflections, she noted that the intervention had succeeded in its goal and that she "could perhaps use the same ideas to develop other aspects of communicative competence that are seldom addressed in the language classroom" (p. 26). McConachy (2013) also wanted to investigate ways in which he could increase his EFL Japanese students' pragmatic awareness. He first constructed a short dialogue focused on complimenting:

(140) Phil: Hi Jane. Wow, have you lost weight?
Jane: Oh, um, I'm not sure ... probably not.
Phil: Oh no ... you really look great!
Jane: Oh. By the way, I have finished checking these documents. (p. 103)

He then encouraged his students to discuss and reflect upon what interpretations they had regarding the appropriateness of the interaction. He also prompted students to elaborate on how the kinds of contextual variables might change their perception of the situation:

(141) T: Okay, so let's imagine it's the same conversation, but we change the place of Phil and Jane. So this time, Jane says "Hi Phil. Wow, have you lost weight?" and Phil says "Oh, I'm not sure... Probably not". Would anything change? Would the conversation still be inappropriate or do you think it might be okay?
Seiji: So, I think it's much more inappropriate because... to say "have you lost weight?" to supervisor is too friendly and...
T: To say that to a supervisor is even more inappropriate? Do you think it's more inappropriate to say to a man or a woman? (p. 107)

### 9.6.1 Student-Collected Research

Of course, students can also collect data on themselves or their own experiences. An example of this is Bell and Attardo (2010) who focus on failed humor. Humor is a fertile area for the investigation of pragmatic failure or misfires. Joke telling, for example, is an activity type or a speech event[1] in which the purpose (or perlocutionary goal) is to amuse the recipient of the joke. As humor can fail at any level of linguistic communication, from phonetics (one may not actually hear parts of the joke) to the metapragmatics of the activity type (one may fail to display appreciation, for whatever reason), it requires both pragmalinguistic and sociopragmatic competence on the part of the L2 learner. Bell and Attardo asked international graduate students to keep a diary for eight weeks in which they recorded their experiences of humor and any reflections they had. Bell also met with the students regularly to discuss their diary entries in more detail. A range of failure types was evident. In one example, the L2 participant recalled a conversation and during an interview described it in these terms:

1 On activity types (Levinson, 1979) and speech events (Hymes, 1972), see Section 8.3.4.

(142) the story was very funny and interesting [to the rest of the class], but I didn't understand at all. (Bell & Attardo, 2010, p. 431)

As it turns out, one of the authors (Bell) had been present and *she* recalled that the funny story revolved around the word *brown-nosing*, which had apparently not been part of the instruction received by the speaker. So, this is a relatively simple example of not knowing the right word, which causes a failure to understand at the lexical level. In the next example, the student explains that the particular context and expected relationship, in this case classroom discourse between teacher and student, caused the failure. The teacher (Bell) is discussing her attempts at teasing one of her students, Masao, who was apparently injury-prone, and Masao explains why he misinterprets the joking as actual concern:

(143) Nancy: how about like when I tease you about like breaking your ankle or when I tease you when I ask you like like "Oh, what's your new injury?"
Masao: oooooooooh! is it humor?
Nancy: I call it- it's teasing.
Masao: teasing.
(...) Masao: to recognize is very difficult for me. (...) because most Japanese teacher don't say humor. so, I think I thought teacher didn't say humor. so "Aaah!" she is, she is worried about me.

Masao interpreted Bell's references to hurting himself as concern, rather than as teases because, according to Masao, in his native culture (Japanese) teachers do not "say" humor. As classroom interaction is not keyed for humor in Japan, Masao failed to "get" the intention to produce humor (teasing), while obviously being able to process the text. Yang (2016) conducted a more formal study in which Chinese FL students in the United States who were participating in self-access online instruction on thanking responses kept weekly e-journals. Students were required to respond to prompts given by the researcher while they reflected on their learning experience. Yang performed a content analysis on these entries and was able to document developments made by the students in their understanding of the different thanking responses possible in Mandarin Chinese and the salient contextual factors that prompted specific choices, for example, "I now pay attention to the context of my thanks. If around friends, my thanking is less formal than it was previously" (p. 199).

In closing, we have shown that there are multiple possible research designs and data collection methods in pragmatics and ultimately, the particular question being asked will drive the specific choice of methodology. Student and teacher-researchers should begin by familiarizing themselves with the work that has already been conducted in their area of interest to see the ways in which design choices have been refined in previous research studies.

## 9.7 Conclusion

In this chapter, we have reviewed the typical research designs that comprise studies of L2 pragmatic phenomena. We have focused on the pros and cons of data collection techniques and common research designs with a view to introducing novice researchers in the field to the kinds of issues that can arise when undertaking these projects. Of course, it is not possible to address every approach to data analysis in one chapter. For example, with regard to interactional data, we have focused on an interactional sociolinguistic approach with which we have a great deal of experience. Other approaches of interest include Conversation Analysis (see Mori & Nguyen, 2019 for an excellent summary) and Institutional Conversation analysis (Heritage, 2005).

# 10

# Metapragmatics

In this chapter we wrap up the discussion of metapragmatics, which started in Chapter 7. In Chapter 7 we considered primarily implicit, grammatical metapragmatics. In this chapter we tackle more theoretical and less grammatical topics, which are also more foundational. We should also clarify that there is a sense of the term "metapragmatics," that is, the discussion of how pragmatics is or should be done, which while perfectly valid in itself, will not be the object of our attention in this chapter, but see Caffi (1998) for a discussion.

## 10.1 Metalanguage and Object Language

Metalanguage is a language used to talk about another language. Consider the following extract from a Latin grammar:

(144) The subject of the first or second person is sometimes a substantive, contrary to the English idiom: as, Hannibal petō pācem, I Hannibal am suing for peace. pars spectātōrum scīs, a part of you spectators knows. exoriāre aliquis nostrīs ex ossibus ultor, from out our bones mayst some avenger spring. trecentī coniūrāvimus, three hundred of us have sworn an oath together. (Lane, 1898, p. 180)

It is quite easy to distinguish the language (Latin) from the metalanguage used to describe it (English) despite the fact that we removed the formatting of the original to make this point. However, it is not always that easy to tell the two apart, especially if we use English, say, to talk about English. So we need to look a little deeper into the language/metalanguage distinction.

### 10.1.1 The Origins of the Language/Metalanguage Distinction

The distinction between object language and metalanguage comes originally from logic. The reason for having the distinction is actually quite important. Bertrand Russell, based on work by Frege, whom you will recall from Chapter 1, was in the process of formalizing all of logic into a coherent system based on the theory of sets. This would become the monumental *Principia Mathematica*. As he was doing so he came across a paradox,

*Pragmatics and Its Applications to TESOL and SLA*, First Edition. Salvatore Attardo and Lucy Pickering.

discovered by Burali-Forti, an Italian mathematician. The formulation of the paradox is technical, but a very relatable equivalent is provided here

(145) In the village there is one barber. The barber shaves all the men who do not shave themselves. Does the barber shave himself?

If you say "yes" you are violating the rule that says he can only shave those who do *not* shave themselves; but if you say "no" then he *should* shave himself! You may think that this is silly, but it is not, as Russell and Frege realized immediately, because if the paradox stands, then it undermines the whole edifice of logic, because if logic contains a self-contradiction then it is useless, mathematically speaking.

So, the problem was fixed by Russell's introduction of the theory of types: essentially, the theory states that there are different levels of language: the object language, then the meta-language, which make statements about the object language, then there is a meta-meta-language, which makes statements about the meta-language, and so on. So the theory of types solves the logical equivalent of the barber's paradox by forbidding statements about statements. It would be like if the police[1] went to the barber and said: "Floyd, from now on, you are shaving everyone."

Thus, "regular" language, language that talks about dogs, houses, and kangaroos, is the object language and language that is about language is metalanguage. So far, so good. However, there is a further concept we need to introduce: self-reference.

It is relatively easy to distinguish between metalanguage and self-reference (or self-reflexiveness). Consider the following example:

(146) English requires an expressed grammatical subject.

since this sentence is about English, it is metalinguistic: it talks about language. In this sense, all sentences about grammar, for example, are metalinguistic. Consider now (147)

(147) This sentence was written by either Pickering or Attardo

This is metalinguistic as well, since we are talking about a sentence, but (147) differs from (146) in that (147) is about none other than (147), or to put it differently it refers to itself, that is, it is self-referential. Metalanguage need not be self-referential, and self-reference need not be metalanguage. When James Bond says

(148) My name is Bond. James Bond.

he is self-referring, but not metalinguistic. He is talking about himself, but not about language. Of course a sentence may be both metalinguistic and self-reflexive.

---

1 Deputy Barney Fife, for example. This example is inspired by the American TV sitcom *The Andy Griffith Show*, which ran in the 1960s. It is considered one of the classics of American sitcoms. Floyd is the fictional Mayberry's town barber.

(149) This sentence has five words.

Finally, one should not confuse self-reflexiveness with truth, as in example (150), which is self-reflexive and false, demonstrably.

(150) This sentence is in German.

### 10.1.2 Uses of Metalanguage in Linguistics

As the reader will recall from Section 6.1.1, Jakobson introduced the "metalanguage" terminology to linguistics. It has been used in Systemic Functional Grammar (Section 6.4.2) and of course it constitutes the foundations of metapragmatics, particularly the work on stance and pragmatic markers which are all metalinguistic (Section 7). Jakobson's examples are primarily of the definitional or "glossing" type: "whenever the addresser and/or the addressee need to check on whether they use the same code, speech is focused on the code: it performs a METALINGUAL, i.e., glossing) function. 'I don't follow you — what do you mean?' asks the addressee." (1960, p. 356)

The idea of reflexivity has also found significant application within metapragmatics. Verschueren (2000) defines reflexivity as the metalinguistic awareness of the choices made by the speaker in their repertoire. As such it should not be confused with self-reflexiveness. Reflexivity is more generally the idea of metalinguistic function in Jakobson, that is, the direction of the use of language toward language itself.

#### Implicit and Explicit Metalanguage

As Verschueren notes, explicitness (and its converse, implicitness) lie on a cline or continuum, so the distinction must not be considered a binary one. On the highest degree of explicitness we find speech act verbs such as "assert" or "deny." At the opposite end, of maximal implicitness, we find tense or pronouns (see Section 7.2). The following examples are intuitively ranked from most to least explicit. The situation would be a parent talking to their child.

(151) Make your bed!
I told you to make your bed!
Can you make your bed?
You could make your bed.
Is your bed made up?
I made your bed up.
Isn't it nice to go to sleep in a nice clean fresh bed?
Orderliness increases productivity and builds character.

In a sense, metapragmatics can be considered a form of monitoring, a "paying attention" to the very act of speaking. Speakers do monitor speech for errors and dysfluencies, but the monitoring extends much further than just making sure that we don't misspeak. First, it is constant: "self-monitoring (...) is always going on" (Verschueren, 2000, p. 444); second, it extends to all forms of pragmatic competence, for example

(152) Pickering: "Here's a donut."
Attardo: "Thank you."
Pickering: "What's wrong?"

In this example, Pickering draws the inference that Attardo must be ill or upset because his normal reaction would be much more enthusiastically grateful. Pickering is not wondering all the time whether Attardo is in a bad mood, rather, she is monitoring all exchanges for anything out of the ordinary, including naturally, pragmatic factors. In this case, the level of politeness did not match the expected (usual) enthusiasm and thus this becomes the basis for inference.

Silverstein (1993, p. 48) and Verschueren (2000, p. 442) in fact describe the metapragmatic monitoring of the speakers as a "calibration." Consider example (153)

(153) A.67 utt1: I'd probably have a different perspective if I actually knew someone that had gone into the Peace Corps.
B.68 utt1: Yeah.
A.69 utt1: But I don't.
B.70 utt1: I, + I, + I don't.
A.71 utt1: and none of my, -
B.72 utt1: Didn't mean to cut you off there.
A.73 utt1: Oh, that's okay. (Switchboard corpus: sw_0325_2171)

In turn B.72, speaker B clearly orients to her previous turn (B.70) as a dispreferred choice, an interruption, and apologizes for it. The metalinguistic reference to the previous turn is not quite explicit, but the description of the error is so. Note how A, by accepting the apology, also implicitly orients to turn B.70 as an interruption hence validating B's perception and by being gracious about it, reinforces that the "correct" behavior in that situation is to not interrupt and if one makes a mistake, to apologize for it. So, in this sense the speakers and the pragmatic system are mutually calibrating one another. Consider that if A had responded differently in turn A.73, for example by saying, *what interruption?* or if they had said *You are interrupting more now, shut up and let me talk!* B would have recalibrated their metapragmatic competence quite differently. The acquisition of politeness particularly, since it is explicitly taught, unlike turn taking, would be a good example of metapragmatic recalibration: think of all the times that a parent has to tell a child *say "thank you"* or *say "please"*.

### 10.1.3 Metadiscourse

The term "metadiscourse" is an umbrella term (Hyland, 2005, p. 16) that covers any non-propositional meaning in a text.[2] Hyland defines metadiscourse as "a coherent set of interpersonal resources used to organize a discourse or the writer's stance toward either its

2 On the difference between propositional meaning and illocution, see Section 3.1 and on the difference between propositional meaning and stance and pragmatic markers, see Chapter 7.

content or the reader" (Hyland, 2018, p. xiv), so as we can see, there is not much difference between metapragmatics and metadiscourse, with the exception that metadiscourse is restricted to writing.

Since the overall meaning of the text, written or otherwise, is ultimately "co-produced" (Hyland, 2005, p. 13), a claim that by now should sound quite familiar, we can think of metadiscourse as primarily audience management, both in the sense that metadiscourse helps the author express their stance vis-à-vis the propositional content of the text, but also to help the readers "understand the material and guide their response to it" (p. 12). In particular, metadiscourse manages the amount of shared knowledge about the subject matter. Consider the following example, from the first line of Kant's *Prolegomena to Any Future Metaphysics*, one of the most influential books of Western Philosophy.

(154) THESE Prolegomena are destined for the use, not of pupils, but of future teachers, and even the latter should not expect that they will be serviceable for the systematic exposition of a ready-made science, but merely for the discovery of the science itself.

First, note how the text refers to itself (i.e., it is self-reflexive); second, note how by excluding students from its audience, Kant both implies that non-academics would have no use for the book at all, and that it is a very advanced textbook, destined for professional philosophers. By so doing, Kant sets a very high bar of expectations of what he will take for granted. Indeed, in the next few paragraphs he uses, without definition, the words "metaphysics," "cause and effect," "*a priori*," and "necessity."

So, on the one hand, metadiscourse is "the means by which propositional content is made coherent, intelligible and persuasive to a particular audience" (Hyland, 2005, p. 39) and, on the other hand, to express the authorial stance. Let us consider an example of academic textbooks, like the one you are reading. Hyland finds that in textbooks one of the functions of metadiscourse is "to reduce the weight of new propositional material for novices and present unfamiliar content more comprehensively" (p. 105). For example, in a biology research article the logical connections between sentences are left for the reader to puzzle out, because "[d]omain knowledge specific to [the discipline] allows the informed reader to unpack the connections between these sentences" (p. 107), whereas in the case of textbooks, the authors "typically signal the intended connections more explicitly" (p. 107). More generally, Hyland concludes that "research writers [...] typically address their readers as experts and use metadiscourse to draw on shared understandings and emphasize solidarity" (p. 111), whereas textbook authors use a style that "clearly orders material and elucidates connections [...] and emphasizes an expert role toward both information and readers" (p. 111).

## 10.2 Deixis, Indexicality, and the Semiotic Turn in Sociolinguistics

### 10.2.1 Deixis

In Section 7.2 we examined deictics or indexicals, as they are also known. These are linguistic expressions that are "pointers" to other parts of text, or to the context. Furthermore, we discussed how some linguistic elements may point at social factors such as familiarity (the T/V pronouns, for example), social class (the use of RP in England), or status (honorifics); see Section 7.2.3.

The time has come to focus squarely on the general process whereby the use of a linguistic item becomes a pointer to an extra-linguistic social factor, so that the speaker who uses that linguistic item, the situation in which it was used, and the linguistic co-text in which it was used, all become linked to each other. So, it is the capacity to associate two items (a linguistic expression and its context, for example) that affords the capacity to derive meaning from the association. In sum, the use of a linguistic feature becomes a signifier and the signified is anything that is associated with the usage. This is known as indexicality.

### 10.2.2 Indexicality

The reader will recall from Section 1.1.1 the discussion of Saussure's definition of the linguistic sign as "something that stands for something else" and the fact that the linguistic sign is arbitrary: there is no good reason for a dog to be called "dog." The existence of completely different words for "dog" (such as Spanish "perro") clearly demonstrate the arbitrariness of the linguistic sign, notwithstanding the existence of onomatopoetic words, which are few and do not affect the general point.

#### Types of Signs

Linguistic signs are not the only type of signs. If you drive a car in most of the world, you will be familiar with the signs in Figure 10.1.

Besides the linguistic elements (the "please no parking" caption (in Chinese) and the "P" letter) the sign includes a non-linguistic visual sign the slashed circle, which has the meaning of "prohibition" in the code of traffic signals. Other shapes have other meanings, such as "warning" for the triangle, for example. Nonetheless, these signs are still arbitrary: there is no special reason why a circle should mean "prohibition." However, consider now the signs in Figure 10.2.

These signs include crucially an arrow. The point of an arrow sign is to point in the direction that the sign means. So, if the road to Dallas is on the left, then the sign will point to the left. This is the opposite of arbitrariness. The arrow *must* point in the direction we mean, otherwise it will not work, in fact, worse, it will send people in the wrong direction. In order to distinguish this type of signs, which are partially[3] motivated, Peirce used the term indexical precisely because they bear some sort of "pointing" relationship to the referent. The last type of sign, in Peirce's typology, are icons. Icons bear a fully motivated relationship to their referent. They resemble it in very specific ways.

Consider Figures 10.3 and 10.4: Figure 10.3 is a representation of the actual physical tower, which uses different shades of color (grey) and Figure 10.4 is a representation of the tower which uses two colors (black and white). However, Figure 10.3 is a photograph and 10.4 is a drawing. Regardless of the medium (two colors vs. several), both images *resemble*

---

3 Partially and not fully motivated, because instead of an arrow we could have a finger (☚). Indeed, we do not even have to have a recognizable object, any graphical representation of directionality will suffice (e.g., the "<" in the top left sign in Figure 10.2).

**Figure 10.1** No parking sign in China. Dr. Ying Zhang.

**Figure 10.2** Directional arrow signs.

**Figure 10.3** The Eiffel Tower. Photograph. Paul Cooper; Public Domain Pictures.net.

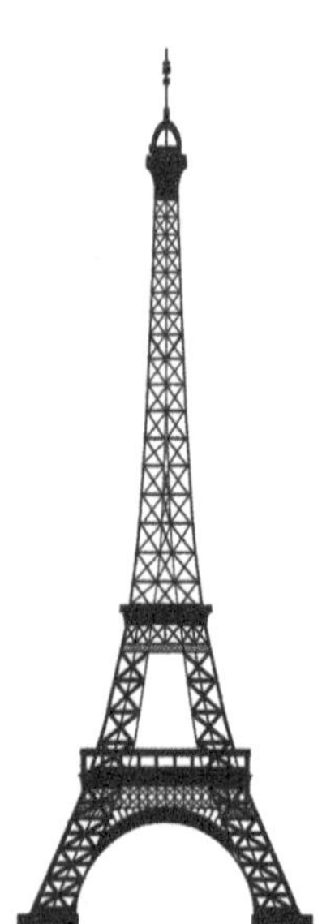

**Figure 10.4** The Eiffel Tower. Drawing.

physically their referent. You could stand in front of the tower in Paris and match detail by detail the real thing to your image.[4] Note that while the picture is more realistic (it resembles its referent more) it still is a representation: the *real* Eiffel tower is made of steel and covered with weather-resistant paint. The photograph is made of ink on a page.

How does this relate to pragmatics? Since the 1980s, pragmatics has been evolving toward a more sociolinguistic view of language, incorporating interactionist and discourse analytic themes and methodologies. At the same time, sociolinguistics had been moving toward semiotics. Hence, the need to address these concerns, to which we turn next.

### 10.2.3 The Semiotic Turn in Sociolinguistics

In the 1990s, sociolinguistics took a "semiotic turn" with the explanation of contextualization in semiotic terms (Silverstein, 1992). Contextualization had been introduced in the 1970s by Gumperz (see Chapter 8) denoting the process whereby sentences received their full interpretation only in context. Silverstein and others (see a discussion in Duranti, 2012) noted that there exists a mutual relationship of indexicality between the utterances and their contexts. Consider the following example.

In Section 4.1.6, we saw the French expression "P'têt ben qu'oui, p'têt ben qu'non" ("maybe yes, maybe no") which has acquired proverbial status (it was even used as a gag in an Astérix cartoon) indexing precisely this regional origin (a related expression is "Une réponse de Normand" ("the answer of a Normand"), that is, an evasive, non-committal

4 You probably should not try that, as you will look stupid doing so and the French already think we are, so we should not encourage them.

answer. So, obviously the region may index the expression (a Normand's response is an evasive response). However, suppose that a person newly moved to Normandy wanted to "blend in" and decided to answer questions evasively to "sound Normand." Now the relationship has reversed: the expression indexes the region: if one is evasive one is a Normand.

**Indexicality and Enregisterment**

Indexicality is defined as the "nondenotational or merely indicative relation of a linguistic token form to some component(s) of the context in which it occurs" (Silverstein, 2016, p. 52). Let us unpack the unquestionably dense definition: the relationship between an item of linguistic performance ("token form") to any aspect of its context (i.e., the speaker, the hearer, the situation, etc.) is not denotational (i.e., it is not a sign which comes with a referent to begin with) but rather it is a pointer, that is, it indicates it. Recall that deictics are pointers.

Let us consider briefly the example of the High Rising Terminal intonation contour, more commonly known as Valley Talk, Uptalk, or Mallspeak. Consider this example in which a speaker with HRT in her repertoire explains that when someone asks her for her name she answers "Amanda" with HRT, despite the fact that she obviously knows her own name. The fragment of dialogue can be heard in the YouTube clip below.

(155) am ⇑ an da vs. am ⇓ an da
https://www.youtube.com/watch?v=n_WM-Af5svs

The HRT that is characteristic of Uptalk has an indexical function: it marks a speaker's affiliation with a particular group, for example, in this case, HRT is stereotypically associated with young women and Australian speakers and with linguistic insecurity (on uptalk in the perspective of indexicality, see Tyler, 2015 and references therein). When the particular linguistic feature of HRT becomes associated with a given group and with value judgments about it, we have what has been described as "enregisterment" (Agha, 2005; Johnstone et al., 2006; Silverstein, 2016).[5]

So, in a nutshell, any linguistic feature that becomes associated with any aspect of the context, becomes a pointer to it. Once it reliably points to it, it becomes a sign of it (see Section 1.1.1), and therefore its use becomes meaningful. This is why adopting stereotypical markers of a given register/variety can be used to signal solidarity (belonging to a group) or conversely can be used to mock (parody) a group. A good example of this would be the Southern drawl, which is stereotypically associated with negative connotations in the United States (slow, stupid; see Section 10.4.1).

Covert or reverse prestige is another example of enregisterment. A classic example of it is the dialect of Martha's Vineyard (a small island in Massachusetts, near Cape Cod), which was studied by Labov (1963). In particular, Labov examined the diphthong [aɪ], which is produced with a more or less raised [a]. The range of the vowel includes the

5 Silverstein claims to have introduced the term in 1992. His work is challenging. Duranti (2012) is a much more accessible introductory treatment of indexicality.

low [aɪ], the [ɐ], an intermediate stage of raising between [a] and [ə], and finally the medial vowel [əɪ]. The low variety [aɪ] is the "standard" North American form, whereas the mid variety [əɪ] is typical of the island's variety. Labov found a pattern of uses that seems odd: both in the older and younger speakers <30 and >60 there is *less* centralization, whereas in the 30–60 age group there is most centralization. Essentially, the people in the 30–60 age group were using the [əɪ] pronunciation as a marker of solidarity with the island's way of life which they felt was being threatened by the influx of tourists who of course did not sound like the islanders. As Labov puts it "when a man says [rɐɪt] (...) ['right'], he is unconsciously establishing the fact that he belongs to the island: that he is one of the natives to whom the island really belongs" (1963, p. 304). Since in general terms, non-standard less common forms are considered less prestigious than standard widespread forms, this is a case of reverse prestige, that is, of a community that attributes prestige to a variant differently than the general population. We should note that Labov himself does not use the term covert prestige in the study. The term was introduced by Trudgill (1972).

Contrast now Received Pronunciation, the quintessential prestige variety, with covert prestige, which is essentially its converse: prestige is attributed to the low variety, with its connotations of working class, rootedness, and manliness. The connotations of Received Pronunciation are of course the opposite: upper class, educated, cosmopolitan, foppish, or stuck up.

While co-occurrence and repetition may trigger indexicality, it would be a mistake to equate them. As Kiesling (2009) argues,

> it is possible to have co-occurrence without indexical meaning. Johnstone and Kiesling (2008) show that in fact the people who use a particular feature of Pittsburgh speech (/aw/ monophthongization) do not necessarily understand that feature as indexing a Pittsburgh identity; rather, other aspects of social discourse must take up this possibility and "point out" to speakers in different ways that the form is local to Pittsburgh. Indexical meaning can thus arise out of statistical commonality or single instances of use that are salient enough to gain meaning for speakers.

Kiesling does not exemplify, but we could take the infamous remark by John Lennon that the Beatles were more popular than Jesus as a good example of a single instance of use that was widely taken to index a sacrilegious stance. For the record, Lennon denied that his intention was such.

## 10.3 Metalinguistic Awareness

Metapragmatics can be defined as the speakers' competence of the appropriateness of their linguistic behavior (Caffi, 1998). Verschueren defines metapragmatics as the reflexive awareness of language use (1995, 2000, p. 445) with different degrees of "consciousness" (implicit/explicit, p. 447).

### 10.3.1 Implicit and Explicit Awareness

A speaker may be aware of their linguistic behavior implicitly or explicitly. The explicit case is easily defined and conceptualized. If the speaker explicitly, that is, in their speech, refers to some feature of language, then it is an explicit case of metalinguistic awareness. Consider the following example:

(156) A.93 utt2: Do you think, you, D Base is more flexible or allows you to do more.
A.93 utt3: Or do you think the others are pretty much compatible these days?
B.94 utt1: Um, I wouldn't say compatible, but –
A.95 utt1: But, uh – -
B.96 utt1: – certainly comparable.
A.97 utt1: – yeah,
A.97 utt2: I didn't mean compatible,
A.97 utt3: <laughter> I meant comparable.
A.97 utt4: My brain is going to mush. (Switchboard corpus: sw_0089_3086)

Here Speaker A uses the word "compatible" and when corrected by B, in turn 97, utterances 2 and 3, she comments metalinguistically that she did not mean "compatible" but in fact "comparable." Similar examples would be someone commenting that a given utterance is rude or impolite or well said.

## 10.4 Ideology, or the Lack of Awareness

We now turn to the last topic we will tackle in our discussion of metapragmatics. We have seen that metapragmatics is a broad category, that encompasses a significant range of issues all connected by a "thread" of reference to pragmatic practice, be it explicit or implicit. The last step is to connect metapragmatics directly with social issues and constructs (such as class, gender, power, etc.). Indeed, as Rosa and Burdick (2016) claim "metalinguistic and metapragmatic commentary serves to connect language use and social structure" (p. 108). This connection is analyzed through the construct of linguistic ideology, that is, a set of beliefs about language that the speakers holds.

### 10.4.1 Definition of Ideology

Ideology can be defined as the lack of awareness, on the speakers' part, of the contingent, "partisan" aspect of their beliefs. Let's try to make this definition more explicit. Eagleton (1991) reviews several definitions of ideology (see also Kroskrity, 2004); the definition that is most relevant in this context is "a set of (false) ideas that help legitimate a (dominant) political power." Let's take apart a few of the aspects of this definition (those we put in parentheses, to indicate that they are optional). First, not all the ideas that constitute an ideology need to be false, for example, Mussolini's Fascism made much of the Roman Empire heritage, and, clearly, modern Rome is ancient Rome two millennia later. So that part of the ideology was actually true. Needless to say, the modern Italian army was nowhere as powerful as the ancient Roman one. So *that* part of the Fascist ideology was false. So, in conclusion, not all the components of an ideology need to be false. Second, while an ideology is in the service of a political power, that political power need not be dominant. Take the Republicans and the Democrats in the United States, around 2020. The two parties have clearly different ideological stances, at least on some topics. The fact that the Republicans are currently in a position of dominance, since they control the presidency and the Senate, does not mean that the Democrats do not have an ideology. In a sense we could summarize this point as any political system is an ideology (to someone who does not share the same set of beliefs).

Eagleton (1991) does an excellent job of showing how the term "ideology" is used in common parlance as a derogatory term. Much like a traitor is the opponent's convert, and freedom fighters are terrorists on the other side of the war, an ideology is something your opponent has, whereas we have systems of belief. We think that our definition of "lack of awareness of the contingency of the set of beliefs" mitigates Eagleton's point. We are not alone in this sort of definition. For example, Verschueren (2000) states:

> In the realm of social life in general, more or less coherent patterns of meaning which are felt to be so commonsensical that they are no longer questioned, thus feeding into taken-for granted interpretations of activities and events, are usually called ideologies. Similarly, when elements of metapragmatic awareness can be seen to form persistent frames of interpretation related to the nature and social functioning of language which are no longer subject to doubt or questioning, it becomes possible to talk about ideologies of language.
>
> *(p. 450)*

The ideological aspect of no longer being doubted or questioned is called in philosophical circles "naturalizing" a belief. A joke, attributed to David Foster Wallace, explains it best:

(157) Two fish are swimming when they come across a third fish, who greets them by saying "Hey, how's the water?" The two fish swim away and then one turns to the other and says, "What the hell is water?"

If you are a fish, you spend your entire life in water and so you end up not noticing the water. Water is perfectly natural to fish. That the nobility was innately superior to the peasantry was obvious, natural or divinely ordained in the middle ages. It took the French revolution to get people to think otherwise and to start believing that everyone is equal, in principle.

The really crucial points in the definition, the two that must be there, are that an ideology is

1. a set of ideas, and
2. that these ideas *legitimize* a group, leadership, or political force.

### Legitimizing

Let's briefly consider what "legitimizing" entails: to make something legitimate (lawful, and hence valid) presupposes that whatever we are legitimizing *was not so to begin with*. Either something *is* legitimate and therefore does not need legitimization, or something is *not* legitimate and thus it is in need of "repair" which comes from some activity that carries legitimacy. A few decades ago, a child born out of wedlock was called "illegitimate." The way the child could be legitimized was by the two parents marrying each other.[6] If you transfer this analogy to beliefs, you get that an irrational belief (i.e., not justified by fact) needs to be legitimized by changing the status of the fact from that of a questionable fabrication to something that is naturally the case, so obvious that it will no longer be questioned. So in conclusion, legitimizing involves to some degree of deception. Silverstein (1979) defines ideology as "rationalization or justification" of speakers' beliefs, along the same lines. This does not entail that the speakers are aware of the process. Bourdieu speaks of their "complicity" by which he means the *habitus* that has been inculcated in the speakers (1991, p. 51) from birth and therefore is acquired subconsciously.

### The National Language Ideology

Let's consider briefly an example of language ideology. In the 1800–1900 period many European countries came under the influence of the idea of "nationhood" and countries like Germany and Italy became unified. Language played a relatively small role, but the case of Italy is remarkable because the country was split among numerous local languages, some conducting full-blown legal, administrative, and literary activities in the local language (e.g., Neapolitan, Sicilian, Lombard). Some regions presented a diglossic situation: for example in Piedmont, the acrolect was French. Cavour, the prime minister who was responsible for the unification of Italy under the monarchy of the Savoia dynasty, spoke and wrote in French. Once Italy was largely unified (1861) Cavour faced the problem of unifying the army and administration. To do so, the dialect of Tuscany was chosen, in the form used by the three greatest Italian writers (Dante, Petrarch, and Boccaccio) in the 14th century. So, in other words, a variety of Tuscan which had not been spoken for about 500 years was resuscitated and made by fiat (pun intended) the national language, to be taught in schools, used by bureaucracy, and spoken in the military. This was accomplished in a relatively short amount of time, by fostering a linguistic ideology that, on the one hand exalted the "three crowns" as the highest accomplishments of the (until then, non-existent) Italian language, and on the other hand devalued the local languages as mere "dialects" and made using them in school a "mistake." In particular, the practice in the military to send young men to serve the compulsory draft in regions away from the one they were from, forced them to learn at least some Italian to get by. The outcome, about 150 years later, has been a significant standardization over Italian, with the almost complete abandonment of the local varieties, which even where they persist have been heavily influenced by the national language. Let's add one last consideration: the ideology of the national language is so entrenched in Western culture that one often encounters arguments that make "full citizenship" dependent on speaking the national

6 Technically as long as the mother was married to *someone* and that someone recognized the child, the problem was solved. In the text we go for the slightly less sordid narrative.

language (think of the English-only movement in the United States). Needless to say, in quadrilingual Switzerland (German, French, Italian, Romansh[7]) or in multilingual societies, such as Nigeria, such arguments are heard less frequently. On multilingualism, see Section 11.2.

### Hegemony and *habitus*

When a national language and its related ideology of superiority over other varieties is well established it achieves the status of hegemony: in a hegemonic situation, the group in power achieves such complete control of the public discourse that even those groups that are disenfranchised believe the ideology and propound it themselves. In a hegemonic situation, the oppressed actively participate in their oppression. The process whereby an ideology becomes hegemonic and thus appears natural is called naturalization. This is very close to Bourdieu's (1991) concept of *habitus* which consists of all the experiences that an individual is exposed to, starting from birth, so socialization, schooling, social connections, cultural consumption (television, films, music, books, news reporting), and so on. These experiences slowly and imperceptibly accrete into a world view, an ideology. So deep goes *habitus* that Bourdieu considers that it is reflected in the way people behave, the way they walk, hold themselves upright, the physical stances they take when speaking, etc. If this seems excessive, consider how teenagers famously enraged their parents by "slouching" (i.e., not sitting properly) just a few years ago or how in Victorian times girls were taught to walk holding a book on their heads (which makes you keep your head up). The term for this is "embodiment" and we will return to it in Chapter 11.

One of the subtle and hardly perceptible forms whereby *habitus* is engendered in the speaker is *condescension*. Let's quote Bourdieu, for a French example:

> [A] French-language newspaper published in Béarn (a province of south-west France) wrote of the mayor of Pau who, in the course of a ceremony in honour of a Béarnais poet, had addressed the assembled company in Béarnais: "The audience was greatly moved by this thoughtful gesture".[...] In order for an audience of people whose mother tongue is Béarnais to perceive as a "thoughtful gesture" the fact that a Béarnais mayor should speak to them in Béarnais, *they must tacitly recognize the unwritten law which prescribes French as the only acceptable language for formal speeches in formal situations.*
>
> *(1991, p. 68; our emphasis, SA/LP)*

French is of course the national language of France, also in a hegemonic position vis-à-vis the other linguistic varieties in France (and this despite official support for other languages such as Occitan). Bourdieu continues to note how the condescension reinforces the hegemony of the national language even as the mayor chooses not to speak it, precisely because it frames it as a "thoughtful gesture" (i.e., the mayor is somehow doing a favor to the audience by addressing them in their shared mother tongue). Notice how the whole exchange only works if all the people involved accept that in formal, official situation one should use the official language, that is, French.

---

7 Romansh is a Romance language (i.e., a descendant of Latin) spoken primarily in the Grisons canton of Switzerland.

### Naturalization

Naturalization thus takes place when new meanings are attached to linguistic forms, below the threshold of the consciousness of the speakers. Within the various ways in which naturalization is effected, two stand out: recursion and erasure. We will consider them through the work of Gal and Irvine (1995).

Recursion is an extension of the meaning of a sign. For example, in the Martha's Vineyard example in Section 10.2.3 the pronunciation of *right* as [rɐɪt] as opposed to [aɪ], in the context of Martha's Vineyard connotes (is indexed for) "local." To this meaning ulterior meanings are added, such as "authentic" or "genuine." This is the process of recursion. Note how, despite the fact that linguistic signs are symbolic and hence arbitrary,[8] their relationship with the socio-economic-cultural context is treated as iconic (i.e., motivated) and is thus called "iconicity" (Gal & Irvine, 1995, p. 963).[9] Think of the association of Southern dialect features, such as the southern drawl, in the United States with the feature of "low intelligence" (see Hamilton, 2009, delightfully titled "Y'all Think We're Stupid: Deconstructing Media Stereotypes of The American South"); as Gal and Irvine would have it "[by] picking out qualities supposedly shared by the social image and the linguistic image, the ideological representation [...] binds them together in a linkage that appears to be inherent." (pp. 973–974).

Erasure is defined as "the process in which ideology, in simplifying the field of linguistic practices, renders some persons or activities or sociolinguistic phenomena invisible. Facts that are inconsistent with the ideological scheme may go unnoticed or get explained away" (p. 974). For example, Gal and Irvine note that in Macedonia, a region including northern Greece and Northern Macedonia, after World War I, the presence of Slavic speakers in Macedonia was denied and the census asked only if the person spoke Greek (p. 984). A more familiar example may be L2 speakers who may be quite fluent in their L1 but find themselves assigned to remedial sections of classes, that is, their linguistic performance is seen as "lacking," because their knowledge of another language is simply ignored (erased). Another example, still in the US context, is the English only movement which conveniently ignores that there are literally hundreds of Native American languages still spoken in the United States, not to mention that some states, such as Texas, were originally Spanish speaking. In fact, when Texas was part of Mexico, in 1834 both Spanish and English were recognized as the official languages of the area. In 1925, it was made a *criminal offense* to teach Spanish in public schools.[10]

Thus, in conclusion, taken together, iconicity, recursion, and erasure yield the naturalization of a hegemonic ideology, such as the superiority and essential status of a national language.

---

8 It should be noted that whereas linguists agree that linguistic signs are fundamentally arbitrary, there are plenty of behaviors on the speakers' part which show that they believe the contrary, that is, that language is somehow motivated. This is not the place to pursue this (but see Attardo, 1994, pp. 149–169), however, the fact that speakers assume a non-arbitrary, motivated theory of the sign goes a long way in explaining why speakers treat the signs–context connection as motivated.

9 Coupland (2016) assumes that the connection may also be indexical, that is, partially motivated.

10 The historical information on Texas comes from the Portal for Texas History, hosted at the University of North Texas Libraries.

The following are some examples of ideological statements:

- The standard variety is a language and the non-standard varieties are dialects.
- Standard varieties are better than dialects.
- Speakers of non-standard varieties are worse than speakers of standard varieties.
- English became a world-language (lingua franca) because it is easier to learn.
- English is better than other languages.

Think about them. You probably believe some of them to be true. A good survey of the field of linguistic ideologies can be found in Rosa and Burdick (2016).

Finally, you might wonder: aren't the ideas presented in this book or this chapter also contingent and hence ideological? Indeed, science recognizes the partial, always questionable, work-in-progress status of our theories and conceptualizations. As scientists we are well aware of this. However, science comes with a nice side effect: it works. Science can make predictions that can be tested. Science builds rockets that fly into space and even leave the solar system, science cures diseases, science builds microwave ovens that warm up your dinner. In short, science is empirically testable, in a way that ideologies are not.[11]

## 10.5 Conclusion

This chapter, and the following one, called "frontiers" give an idea of what the most recent developments of the field are. In other words, what scholars are working on more or less "right now." We provided some introductory background on the concepts of metalanguage and indexicality, which are central to these trends and discussed the "semiotic turn" of sociolinguistics (and pragmatics along with it) as well as the notions revolving around linguistic ideologies. These are among the most exciting new areas of research in the field.

Unlike most of the previous chapters, we do not include a section on the impact of the subject matter on SLA and TESOL. This is due to the fact that it is a little too early to do so. The field is still assessing and "digesting" these ideas. No doubt its effects will be profound. For those wanting to "peek" ahead, we can recommend Ortega (2011) and Hall (2018). These sources will give an idea of the complexity of the matter and of how the cutting edge of the field is evolving.

11 If you are smart enough to ask whether this last statement is a form of ideological belief in scientism, then you are also smart enough to figure out why the answer to this question cannot be included in an introductory textbook.

# 11
# Frontier

This final chapter briefly outlines several of the most recent developments in pragmatics. These are not chapter meant to be comprehensive treatments, like the previous chapters, but just "appetizers" so to speak to give the reader an idea of some of the directions that pragmatics is moving toward.

## 11.1 Pragmatic Resources in English as a Lingua Franca

English as a Lingua Franca (ELF) is defined as "a vehicular language spoken by people who do not share a native language" (Mauranen, 2003, p. 513) or similarly as a context in which communication occurs "between fairly fluent interlocutors from different L1 backgrounds, for whom English is the most convenient language" (Breiteneder et al., 2006). Prompted largely by researchers in the European context (e.g., Jenkins, 2000; Seidlhofer, 2007), the investigation of ELF looks at how linguistic systems might be used similarly or differently by interlocutors in this particular context as opposed to any other. One common finding is that interaction in ELF is characterized by an inherent robustness; that is, atypical linguistic behavior is better tolerated than in other contexts. Early work by Firth (1996) describes these behaviors as falling under a "Let it Pass Principle" in which "the hearer lets the unknown or unclear action, word or utterance 'pass' on the (common-sense) assumption that it will either become clear or redundant as talk progresses" (p. 243). Thus in general, linguistic features, including those that fall under the umbrella of pragmatics, are thought to be more open to negotiation than in native speaker-based contexts. Other features of ELF interaction attest to an important transparency principle also. There is a recognition of a lack of common ground and a desire to enhance communicative efficiency. Kecskes (2006) notes that interactants prefer to use "semantically analyzable formulas" that have clear compositional meaning. Pickering (2009) and Pickering and Litzenberg (2011) found this to be the case with the use of intonation in ELF. While in native speaker-based interaction, intonational features have been shown to cue both informational and social convergence (see Chapter 8), this was not the case in the ELF examples. Specifically, there was no evidence for what has been described as "socially integrative" uses of tone choice found in NS-based interaction (Hewings, 1995). For example, typically, when contradicting a previous speaker, NS participants will use a rising tone to avoid the appearance of overt

*Pragmatics and Its Applications to TESOL and SLA*, First Edition. Salvatore Attardo and Lucy Pickering.

contradiction and perception of rudeness or abruptness that may be inferred from a falling tone (see the earlier discussion of rising and falling tones in Chapter 8 and Example 1.2). There is no evidence of this "face-saving" function of tone choice in our ELF data; in fact, participants appeared to have no expectation of this kind of use of intonation. The following example demonstrates the low, falling tones that typically occurred when these speakers disagreed and which would strike the NS ear as unnecessarily abrupt and rude.

(158) Thai L1 speaker (T) and Korean L1 speaker (K)
T: //⇗ do you have TAble//
K: //⇗ yeah like TElevision//
T: //⇘ NO// //⇘ TAble//

This is not just the case for phonological "softeners" or mitigating strategies but also includes lexical and syntactic markers as McKay (2009) notes:

> When speakers did disagree, they tended not to use any phrases to soften the disagreement such as "I hate to disagree with you but" Rather they used raw negation, rejection and disagreement, shunning the use of face-saving strategies.
>
> *(p. 237)*

Finally, there is evidence that interlocutors will also adapt linguistic devices to match their needs. For example, House (2009, 2013) examines the use of short pragmatic markers (e.g., *you know, yes/yeah, so* and *ok*) in academic advising sessions and finds that ELF speakers re-interpret them for their own purposes and argues that they perform different functions. For example, she suggests that *you know* and *yeah* which are considered to primarily be interpersonal markers, are used in a "more self-referenced way" by ELF speakers to gain time in discourse planning and production or to act as a kind of coherence marker when there are language formulation difficulties. What seems clear is that informational and social convergence are differently achieved in cross-varietal contexts of interaction and context of use is crucial. It also seems unlikely that strategies developed over time for use in one context will easily transfer to another context, and some features of ELF interaction may conflict with the ways in which NSs typically negotiate understanding. It may be that NSs and NNSs who bring their primary strategies to all interactions will find themselves listening for very different things.

## 11.2 Multilingualism

Directly related to ELF is multilingualism, that is, the use of multiple languages by a single speaker. This is a phenomenon which a generation ago would have been the province of sociolinguistics. That it is now considered mainstream pragmatics is a testament to the evolution of the field toward sociopragmatics, which started in the 1980s. Many scholars argue that we have entered a historical period, variously called "post modernity" or "late modernity" which is characterized by:

1. the consequences of the end of colonialism, which include the widespread use of English worldwide, both as expanding and outer circles (Kachru, 1985) but also of English as a Lingua Franca.

2. a significant increase of migratory phenomena, due to political (e.g., war) or economic reasons (famine, unemployment, etc.) (Blommaert, 2015; Blommaert & Rampton, 2011). Not all migratory phenomena are limited to the dispossessed, we can also include the so-called *brain-drain* (human capital flight) which results in significant numbers of educated, middle-class professionals leaving their home country and moving to privileged regions, such as the United States or Northern Europe, in search of better compensation or opportunity. In some cases, such as Jewish scientists fleeing Nazi-controlled Europe, the two types of migration converge.
3. superdiversity. It has been argued (e.g., Blommaert, 2015) that in the past 30 years, that is, since the end of the Cold War, we have entered a period called "superdiversity," defined as "the extraordinary complexity of contemporary social configurations due to post-cold war migration patterns and the digital revolution" (p. 23). The term was introduced by Vertovec (2007, 2019).
4. economic globalization, which obviously favors the spread of English, both in the sense that more people become incentivized to learn it, but also its use as a lingua franca. Furthermore, it increases and facilitates brain drain and depresses economies in the countries from which brain drain originates, in advanced capitalism.
5. mediatic globalization, for example, Hollywood films and cartoons, music (rock-n-roll, but also dance music), the internet, and social media favors the spread of ubiquitous multilingualism, not only because they expose increasingly large numbers of people to speakers of other languages to English but also because other centers of cultural diffusion take advantage of these increased opportunities for global distribution. Think for example of Bollywood movies, produced in India, or of the fact that Franco-Belgian cartoons are known and translated worldwide, as are Japanese manga and the phenomenon of cosplay, which has been successfully exported to many countries.

Fishman (1998) notes that the prominence of English is accompanied by increased standardization and local support for other languages, so that, while the smaller languages are at risk of extinction, those of intermediate size will likely prosper. In other words, there is no risk of English becoming the only language spoken. In fact, Chinese, Swahili, Hausa, Spanish, and Arabic are growing as auxiliary languages. The "unprecedented" prominence of English worldwide has led to the theorization of a hierarchy of languages, visually represented in Figure 11.1.

An important point, stressed by Aronin et al. (2013, p. 10), is that the ubiquitous diffusion of multilingualism (which they label "suffusiveness") does not imply that this is a uniform phenomenon. On the contrary, the globalization of multilingualism is a "patchy" phenomenon: consider that the use of English as medium of instruction in higher education is spreading worldwide, even in countries like Spain or Italy, which have rich linguistic and research traditions, and no colonial connection to the British empire (which of course explains why the practice is common in India, for example). While this is unquestionably true, it is also true that in large parts of South America the penetration of English is marginal and Spanish and Portuguese remain entrenched as auxiliary languages. To use another example, in Europe, Northern European countries (such as Sweden, Norway, and Denmark) have been historically at the vanguard of the adoption of English in higher education, but in a rural context the presence of English has been much more limited.

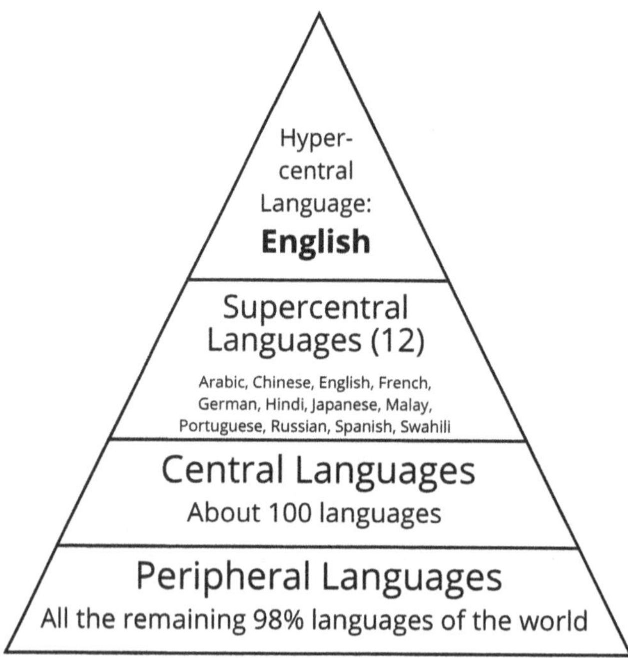


**Figure 11.1** The hierarchy of world languages; adapted from de Swaan (2001) and Cook (2013, p. 190).

Trilingualism and multilingualism gain from being studied from a complexity theory perspective, because, as noted by Aronin (2015, pp. 15–16), multilingualism is a complex phenomenon, in the technical sense of complexity theory (see Section 11.4), that is, it has multiple agents, emergent features, sensitivity to initial conditions (a.k.a., the butterfly effect, see Section 11.4.1), and more.

The following are some implications for teaching in multilingual environments:

1. Replacement of the monolingual native speaker as the *norm* with the model of a multilingual, proficient speaker.
2. Recognition of the advantages of multilingualism in socio-economical terms but also at the neurological level, with the caveat that not all effects are positive (see Section 11.6.1).
3. The acquisition of an L3 is different than the acquisition of both L1 *and* L2. (e.g., Green, 2017; Safont and Portolés, 2015; Westegaard et al., 2017) Under certain circumstances, trilingual children outperform bilingual ones, for example, in the learning of the *ser/estar* difference in Spanish, if L2 is a language that shares the distinction (e.g., Catalan) versus one that does not (e.g., German, Italian) (Arnaus Gil, 2015). In other situations, L3 shows a non-facilitative effect (Westegaard et al., 2017), that is, it makes it *harder* to acquire a new linguistic feature.
4. L3 speakers undergo cognitive restructuring, to various extents, which may range from the influence of L1 on L2 to attrition, that is, loss of L1 features (Pavlenko, 2011).

Aspects of multilingualism that may differentiate it from L2 acquisition are generating more interest including in the field of pragmatics (e.g., the 2013 special issue of the *Journal of Pragmatics* (Vol. 59)). Questions such as "do the developmental paths of production and comprehension differ or converge as the multiple languages are acquired?" are being asked. In other words, is the path of a bilingual learning a third language different from that of a monolingual speaker learning a second language? Is there a "multilingualism factor" (also called an M-factor)? The work of Safont-Jordà and her colleagues in Catalan, Castilian, and English is a good example of the kind of research that can be undertaken (Portolés & Safont, 2018; Safont & Portolés, 2016; Safont-Jordà, 2005). They have focused on the speech acts of requests and tested both adult and child learners using mixed methods studies including a longitudinal case study of a single L3 child learner (Safont-Jordà, 2003). Overall, their findings suggest that L3 learners (bilingual speakers of Catalan and Castilian learning English) employed more varied and more frequent request modifiers (e.g., *please, if possible could you?*) than their L2 counterparts (monolingual speakers of Castilian learning English). In the case of the single child learner, Pau, the introduction of the third language appeared to positively affect his pragmatic development in an increased use of indirect requests across all three of his languages. This increase in pragmatic formulas was also found in a much larger study of 184 primary and infant school learners (Safont & Portolés, 2016). The researchers suggest that these findings call for further research on the pragmatic development of third language learners including both different aspects of pragmatics and different linguistic backgrounds (2005, p. 84). Further discussions of multilingualism can be found in an edited collection (Singleton et al., 2013).

## 11.3 Embodied Cognition

There are various definitions of embodiment. A pretty standard one is

> Cognition is embodied when it is deeply dependent upon features of the physical body of an agent, that is, when aspects of the agent's body beyond the brain play a significant causal or physically constitutive role in cognitive processing.
>
> *(Wilson & Foglia, 2017)*

which is the general use that psychologists and philosophers make of the term. Some define embodied meaning as gestures or physical posture (e.g., Goodwin & Goodwin, 2004). This is the sense in which Looney (2019) speaks of the "embodied nature of co-operative action" (see Section 8.5).

Bourdieu's (1991) embodied *habitus* (which we discussed in Section 10.4) means that a certain cultural item has been assimilated by the person, but there is no particular "physical" sense. So, we may consider this sort of use of "embodiment" as metaphorical. There is no real reference to the physical body.

There is a last use of the term embodiment, found primarily within cognitive linguistics (Lakoff, 1987; Langacker, 1987). Cognitive linguistics maintains that conceptual organization arises from embodiment, that is, it reflects the fact that perception happens through the body. Thus, at a mundane level, since humans cannot see infrared and ultraviolet light, our visual "space" is limited to visible wavelengths. More importantly, consider that human bodies are asymmetrical, we have one head, and it is on top of our bodies. From this fact, argues cognitive linguistics, comes the metaphorical schema up/down, which is then axiologically interpreted as good versus bad (we feel "up" when we are in a good mood and "down" when we are sad; Lakoff & Johnson, 1980, pp. 14–18). Another example is images such as "a heated argument." Wilkowski et al., (2009) find that conceptualizations of anger and of heat are conceptually related and affect the physical perception of the temperature by the subjects (i.e., mentioning anger causes the subjects to experience the room as warmer). This would be related to the fact that anger causes the release of stress hormones, such as adrenaline, which cause the body temperature to rise.

## 11.4 Complexity Theory

The ominously named complexity theory is an approach to complex systems (in a mathematical sense, i.e., meaning that they cannot be modeled with a linear equation).[1] So, complex does not (necessarily) mean complicated, although, as we will see, often complex systems are complicated too. Indeed, the typical examples of complex systems that baffle mathematical models are the weather and the stock market, which require taking into account hundreds of variables (temperature, wind speed, humidity, daylight, etc.) and in some case are reflexively irrational: in the stock market, notoriously, "panic" selling can be set off for no apparent reason, under the right circumstances, whereby investors sell their shares just because they see "everybody" doing the same thing. In what follows we will present in a non-technical, accessible way complexity theory and its application to linguistic systems.

### 11.4.1 Complex Systems

So, why is the fact that the stock market is not a linear system important? Linear models are predictable: the relationship between the input and the output never changes. So, for starters, complex non-linear models are unpredictable. It would be nice if we had a linear equation describing the price of even only one stock. Then you would be able to plug in into your formula the current price, say, and see what the price of the stock would be tomorrow. Then if the stock was increasing in price, you would hold on to it and sell it tomorrow, at the higher price, or if it was going down, you would sell it now. As one can plainly imagine, if one had such a formula, one would become very rich, very quickly. Or, if one could predict tomorrow's weather from today's, again one would be safe from tornadoes, hail, etc.

Couldn't we have a really complicated formula, with hundreds of variables, say, and that really complicated formula would allow us to predict the behavior of the system? Indeed,

1 A linear equation is a mathematical formula that can be represented as a straight line (hence, linear) on Cartesian axes. A typical linear equation would be $x = 2y$. This simply states that for each value of $x$, $y$ is equal to $x$ times two. This is all the mathematics that we will need in this book. Needless to say, systems theory requires serious mathematics.

people have tried this and, for example, weather forecasting has improved enormously since its early days by incorporating vast amounts of data and using intensive computing which allows the meteorologists to solve thousands of equations to produce models of the weather. Likewise enormous amounts of resources have been poured into building extremely complex computer systems to predict the behavior of stocks. However, there are two problems: (1) the butterfly effect, and (2) emergent properties.

The so-called butterfly effect has been popularized widely. The basic idea is that a very small cause (a butterfly flapping its wings) can have an extremely large effect (a hurricane a continent away). In a sense, this is just another way to look at non-linearity: a linear cause–effect relationship would require that small causes produce small effects. Think of throwing a ball: a lot of force yields a lot of distance.

Emergence is an important property of complex systems. An emergent property of a complex system is a property such that its existence could not be predicted on the basis of just observing the components of the system. Consider traffic jams: if you drive in the center of a big town at rush hour, you are likely to encounter a traffic jam, that is predictable. Also, if there is an accident and the road is closed, obviously there will be a traffic jam. These are predictable events. Consider now the following situation: you are driving on the highway and suddenly you see the drivers ahead of you braking. So you brake too, to avoid hitting them, and you come to a stop. Needless to say, the drivers behind you also see that and stop as well. You are now sitting in a traffic jam. However, once the flow of traffic resumes, you are surprised to see that there is no ambulance or tow truck, and there is no road work either. So what caused the traffic jam? Most likely driver 1 slowed down, perhaps to exit the highway. So, driver 2 behind them, also slowed down, or changed lanes to avoid having to slow down. This caused the drivers behind driver 2 to also slow down or change lanes, which caused the drivers behind them to do so as well. At some point, drivers run out of lanes to move to and so the only option left is to slow down. This forces the drivers behind them to also slow down and after a suitable number of cars are involved, eventually the cars behind them have to come to a stop and this forces all the cars behind them to come to a stop as well. So, there was nothing in the highway (such as roadwork) or in the traffic (such as an accident) that could have led you to predict that there was going to be a traffic jam, but the emergent properties of the traffic (i.e., the individual choices of the drivers wanting to avoid hitting another car) caused the traffic jam. Note that the drivers did not coordinate their behavior or plan to have a traffic jam; it just emerged spontaneously from the traffic conditions and the individual behaviors.

The point of the butterfly effect and the emergent traffic jam is that a complex system cannot be predicted specifically. If the traffic is heavy and the highway has only two lanes, you can predict that the likelihood of traffic jams will be higher than if the highway is five lanes and traffic is light, but you cannot predict when the next traffic jam will be. Now, you may be wondering what butterflies and traffic jams have to do with second language learning and teaching. Much like in the traffic jam situation, we can predict that motivated, intelligent students, under the appropriate conditions, taught by a motivated, intelligent teacher, with appropriate materials will successfully learn a second language to some degree. We'd like to do better than that, for example, determine which combination of factors works best. The point of complexity theory is that a linear model does not work well and in order to do better than that you need a complex systems approach.

It is impossible to summarize all of complexity theory's insights in this context, so we will limit ourselves to listing a few salient themes then the discuss some potential applications to SLA.

- Non-linearity: There is no direct or proportional relationship between cause and effects (butterfly effect). You may despair that you will ever understand how to use the partitive in French, after weeks of practice, and then one day, suddenly, you are using it.
- Language is seen as a dynamic system, that is, as change. In particular, the opposition between synchronic and diachronic is abandoned: language is always in flux, changing. Today's system contains the seed of tomorrow's.
- Context is not seen as external, the speakers and their context are coupled in a never ending feedback cycle (see Section 8.3 and particularly the fact that context is a psychological construct: thus context and the speakers are both *mutually* changing each other).
- Language is seen as emergent and self-organizing. In other words, there need not be a goal shared by agents to result in collective coordinated behavior: think, for example, of birds in huge flocks: no individual bird knows where they are going, they just follow a simple heuristic to follow the birds next to them.

### 11.4.2 Applications to Linguistics

Larsen-Freeman and Cameron (2008, p. 240) argue that the complexity theory view of language acquisition is fully consonant with emergentist and ecological/sociocultural approaches. Indeed that is the case.

Emergentism denotes the idea that there is no underlying universal grammar, to use the Chomskian term, and that instead grammar self-organizes from a number of interdependent factors, which include most notably memory and sensitivity to frequency (Ellis, 2002), that is, if we encounter a pattern more than once we notice this fact and remember it. Obviously this is a very elegant model, since it has great simplicity. This sort of model has been implemented computationally using connectionist models, which have been applied to grammar problems (e.g., Ellis & Schmidt, 1997).

As we saw, complexity theory sees speakers/learners and the context as coupled, that is, as an inseparable dyad. Sociocultural approaches (Lantolf, 2000a) are based on Vygotsky (1978). It is too complex to elaborate on the details of these models, but an example, from Lantolf (2000b), will clarify the "coupling" between learner and the context in which the learning occurs. Lantolf discusses, from a study by Gillette (1994), the case of US college students who were interested in studying a foreign language and those who did not see the point of it. The latter deployed "learning strategies" "not directed at learning the language, but at coping with 'the imposition' of having to study a foreign language" (p. 12). Conversely, the students who were interested in other cultures used strategies directed at learning. Consider now a hypothetical researcher trying to figure out why the performance of a certain group of students is markedly better or worse, *without taking into account the context* of these students' classroom experience. In other words, the data would only make sense *within the dyad student-context.*

Van Lier (2004) defines an approach that relies on three perspectives: ecological, semiotic, and sociocultural. He provides a clear and succinct definition which we quote in full here.

- *Ecological,* in the sense that activity in a meaningful environment generates affordances for enhancing that activity and subsequent activities;
- *Semiotic,* in the sense that meanings rely not just on linguistic but also on all other meaning resources of physical, social and symbolic kinds; and
- *Sociocultural* in the sense that historical, cultural, and social artifacts and activities provide tools and resources to mediate learning and action (*van Lier, 2004, p. 80*).

Let us explicate that van Lier uses "semiotic" in a different, but not unrelated sense than Silverstein did within the discussion of enregisterment (see Section 10.2.3); whereas Silverstein is using a strict Peircean terminology, van Lier is using a broader related sense and namely that physical (embodied, in the Goodwin sense discussed earlier) action, social practices, and linguistic symbols all share a common mechanism to convey meaning, that is, the semiotic process, even though the actual specific ways in which all three types of signs signify are quite different (e.g., gestures can be symbolic, that is, arbitrary (the "thumbs up" sign), indexical (e.g., pointing with your finger or by thrusting the chin in the direction you mean), and iconic (e.g., smiling, or the wide-eyed eyebrows raised expression of surprise).

Finally, the theory of affordances was developed in the psychology of vision by Gibson, (1977, 1979); affordances are what the environment of an "animal" offers as possibilities to the animal itself. Affordances are not limited to the visual aspect of reality. For example,

> if a terrestrial surface is nearly horizontal (instead of slanted), nearly flat (instead of convex or concave), and sufficiently extended (relative to the size of the animal) and if its substance is rigid (relative to the weight of the animal), then the surface affords support.
>
> *(Gibson, 1979, p. 127)*

Another example is "handles" that afford grasping with a human hand (obviously, because they were built with that purpose in mind).

## 11.5 Cyberpragmatics

An interesting development which we have not addressed in any significant way is the development of a field of research dedicated to the pragmatics of online interactions (cyberpragmatics). There can be no question that since 1989, when Tim Berners-Lee invented the World-Wide-Web four decades ago, a whole new domain of communication has come about. If we add to this the introduction of the smart phone around 2000, which allows us to carry a device that is instantly connected to the internet, the penetration and impact of the internet have been nothing short of astonishing.[2] Needless to say, the new medium has spawned a set of new genres (Diltrow & Stein, 2009) and settings that are in part determined by the affordances of the media. Consider the tweet (a message on the Twitter platform) which was initially restricted to 140 characters. Clearly, much like the telegraph, where one paid by the word, had produced the telegraphic style, the limit of 140 characters forced "tweeters" to plan carefully so as not to exceed the limit. Interestingly, the average length of a tweet was 34 characters. When the limit was raised to a whopping 240 characters it dropped to 33![3] Clearly, length was not the issue. Moreover, Twitter allowed users to add a picture. Obviously the affordance of "limited length" conditioned the users to short messages and acronyms. The meme is even more enlightening, as it is a multimodal genre the purpose of which is to "go viral" (i.e., achieve maximum distribution) by being "replicated," that is, being shared by the users. In this sense, it is more akin to graffiti or to chain-letters than to a letter or postcard. On memetics, see Shifman (2014).

Initially, the focus of researchers was mostly on the linguistic changes that the new medium was producing (Baron, 2008; Crystal, 2001; Herring, 1996) and particularly on questions such as whether computer-mediated communication was closer to oral or written language. Among other topics to attract widespread interest were the acronyms (such as LOL (laughing out loud), ROTFL (rolling on the floor laughing), TTYL (talk to you later), etc.), the use of hashtags (which are technically metadata allowing algorithms to find messages related by topic, so that by writing #lizzo one can find all information related to Melissa Viviane Jefferson, provided it has been tagged as such), and the use of emojis and emoticons (little images that have semi-conventionalized meaning). On emojis, see Danesi (2017) and Evans (2017). Chapter 9 of Danesi's book is specifically on the pragmatics of emojis.

Gradually, however, the focus broadened to more "pragmatic concerns (Herring et al., 2013; Yus, 2011, 2019). For example, Yus (2019) notes that a very large part of the purpose of online communication of the type done on Facebook, Foursquare, or Pinterest is almost entirely phatic (see Section 6.1.1). Think of the "like" button on Facebook. Apart from a vague "positive" denotation, the purpose of the like is to communicate that one has seen the post and approves of it. Other uses are more akin to "conspicuous consumption" (Veblen, 1899), that is, they serve the purpose to represent a "curated" self which has precisely the purpose to display one's wealth (by showing that one can afford to travel to exotic locations, eat at expensive restaurants, etc.). Be that as it may, Yus (2019) highlights that the majority of the communication taking place is non-propositional, which has significant consequences for the status of the information being conveyed (for one, it is much harder to refute non-propositional information).

This brings about a darker side of cyberpragmatics, which is the issue of the veracity of the information that is circulated. There was always an issue on the internet that one could easily disguise one's identity (the famous New Yorker cartoon displaying a dog in front of a

---

2 However, we must not forget that there are significant differences in accessibility between the so-called developed world and the rest of the world. Furthermore, a significant percentage of all information on the web is in a few super-central (see above) languages. These issues are largely unaddressed.

3 https://techcrunch.com/2018/10/30/twitters-doubling-of-character-count-\-from-140-to-280-had-little-impact-on-length-of-tweets/

computer and the caption says "On the internet, nobody knows you're a dog." sums up the issue as clearly as 1000 words), but recent events have topicalized the possibility that a message or meme that one is reacting to was in fact produced by a bot (i.e., a software program designed to interact with users for example by answering their questions) or by someone hired to pretend to be a "normal user" while in fact spreading propaganda.

We could continue to list new topics that have appeared in the past four decades and that are in great need of analysis. For example, some videogames allow players to talk (either via text but actually in some cases using video and sound). As a new medium, it deserves to be investigated, if for no other reason than since sexual predators use these features to recruit victims, it would be useful to be able to monitor them. Another final example: platforms such as Facebook, Netflix, or Amazon use statistical information on users' preferences to "filter" what information gets served to the user. How does that affect the nature of discourse, when we are mostly presented with the opinions and comments of those we have a statistical affinity with? The phenomenon of the political echo-chamber has been the object of some discussion, for example, Mclennan (2018), but a pragmatic treatment awaits. Finally, an important area which has seen some work is the pragmatics of human–computer interaction (e.g., Krämer et al., 2012). Here as well, the field is wide open.

## 11.6 Neuropragmatics

Neuropragmatics is concerned with the processing of pragmatics by the brain. We can examine the brain of subjects affected by pathologies or physical injuries or neurotypical subjects (i.e., who have not suffered injuries of pathologies). We will start by examining the latter and will address pragmatic disorders below.[4]

The first studies in neurolinguistics at large were based on pathologies, particularly traumatic injuries to the head. Nonetheless, they led to the identification of Broca's and Wernicke's areas (Figure 11.2), when researchers found that injuries to those areas caused language loss. It wasn't until the introduction of electroecephalography (EEG) and functional magnetic resonance imaging (fMRI) and other non-invasive methods to assess brain activity, that pragmatic concerns became their own subdiscipline. Too many areas of cognition have been investigated to list here; an area that is particularly interesting is the difference between hot and cold cognition. Cold cognition is, for example, word and sentence meaning. Hot cognition includes prosody, gestures, and facial expressions. Hot cognition is processed faster than cold cognition (Ahlsén 2017). Pragmatics would fall under the hot cognition category, presumably.

Neuropragmatics has focused on several areas of direct pragmatic interest, but by all means not all: most neurolinguistic studies are limited to syntax, semantics, and phonology, and do not *not* address pragmatics. Nonetheless, there have been studies about the processing of figurative speech, such as metaphors. For example, McDonald (1992, 1999)

4 It should be noted that there is a branch of psycholinguistics called experimental pragmatics (e.g., Noveck, 2018) which has tested primarily Gricean and Relevance Theoretic claims, with interesting results. Of course, psycholinguistics has addressed pragmatic concerns before, see a synthesis in Giora (2003).

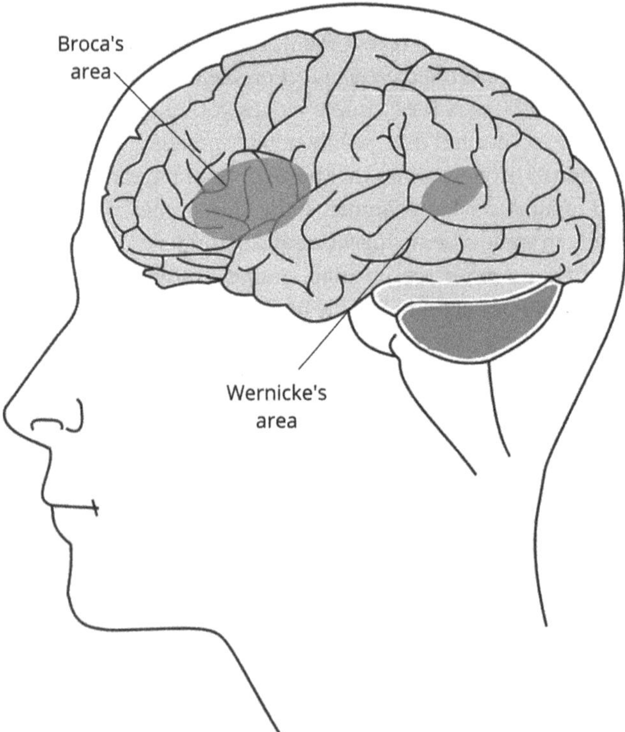


**Figure 11.2** Broca's and Wernicke's areas.

has examined the processing of indirect speech, in particular the violation of Grice's maxims, the capacity to draw inferences and access presuppositions, the capacity to access scripts and frames of knowledge, idiomatic expressions, and conversational turns management. More recent work (e.g., McDonald, 2017) has focused on emotions. Rapp et al. (2012) provide a meta-analysis of figurative meaning, mostly on metaphor, idioms, and irony. They conclude that "a predominantly left lateralised network, including the left and right inferior frontal gyrus; the left, middle, and superior temporal gyrus; and medial prefrontal, superior frontal, cerebellar, parahippocampal, precentral, and inferior parietal regions, is important for non-literal expressions" (p. 600). They find that contrary to expectations the right hemisphere is not predominant in the processing of figurative language, although there was some activation. Another more recent meta-analysis is Reyes-Aguilar et al. (2018). It also includes, beyond the topics discussed earlier, speech acts. Reyes-Aguilar et al. (2018) found a "bilateral fronto-temporal network that included the [medial prefrontal cortex]" (p. 64) which is associated with social cognition. The network consists of "Three significant clusters [...] centered in the left inferior frontal gyrus, pars opercularis (BA 44); anterior middle cingulate cortex (BA 32); and right inferior frontal gyrus, pars orbitalis (BA 47)" (p. 65).

### 11.6.1 Lateralization and Specialization

The right and left hemispheres of the brain have different functions. This is called lateralization. The idea is that one side of the brain specializes in some functions. We know, for example, that the right size of the brain controls the left side of the body and vice versa. An example of lateralization are Broca's and Wernicke's areas, which are found, generally speaking, on the left side of the brain (but see below). We should point out that there is variability in lateralization, at the individual level; moreover, neuroplasticity (i.e., the capacity of the brain to regenerate and retrain itself) shows that these functions are not necessarily fixed.

Interestingly, lateralization is connected to left- and right-handedness. Right-handed people have 90% lateralization in the left hemisphere for language, whereas left-handed people have 50% lateralization and bilateralization (i.e., on both sides). Broca's and Wernicke's areas are found in the left hemisphere for 95% of right-handed people and for 70% of left-handed people.

There has been significant debate on language-specific areas of the brain in bilinguals. For example, Lucas et al. (2004) found that in bilinguals "there are distinct cortical representations for multiple languages within the same brain" (p. 452), that is, bilinguals have different areas of the brain allocated to each language. About 60% of the subjects showed overlapping sites (i.e., the two languages shared some areas of the brain), but about 40% did not. Another interesting finding is that "the acquisition of a second language does not appreciably alter the organization of the first" (p. 454). Conversely, Sulpizio et al. (2020) find that L1 and L2 speakers use the same areas of the brain for both languages: "overall, first and second language are processed through the same neural structures" (p. 849). Executive control, that is, deciding which language to use "is accomplished by relying by a widespread and domain-general executive network involving structures such as the prefrontal cortices, the inferior parietal lobules, and the left caudate nucleus" (p. 849).

Perani and Abutalebi (2005) report that bilinguals who acquired both languages in early childhood activate the same brain areas for both L1 and L2, whereas Late bilinguals activate some different areas. Figure (11.3) shows the *differences* in activation, hence the blank image on the left (Early bilinguals: same activations). Contrast Late bilinguals with high proficiency (center image) and Late bilinguals with low proficiency (right image).

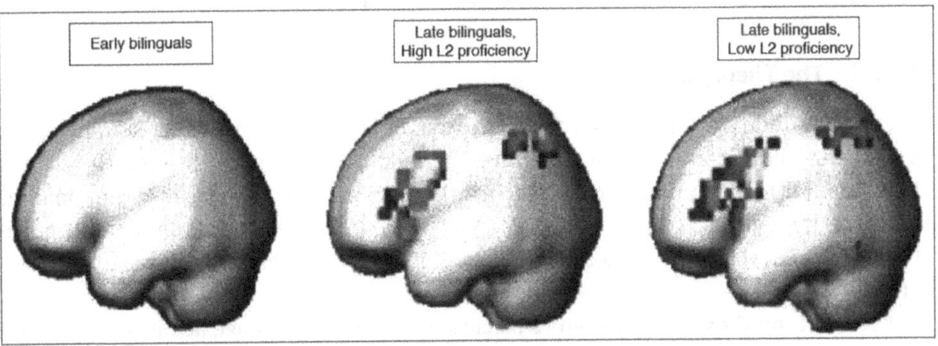


**Figure 11.3** Brain activity patterns in bilinguals (from Perani & Abutalebi, 2005, p. 203.)

### Linguistic Consequences of Damage to the Brain

Aphasia is the partial or total loss of the capacity of speech, writing, and/or reading due to an injury to the brain, such as trauma, a stroke, or a tumor. Injuries to the brain have been shown to affect the two hemispheres differently and in fact injury to specific areas of the brain results in different kinds of aphasia. For example, Broca's aphasia, which obviously affects Broca's area, is characterized by trouble with speech production but well-preserved understanding, unlike Wernicke's aphasia which displays fluent speech but trouble understanding (see Figure 11.2). Bibby and McDonald (2005) consider the effect of traumatic brain injury on theory of mind and finds that affected patients suffer from loss of theory of mind capacity. Cummings (2015) also addresses the interplay between theory of mind (see Section 11.6.2) and pragmatic disorders.

#### Left hemisphere

Damage to the left hemisphere generally results in aphasia, as seen earlier (Broca's and Wernicke's aphasias). Cummings (2005, p. 282) notes that specifically pragmatic impairment is present in left hemisphere damaged patients, and not just "structural" aphasia. Also, Cummings notes that patients who suffer from left hemisphere aphasia can often use pragmatic strategies to compensate in part of the language problems they experience. For example, they can rely on context to compensate for problems of understanding.

#### Right hemisphere

Right hemisphere damage was considered to be mostly cognitive, affecting attention, memory, problem-solving skills, and more generally reasoning. Most significantly, researchers believe that language was not really affected by right-hemisphere damage. However, according to Cummings (2005, p. 185), with the advent of relevance theory and its interest in inferencing, a new trend of research emerged that was concerned with how much right hemisphere damage affected the capacity to draw inferences. The studies reviewed in Cummings show that patients with right hemisphere damage relied on encyclopedic information to draw inferences and when this was missing they were unable to rely on the inferences provided by the text. Parola et al. (2016) describe the negative impact of right hemisphere damage on pragmatic processing.

## 11.6.2 The Theory of Mind

Simplifying quite a bit, we could say that the theory of mind is the representation that one speaker has of the state of mind of another speaker. Theory of mind is acquired relatively late in childhood, but children of two can already distinguish between intentional and unintentional actions; however, deception and irony, which require dissimulation and distinguishing between one's beliefs and the interlocutor's are not fully acquired until ages 12 and up.

Theory of mind has been shown to be closely related to language acquisition (Milligan et al., 2007). It is also related to the "mirror neurons" and thus it has been suggested that the mirror neurons may underlie the brain's capacity to model other minds. Mirror neurons are also related to the embodiment of cognition (Arvalo et al., 2015).

### 11.6.3 Pragmatic Disorders

The relationship between pragmatics and neuroscience "goes both ways": neuroscience can answer questions about pragmatics (e.g., the processing of indirect speech), but pragmatics can be used for diagnostic purposes in case of pathology. For example, speech acts are widely used in a clinical setting to assess patients for autism or Alzheimer's disease. Problems with theory of mind are significantly associated with schizophrenia (Sprong et al., 2007) and thus can be used as a diagnostic tool. However, in what follows we will focus on the contributions of neurolinguistics to pragmatics. Cummings (2014, 2017) provide overviews of the field. Our treatment of pragmatic disorders is largely based on her work.

#### The Autism Spectrum

Autism spectrum disorder[5] is a genetic[6] developmental disorder which includes socialization issues, such as indifference to others, indifference to play with other children, lack of theory of mind, and preference for nonverbal interaction. Other issues affect imagination, such a lack of making up stories or the fact that autistic children dislike changes in routine and will repeat the same activity over and over. Finally, communication is an issue as well: 50% of autistic children are non-verbal and those children who do acquire language do so with delays in the standard milestones. Children with autism also manifest abnormal linguistic/communicative behavior such as echolalia (repeating meaningless syllables) and the absence of gestures. Baron-Cohen (2000) shows how theory of mind is severely affected by autism. For example, autistic children find it difficult to understand irony and deception.

#### Specific Language Impairment

Specific Language Impairment (SLI) is a developmental disorder that affects 7–8% of children, which makes it one of the most common developmental disorders.

> Specific language impairment (SLI) is a communication disorder that interferes with the development of language skills in children who have no hearing loss or intellectual disabilities. SLI can affect a child's speaking, listening, reading, and

---

5 Asperger's syndrome and pervasive developmental disorder are part of the autism spectrum. They are now considered to be part of the same phenomenon. Our treatment of autism spectrum disorder relies on https://www.cdc.gov/ncbddd/autism/facts.html.

6 In a metanalysis of 40 studies, Gardener et al. (2011) find that, given that twin studies have established the genetic basis of the disorder, there is a small degree of variance which points to the fact that environmental factors may increase the possibility of manifestation. Among the factors listed are "abnormal presentation, umbilical-cord complications, fetal distress, birth injury or trauma, multiple birth, maternal hemorrhage, summer birth, low birth weight, small for gestational age, congenital malformation, low 5-minute Apgar score, feeding difficulties, meconium aspiration, neonatal anemia, ABO or Rh incompatibility, and hyperbilirubinemia" (p. 344), but there is not enough evidence to actually link any of them to the development of the disorder. (p. 344).

writing. SLI is also called developmental language disorder, language delay, or developmental dysphasia.[7]

The following are the symptoms of SLI in early childhood:

1. Delayed acquisition (reaches language milestones later than peers), particularly
2. Delay in grouping words together into sentences (syntax)
3. Struggle to learn new words and make conversation
4. Have difficulty following directions
5. Frequent grammatical errors when speaking

SLI persists in adulthood. Older children and adults with SLI show the following behaviors:

1. Limited use of complex sentences
2. Difficulty finding the right words
3. Difficulty understanding figurative language
4. Reading problems
5. Disorganized storytelling and writing
6. Often do not respond to comments or questions in conversation, or respond inappropriately
7. Frequent grammatical and spelling errors

From a linguistic standpoint, SLI has been the object of significant attention, because it seems to show a syntax-specific problem, and it is genetically transmitted (e.g., Gopnik & Crago, 1991) and thus can be argued to support a modular organization of cognition. For example, Creemers and Schaeffer (2016) argue that SLI and autism are distinct disorders and that the symptomatology of both point in the direction of a syntactic module affected in SLI and a pragmatic module affected in autism. In the opposite corner, we find scholars who argue that the problem is broadly pragmatic, from an interactionist stance (e.g., Craig, 1991).

## 11.7 Conclusion

The image that we think emerges from this final chapter is that pragmatics has reached maturity as a discipline. We now have a plethora of competing, more or less related areas of research that are only partially overlapping and share some tools and methodologies, but that are being reshaped by new tools, methodologies, and areas of interest that would have been impossible to predict in 1977 when the *Journal of Pragmatics* was started, or in 1985 when the International Pragmatics Association was founded. Pragmatics is changing; it is evolving and incorporating issues and tools that are increasingly specialized and that increasingly require expert training to use (corpora, eye-tracking, fMRI, meta-analyses,

7 The symptomatology and definition of Specific Language Impairment is taken, with slight modifications and additions, from https://www.nidcd.nih.gov/health/specific-language-impairment

etc.). In one direction it is becoming more “scientific” and in another it is becoming truly “humanistic” by embracing ideas of social justice (e.g., critical discourse analysis, analysis of ideology, or of the language of racism, etc.). We find this variety and ebullience of ideas exhilarating, but our task in this book was merely to show to the student and to the reader that pragmatics is a set of tools that can help achieve the goal of language learners. We can only hope to have succeeded in doing so and close with a felicitous speech act of thanking. We truly are grateful to our readers for staying with us all the way.

# Bibliography

Abdelhafez, A. M. (2016). The effect of conversational implicature instruction on developing TEFL students' pragmatic competence and language proficiency. *US-China Education Review*, *6*(8), 451–465.

Abu-Al-Makarem, A., & Petrosino, L. (2007). Reading and spontaneous speaking fundamental frequency of young Arabic men for Arabic and English languages: A comparative study. *Perceptual and Motor Skills*, *105*(2), 572–580.

Agha, A. (2005). Voice, footing, enregisterment. *Journal of Linguistic Anthropology*, *15*(1), 38–59.

Ahlsén, E. (2017). Pragmatics and neurolinguistics. In A. Barron, Y. Gu, & G. Steen (Eds.), *The Routledge handbook of pragmatics*. New York: Taylor & Francis.

Aikhenvald, A. (2006). *Evidentiality*. Oxford: Oxford University Press.

Alcón Soler, E., & Pitarch, J. R. G. (2013). The effect of instruction on learners' use and negotiation of refusals. In O. Martí-Arnándiz & P. Salazar-Campillo (Eds.), *Refusals in instructional contexts and beyond* (pp. 41–63). Brill Rodopi.

Alotaibi, H. 2013 Research article abstracts and introductions: A comparative genre-based study of Arabic and english in the fields of educational psychology and sociology. Unpublished PhD dissertation. Texas A&M-Commerce, Texas.

Andrews, E. (1990). *Markedness theory*. Durham, NC: Duke University Press.

Anscombre, J. C., & Ducrot, O. (1976). L'argumentation dans la langue. *Langages*, *10*(42), 5–27.

Anscombre, J. C., & Ducrot, O. (1983). *L'argumentation dans la langue*. Paris: Mardaga.

Armstrong, S. J. (2007). Grice's cooperative principle at work in an ESL classroom: A case for teaching implicature. *Journal of Inquiry and Research*, *86*, 77–95.

Arévalo, A., Baldo, J., González-Perilli, F., & Ibáñez, A. (2015). Editorial: What can we make of theories of embodiment and the role of the human mirror neuron system? *Frontiers in Human Neuroscience*, *9*, 500. doi:10.3389/fnhum.2015.00500

Ariel, M. (2008). *Pragmatics and grammar*. Cambridge: Cambridge University Press.

Aronin, L. (2015). Current multilingualism and new developments in multilingualism research. In Safont-Jordà, M. P. & Portolés-Falomir (Eds.), *Learning and using multiple languages: Current findings from research on multilingualism* (pp. 1–28). Newcastle upon Tyne: Cambridge Scholars Publishing.

*Pragmatics and Its Applications to TESOL and SLA*, First Edition. Salvatore Attardo and Lucy Pickering.

Aronin, L., Fishman, J. A., Singleton, D., & Ó Laoire, M. (2013). Current multilingualism: a new linguistic dispensation. In D. Singleton, J. A. Fishman, L. Aronin, & M. Ó Laoire (Eds.), *Current multilingualism: A new linguistic dispensation* (pp. 3–23). Berlin: de Gruyter.

Arnaus Gil, L. (2015). Chapter six acquisitional advantages of simultaneous trilingual children: The Spanish Copulas Ser and Estar. In Safont-Jordà, M.P., & Portolés-Falomir, (Eds.), *Learning and using multiple languages: Current findings from research on multilingualism* (pp. 134–154). Newcastle-upon-Tyne: Cambridge Scholars.

Attardo, S. (1994). *Linguistic theories of humor*. Berlin: Mouton de Gruyter.

Attardo, S. (2000). Irony as relevant inappropriateness. *Journal of pragmatics, 32*(6), 793–826.

Attardo, S. (2016). Context as relevance-driven abduction and charitable satisficing. *Frontiers in Psychology, 7*. http://dx.doi.org/10.3389/fpsyg.2016.00305

Bach, K. (1994). Conversational impliciture. *Mind & Language, 9*(2), 124–162.

Bagherkazemi, M. (2014). Short-term and long-term impact of video-driven meta-pragmatic awareness raising on speech act production: A case of Iranian intermediate EFL learners. *Journal of Language and Translation 4*, 25–36.

Bara, B. G. (2010). *Cognitive pragmatics: The mental processes of communication*. Cambridge, MA: MIT Press.

Bardovi-Harlig, K. (2013). Developing L2 pragmatics. *Language Learning, 63*, 68–86.

Bardovi-Harlig, K. (2015). One functional approach to SLA. In B. VanPatten & J. Williams (Eds.), *Theories in second language acquisition: An introduction* (pp. 54–74). New York: Routledge.

Bardovi-Harlig, K., & Mahan-Taylor, R. (2003). Introduction to teaching pragmatics. *English Teaching Forum, 41*(3), 37–39.

Barsony, O. (2003). "Actually, Steve, the deadline was Friday of last week, not this week." Polite ways of correcting or *contradicting* our conversation partner's assumptions. In: Bardovi-Harlig, K, Mahan-Taylor, R. (Eds.), *Teaching Pragmatics*. United States Department of State, Washington, DC.

Baron, N. S. (2008). *Always on: Language in an online and mobile world*. Oxford: Oxford University Press.

Baron-Cohen, S. (2000). Theory of mind and autism: A review. *International Review of Research in Mental Retardation, 23*, 169–184).

Bateson, G. (1955). A theory of play and fantasy: A report on theoretical aspects of the project of study of the role of the paradoxes of abstraction in communication. *Psychiatric Research Reports, 2*, 39–51.

Battistella, E. L. (1990). *Markedness: The evaluative superstructure of language*. Albany, NY: SUNY Press.

Battistella, E. L. (1996). *The logic of markedness*. Oxford: Oxford University Press.

Bauman, R., & Sherzer, J. (1975). The ethnography of speaking. *Annual Review of Anthropology, 4*(1), 95–119.

Bazzanella, C., (1985). L'uso dei connettivi nel parlato: Alcune proposte. In A. Franchi De Bellis & L. M. Savoia (Eds.), *Sintassi e morfologia della lingua italiana d'uso. Teorie e applicazioni descrittive* (pp. 83–94). Rome: Bulzoni.

Bazzanella, C., (1990). Phatic connectives as interactional cues in contemporary spoken Italian. *Journal of Pragmatics, 14*, 629–647.

Bazzanella, C., (2006). Discourse markers in Italian: Towards a 'compositional' meaning. In K. Fischer (Ed.), *Approaches to discourse particles*. Leiden: Brill.

Bazzanella, C., Bosco, C., Garcea, A., Fivela, B. G., Miecznikowski, J., & Brunozzi, F. T. (2007). Italian allora, French alors: Functions, convergences and divergences. *Catalan Journal of Linguistics, 6*(1), 9–30.

Beers-Fägersten, K., & Stapleton, K. (Eds.). (2017). *Advances in swearing research: New languages and new contexts.* Amsterdam: Benjamins.

Belcher, D., & Nelson, G. (Eds.). (2013). *Critical and corpus-based approaches to intercultural rhetoric.* Ann Arbor, MI: Michigan University Press.

Bell, N., & Attardo, S. (2010). Failed humor: Issues in non-native speakers' appreciation and understanding of humor. *Intercultural Pragmatics, 7*(3), 423–447.

Belz, J., & Kinginger, C. (2002). The cross-linguistic development of address form use in telecollaborative language learning: Two case studies. *Canadian Modern Language Review, 59*(2), 189–214.

Belz, J., & Vyatkina, N. (2008). The pedagogical mediation of a developmental learner corpus for classroom-based language instruction. *Language Learning and Technology, 12*(3), 33–52.

Bernstein, B. (1964). Elaborated and restricted codes: Their social origins and some consequences. *American Anthropologist, 66*(6), 55–69.

Biber, D. (2006). Stance in spoken and written university registers. *Journal of English for Academic Purposes, 5*(2), 97–116.

Biber, D., & Conrad, S. (1999). Lexical bundles in conversation and academic prose. In H. Hasselgard & S. Oksefjell (Eds.), *Out of corpora: Studies in honor of Stig Johansson* (pp. 181–189). Amsterdam: Rodopi.

Biber, D., Conrad, S., & Cortes, V. (2004). 'If you look at': Lexical bundles in university teaching and textbooks. *Applied Linguistics, 25*(3), 371–405.

Biber, D., & Finegan, E. (1989). Styles of stance in English: Lexical and grammatical marking of evidentiality and affect. *Text-Interdisciplinary Journal for the Study of Discourse, 9*(1), 93–124.

Biber, D., Johansson, S., Leech, G., Conrad, S., & Finegan, E. (1999). *Longman grammar of spoken and written English. London: Longman.*

Bibby, H., & McDonald, S. (2005). Theory of mind after traumatic brain injury. *Neuropsychologia, 43*(1), 99–114.

Blakemore, D. (2002). *Relevance and linguistic meaning: The semantics and pragmatics of discourse markers.* Cambridge: Cambridge University Press.

Blight, R. (2002). Classroom procedure for explicit instruction in conversational implicature. In *JALT Conference Proceedings*, (pp. 142–148).

Blom, J., & Gumperz, J. (1972). Social meaning in linguistic structure: Code-switching in Norway. In J. Gumperz & D. Hymes (Eds.), *Directions in sociolinguistics: The ethnography of communication* (pp. 407–434). New York: Holt, Rinehart and Winston.

Blommaert, J. (2015). Commentary: Superdiversity old and new. *Language & Communication, 44*, 82–88.

Blommaert, J., & Rampton, B. (2011). Language and superdiversity. *Diversities, 13*(2).

Blum-Kulka, S., House, J., & Kasper, G. (Eds.), (1989). *Cross-cultural pragmatics: Requests and apologies.* Norwood, NJ: Ablex Publishing.

Blum-Kulka, S., & Olshtain, E. (1984). Requests and apologies: A cross-cultural study of speech act realization patterns (CCSARP). *Applied Linguistics, 5*(3), 196–213.

Blum-Kulka, S., & Olshtain, E. (1986). Too many words: Length of utterance and pragmatic failure. *Studies in Second Language Acquisition, 8*(2), 165–179.

Bonnie, K. E., & de Waal, F. B. (2004). Primate social reciprocity and the origin of gratitude. In R. A. McCullough & M. E. Emmons (Eds.), *The psychology of gratitude* (pp. 213–229). Oxford: Oxford University Press.

Bourdieu, P. (1991). *Language and symbolic power*. Cambridge, MA: Harvard University Press.

Bousfield, D. (2007). Beginnings, middles, and ends: A biopsy of the dynamics of impolite exchanges. *Journal of Pragmatics, 39*, 2185–2216.

Bouton, L. F. (1988). A cross-cultural study of ability to interpret implicatures in English. *World Englishes, 7*(2), 183–196.

Bouton, L. F. (1994). Conversational implicature in a second language: Learned slowly when not deliberately taught. *Journal of Pragmatics, 22*(2), 157–167.

Boxer, D., & Pickering, L. (1995). Problems in the presentation of speech acts in ELT materials: The case of complaints. *ELT Journal, 49*(1), 44–58.

Breiteneder, A., Pitzl, M., Majewski, S., & Klimpfinger, T. (2006). VOICE recording: Methodological challenges in the compilation of a corpus of spoken ELF. *Nordic Journal of English Studies, 5*(2), 161–187.

Brezina, V., & Gablasova, D. (2015). Is there a core general vocabulary? Introducing the new general service list. *Applied Linguistics, 36*(1), 1–22.

Brinton, L. J. (2008). *The comment clause in English: Syntactic origins and pragmatic development*. Cambridge: Cambridge University Press.

Brown, J. D. (2001). Pragmatics tests. Different purposes, different tests. In K. Rose & G. Kasper (Eds.), *Pragmatics in language teaching* (pp. 301–325). Cambridge: Cambridge University Press.

Brown, J. D. (2008). Raters, functions, item types and the dependability of L2 pragmatics tests. In E. Alcón Soler, & A. Martínez-Flor (Eds.), *Investigating pragmatics in foreign language learning, teaching and testing* (pp. 224–248). Clevedon, UK: Multilingual Matters.

Brown, P. (2015). Politeness and language. *International Encyclopedia of the Social & Behavioral Sciences, 18*, 326–330.

Brown, P., & Levinson, S. C. (1987). *Politeness: Some universals in language usage* (Vol. 4). Cambridge University Press.

Brown, R., & Gilman, A. (1960). The pronouns of power and solidarity. In T. A. Sebeok (Ed.), *Style in language* (pp. 253–275). Cambridge, MA: MIT Press.

Browne, C. (2013). The new general service list: Celebrating 60 years of vocabulary learning. *The Language Teacher, 37*(4), 13–16.

Bühler, K. (1934). *Sprachtheorie*. Fischer: Jena.

Burkhardt, A. (Ed.). (1990). *Speech acts, meaning and intentions: Critical approaches to the philosophy of John Searle*. Berlin: Mouton de Gruyter,

Burns, A. (2009). *Doing action research in English language teaching: A guide for practitioners*. Routledge.

Burns, A. (2011). Action research in the field of second language teaching and learning. *Handbook of Research in Second Language Teaching and Learning, 2*, 237–253.

Burton, G. (2012). Corpora and coursebooks: Destined to be strangers forever? *Corpora, 7*(1), 91–108.

Busch, B. (2012). The linguistic repertoire revisited. *Applied Linguistics, 33*(5), 503–523.

Busch, B. (2017). Expanding the notion of the linguistic repertoire: On the concept of Spracherleben-The lived experience of language. *Applied Linguistics, 38*(3), 340–358.

Butler, C. S. (2003). *Structure and function-A guide to three major structural-functional theories.* Amsterdam: Benjamins.

Butler, C. S., & Gonzálvez-García, F. (2014). *Exploring functional-cognitive space.* Amsterdam/ Philadelphia: Benjamins.

Bybee, J. (1999). Usage-based phonology. In M. Darnell, E. A. Moravcsik, M. Noonan, F. J. Newmeyer, & K. Wheatley (Eds.), *Functionalism and formalism in linguistics* (pp. 211–242). Amsterdam: Benjamins.

Byrd, P., & Coxhead, A. (2010). On the other hand: Lexical bundles in academic writing and in the teaching of EAP. *University of Sydney Papers in TESOL, 5*, 31–64. Available at: http:// faculty.edfac.usyd.edu.au/projects/usp_in_tesol/pdf/volume05/Article02.pdf

Caffi, C. (1998). Metapragmatics. In J. Mey (Ed.), *Concise encyclopedia of pragmatics* (pp. 581–586). Amsterdam: Elsevier.

Canagarajah, S. (2011). Codemeshing in academic writing: Identifying teachable strategies of translanguaging. *The Modern Language Journal, 95*(3), 401–417.

Canagarajah, S. (2015). Clarifying the relationship between translingual practice and L2 writing: Addressing learner identities. *Applied Linguistics Review, 6*, 415–440.

Carroll, M., & Lambert, M. (2006). Reorganizing principles of information structure in advanced L2s. In H. Byrnes, H. D. Weger, & K. A. Sprang (Eds.), *Educating for advanced foreign language capacities: Constructs, curriculum, instruction, assessment* (pp. 54–73). Washington, DC: Georgetown University Press.

Carston, R. (1997). Relevance-theoretic pragmatics and modularity. *UCL Working Papers in Linguistics, 9*, 29–53.

Celce-Murcia, M., Dörnyei, Z., & Thurrell, S. (1995). Communicative competence: A pedagogically motivated model with content specifications. *Issues in Applied Linguistics, 6*(2), 5–35.

Chafe, W. L. (1970). *Meaning and the structure of language.* Chicago: University of Chicago Press.

Chafe, W. L. (1974). Language and consciousness. *Language, 50*(1), 111–133.

Chafe, W. L. (1976). Givenness, contrastiveness, definiteness, subjects, topics, and point of view. In C. Li (Ed.), *Subject and Topic*, (pp. 25–55). New York: Academic Press.

Chafe, W. L. (1994). *Discourse, consciousness, and time: The flow and displacement of conscious experience in speaking and writing.* Chicago: University of Chicago Press.

Chafe, W. L. (2002). Searching for meaning in language: A memoir. *Historiographia Linguistica, 29*(1), 245–261.

Chapman, S. (2005). *Paul Grice, philosopher and linguist.* New York: Palgrave Macmillan.

Chen, R. (1993). Responding to compliments: a contrastive study of politeness strategies between American English and Chinese speakers. *Journal of Pragmatics, 20*(1), 49–75.

Chen, R. (2010). Compliment and compliment response research: A cross-cultural survey. In A. Trosborg (Ed.), *Pragmatics across languages and cultures* (pp. 79–101). Berlin: Walter de Gruyter.

Cheng, D. (2011). New insights on compliment responses: A comparison between native English speakers and Chinese L2 speakers. *Journal of Pragmatics, 43*(8), 2204–2214.

Cheng, D. (2017). Students' self-perceptions of apologies to instructors. *Language Awareness, 26*(4), 261–281.

Cheng, W., & Warren, M. (2007). Checking understandings: Comparing textbooks and a corpus of spoken English in Hong Kong. *Language Awareness, 16*(3), 190–207.

Chomsky, N. (1971). Deep structure, surface structure, and semantic interpretation. In D. Steinberg & L. Jakobovits (Eds.), *Semantics: An interdisciplinary reader in philosophy, linguistics, and philosophy* (pp. 183–216). Cambridge: Cambridge University Press.

Celce-Murcia, M., Dörnyei, Z., & Thurrell, S. (1995). Communicative competence: A pedagogically motivated model with content specifications. *Issues in Applied linguistics, 6*(2), 5–35.

Cignetti, L. M., & Di Giuseppe, M. S. (2015). Pragmatic awareness of conversational implicatures and the usefulness of explicit instruction. *Revista Nebrija de Lingüística Aplicada a la Enseñanza de Lenguas, 19*, 42–70.

Clark, B. (2013). *Relevance theory*. Cambridge: Cambridge University Press.

Clark, H. H., & Haviland, S. E. (1974). Psychological processes as linguistic explanation. In D. Cohen (Ed.), *Explaining linguistic phenomena* (pp. 91–124). Washington, DC: Hemisphere Publishing.

Clark, H. H., & Haviland, S. (1977). Comprehension and the given-new contract. In R. O. Freedle (Ed.), *Discourse production and comprehension* (pp. 1–40). Norwood, NJ: Ablex.

Clark, H. H. (1996). *Using language*. Cambridge: Cambridge University Press.

Cook, V. (2013). *Second language learning and language teaching*. New York, NY: Routledge.

Cohen, A. D. (1997). Developing pragmatic ability: Insights from the accelerated study of Japanese. In H. M. Cook, K. Hijirida, & M. Tahara (Eds.), *New trends and issues in teaching Japanese language and culture*. (pp. 137-163). Honolulu: University of Hawai'i, Second Language Teaching and Curriculum Center.

Cook, M., & Liddicoat, A. J. (2002). The development of comprehension in interlanguage pragmatics. *Australian Review of Applied Linguistics, 25*(1), 19–39.

Connor, U. (1996). *Contrastive rhetoric: Cross-cultural aspects of second language writing*. Cambridge: Cambridge University Press.

Connor, U. (2004). Intercultural rhetoric research: Beyond texts. *Journal of English for Academic Purposes, 3*(4), 291–304.

Connor, U. (2011). *Intercultural rhetoric in the writing classroom*. Ann Arbor: University of Michigan Press.

Connor, U., & Farmer, M. (1990). Teaching topical structure analysis as a revision strategy. In B. Kroll (Ed.), *Second language writing: Research insights for the classroom* (pp. 129–135). New York: Cambridge University Press.

Conrad, S., & Biber, D. (2004). The frequency and use of lexical bundles in conversation and academic prose. *Lexicographica, 20*, 56–71.

Cortes, V. (2004). Lexical bundles in published and student disciplinary writing: Examples from history and biology. *English for Specific Purposes, 23*, 397–423.

Cortes, V. (2013). The purpose of this study is to: Connecting lexical bundles and moves in research article introductions. *Journal of English for Academic Purposes, 12*(1), 33–43.

Coupland, N. (2016). Introduction: Sociolinguistic theory and the practice of sociolinguistics. In N. Coupland (Ed.), *Sociolinguistics: Theoretical debates* (pp. 1–34). Cambridge: Cambridge University Press.

Coxhead, A., & Byrd, P. (2007). Preparing writing teachers to teach the vocabulary and grammar of academic prose. *Journal of Second Language Writing, 16*(3), 129–147.

Craig, H. K. (1991). Pragmatic characteristics of the child with specific language impairment: An interactionist perspective. In T. M. Gallagher (Ed.), *Pragmatics of language* (pp. 163–198). Boston, MA: Springer.

Creemers, A., & Schaeffer, J. C. (2016). Specific language impairment and high functioning autism: Evidence for distinct etiologies and for modularity of grammar and pragmatics. In *Proceedings of the 6th Conference on Generative Approaches to Language Acquisition North America (GALANA 2015)* (pp. 1–12). Somerville, MA: Cascadilla Proceedings Project.

Crystal, D. (1975). *The English tone of voice: Essays in intonation, prosody and paralanguage.* London: Edward Arnold.

Crystal, D. (2001). *Language and the internet.* Cambridge University Press.

Cuenca, M. J. (2003). Two ways to reformulate: A contrastive analysis of reformulation markers. *Journal of Pragmatics, 35*(7), 1069–1093.

Cuenca, M. J., & Bach, C. (2007). Contrasting the form and use of reformulation markers. *Discourse Studies, 9*(2), 149–175.

Culpeper, J. (1996). Towards an anatomy of impoliteness. *Journal of Pragmatics, 25*: 349–67.

Culpeper, J. (2010). Conventionalized impoliteness formulae, *Journal of Pragmatics, 42,* 3232–3245.

Culpeper, J. (2011). *Impoliteness: Using language to cause offence.* Cambridge: Cambridge University Press.

Culpeper, J. (2015). Impoliteness. In K. Tracy (Ed.), *The international encyclopedia of language and social interaction.* Hoboken, NJ: Wiley. Retrieved from https://search.credoreference.com/content/entry/wileylasi/impoliteness/0

Cummings, L. (2005). *Pragmatics: A multidisciplinary perspective.* Edinburgh: Edinburgh University Press.

Cummings, L. (2014). *Pragmatics disorders.* Dordrecht: Springer.

Cummings, L. (2015). Theory of mind in utterance interpretation: The case from clinical pragmatics. *Frontiers in Psychology, 6,* 1286.

Cummings, L. (Ed.) (2017), *Research in clinical pragmatics.* New York: Springer.

Cunningham, D. J., & Vyatkina, N. (2012). Telecollaboration for professional purposes: Towards developing a formal register in the foreign language classroom. *Canadian Modern Language Review, 68*(4), 422–450.

Dahl, O. (1974). Topic-comment structure revisited. In O. Dahl (Ed.), *Topic and comment, contextual boundedness and focus* (pp. 1–24). Hamburg: Buske.

Danesi, M. (2004). *Messages, signs, and meanings: A basic textbook in semiotics and communication.* Canadian Scholars' Press.

Danesi, M. (2016). *The semiotics of emoji: The rise of visual language in the age of the internet.* London: Bloomsbury Publishing.

Daneš, F. (2003). The double basis of the Prague functional approach: Mathesius and Jakobson. In J. Hladký (Ed.), *Language and function: to the memory of Jan Firbas* (pp. 57–69). Amsterdam: Benjamins.

Dang, T. N. Y. (2019). Corpus-based wordlists in second language vocabulary research, learning, and teaching. In S. Webb (Ed.), *The Routledge handbook of vocabulary studies* (pp. 288–303). New York: Routledge.

Davies, C. E. (2018). Culture, gender, ethnicity, identity in discourse: Exploring cross-cultural communicative competence in American university contexts. In L. Pickering & V. Evans (Eds.), *Language learning, discourse and cognition* (pp. 11–36). Amsterdam: Benjamins.

Davies, C. E., & Tyler, A. (1994). Demystifying cross-cultural (mis)communication: Improving performance through balanced feedback in a situated context. In C. Madden & C. Myers (Eds.), *Discourse and performance of international teaching assistants* (pp. 201–220). Alexandria, VA: TESOL.

DeKeyser, R. (2007). Skill acquisition theory. In B. VanPatten & J. Williams (Eds.), *Theories in second language acquisition: An introduction* (pp. 94–113). Erlbaum.

Dewaele, J. M. (2004). The emotional force of swearwords and taboo words in the speech of multilinguals. *Journal of Multilingual and Multicultural Development, 25*(2–3), 204–222.

Dewaele, J. (2010). *Emotions in multiple languages.* Basingstoke: Palgrave Macmillan.

Dik, S. C. (1978). *Functional grammar.* Amsterdam: North-Holland.

Dik S. C. (1989). *The theory of functional grammar.* Berlin: Mouton de Gruyter.

Dik, S. C. (1991). Functional grammar. In F. G. Droste & J. E. Joseph (Eds.), *Linguistic theory and grammatical description: Nine current approaches* (pp. 247–274). Amsterdam: Benjamins.

Dik, S. C. (1997). *The theory of functional grammar* (K. Hengeveld, Ed.), Berlin: Mouton.

Donaldson, B. (2011). Nativelike right-dislocation in near-native french. *Second Language Research, 27*(3), 361–390. doi:10.1177/0267658310395866

Du Bois, J. W. (2007). The stance triangle. In R. Englebretson (Ed.), *Stancetaking in discourse: Subjectivity, evaluation, interaction* (pp. 139–182). Amsterdam: Benjamins.

Du Bois, J. W., & Kärkkäinen, E. (2012). Taking a stance on emotion: Affect, sequence, and intersubjectivity in dialogic interaction. *Text & Talk, 32*(4),433–451.

Duranti, A. (1997). Universal and culture-specific properties of greetings. *Journal of Linguistic Anthropology, 7*(1), 63–97.

Duranti, A. (2012). Anthropology and linguistics. In R. Fardon, O. Harris, T. H. Marchand, C. Shore, V. Strang, R. Wilson, & M. Nuttall (Eds.), *The SAGE handbook of social anthropology* (pp. 12–26). Los Angeles: Sage.

Duranti, A., & Goodwin, C. (1992). *Rethinking context language as an interactive phenomenon.* Cambridge: Cambridge University Press.

Eagleton, T. (1991). *Ideology.* New York: Routledge.

Eckman, F. R. (2018). Markedness and advanced development. In P. A. Malovrh & A. G. Benati (Eds.), *The Handbook of advanced proficiency in second language acquisition* (pp. 264–281). Hoboken, NJ: Wiley.

Eco, U. (1976). *A theory of semiotics.* Bloomington, IN: Indiana University Press.

Economidou-Kogetsidis, M. (2011). “Please answer me as soon as possible”: Pragmatic failure in non-native speakers'e-mail requests to faculty. *Journal of Pragmatics, 43*(13), 3193–3215.

Eelen, G. (2001/2014). *A critique of politeness theory.* New York: Routledge. [Original pub. 2001, St. Gerome Press].

Ellis, N. C. (2002). Frequency effects in language processing: A review with implications for theories of implicit and explicit language acquisition. *Studies in Second Language Acquisition, 24*(2), 143–188.

Ellis, N. C., & Schmidt, R. (1997). Morphology and longer distance dependencies: Laboratory research illuminating the A in SLA. *Studies in Second Language Acquisition, 19*(2), 145–171.

Ene, E., McIntosh, K., & Connor, U. (2019). Using intercultural rhetoric to examine translingual practices of postgraduate L2 writers of English. *Journal of Second Language Writing, 45*, 100664.

Eslami, Z., & Liu, C. N. (2013). Learning pragmatics through computer-mediated communication in Taiwan. *International Journal of Society, Culture & Language, 1*(1), 52–73.

Eslami, Z. R., Mirzaei, A., & Dini, S. (2015). The role of asynchronous computer mediated communication in the instruction and development of EFL learners' pragmatic competence. *System, 48*, 99–111.

Eslami-Rasekh, Z. (2005). Raising the pragmatic awareness of language learners. *ELT Journal, 59*(3), 199–208.

Eslami-Rasekh, Z., Eslami-Rasekh, A., & Fatahi, A. (2004). The effect of explicit metapragmatic instruction on the speech act awareness of advanced EFL students. *TESL-EJ, 8*(2), n2.

Evans, V. (2017). *The emoji code: The linguistics behind smiley faces and scaredy cats.* New York: Picador USA.

Ezard, J. (2001). Needless battle caused by uncommon language. The Guardian. https://www.theguardian.com/uk/2001/apr/14/johnezard

Fillmore, C. J. (1968). The case for case. In E. Bach & R. T. Harms (Eds.), *Universals in linguistic theory* (pp. 1–90). New York: Holt, Rinehart & Winston.

Fillmore, C. J. (1971/1997). *Lectures on deixis.* Stanford, CA: CSLI Publications.

Fine, G. A., & Manning, P. (2003). Erving Goffman. In G. Ritzer (Ed.), *The Blackwell companion to major contemporary social theorists* (pp. 34–62). Malden, MA: Blackwell.

Firbas, J. (1987). On some basic issues of the theory of functional sentence perspective. II, On Wallace L. Chafe's views on new and old information and communicative dynamism. *Brno Studies in English, 17*(1), 51–59.

Firbas, J. (1992). *Functional sentence perspective in written and spoken communication.* Cambridge: Cambridge University Press.

Firbas, J. (1995). Retrievability span in functional sentence perspective. *Brno Studies in English, 21*(1), 17–45.

Firth, A. (1996). The discursive accomplishment of normality: On 'lingua franca' English and conversation analysis. *Journal of Pragmatics, 26*, 237–259

Fischer, K. (Ed.). (2006). *Approaches to discourse particles*, Berlin: Brill.

Fishman, J. A. (1998). The new linguistic order. *Foreign Policy, 113*, 26–40.

Flowerdew, J., & Tauroza, S. (1995). The effect of discourse markers on Second Language Lecture Comprehension. *Studies in second language acquisition, 17*(4), 435–458.

Fodor, J. A. (1985). Precis of the modularity of mind. *Behavioral and Brain Sciences, 8*(1), 1–5.

Foolen, A. (2011). Pragmatic markers in a sociopragmatic perspective. In G. Andersen, & K. Aijmer (Eds.), *Pragmatics of society* (pp. 217–282). Berlin: Mouton de Gruyter.

Fordyce, K. (2013). The differential effects of explicit and implicit instruction on EFL learners' use of epistemic stance. *Applied Linguistics, 35*(1), 6–28.

Frankenhuis, W. E., & Ploeger, A. (2007). Evolutionary psychology versus Fodor: arguments for and against the massive modularity hypothesis. *Philosophical Psychology, 20*(6), 687–710, doi: 10.1080/09515080701665904

Fraser, B. (1990). Perspectives on politeness. *Journal of Pragmatics, 14*(2), 219–236.

Fraser, B. (1998). Contrastive discourse markers in English. In A. H. Jucker & Y. Ziv (Eds.), *Discourse markers: Descriptions and theory* (pp. 301–326). Amsterdam: Benjamins.

Fraser, B. (2006). Towards a theory of discourse markers. Approaches to discourse particles, In K. Fischer (Ed.), *Approaches to discourse particles* (pp. 189–204). Amsterdam: Elsevier.

Fraser, B. (2009). An account of discourse markers. *International Review of Pragmatics, 1*(2), 293–320.

Friedrich, P. (1972). Social context and semantic feature: The Russian pronominal usage. In J. J. Gumperz & D. Hymes (Eds.), *Directions in sociolinguistics: The ethnography of communication* (pp. 270–300). New York: Holt, Rinehart and Winston.

Fukushima, S., & Sifianou, M. (2017). Conceptualizing politeness in Japanese and Greek. *Intercultural Pragmatics*, *14*(4), 525–555.

Fuller, J. M. (2003). Discourse marker use across speech contexts: A comparison of native and non-native speaker performance. *Multilingua*, *22*, 185–208.

Fung, L., & Carter, R. (2007). Discourse markers and spoken English: Native and learner use in pedagogic settings. *Applied Linguistics*, *28*(3), 410–439.

Gablasova, D., Brezina, V., McEnery, T., & Boyd, E. (2017). Epistemic stance in spoken L2 English: The effect of task and speaker style. *Applied Linguistics*, *38*(5), 613–637.

Gal, S., & Irvine, J. T. (1995). The boundaries of languages and disciplines: How ideologies construct difference. *Social Research*, *62*(4), 967–1001.

Gallese, V., & Goldman, A (1998). Mirror neurons and the simulation theory of mind-reading. *Trends in Cognitive Sciences*, *2*(12), 493–501.

Garcia, P. (2004). Pragmatic comprehension of high and low level language learners. *TESL-EJ*, *8*(2), n2.

Gardener, H., Spiegelman, D., & Buka, S. L. (2011). Perinatal and neonatal risk factors for autism: A comprehensive meta-analysis. *Pediatrics*, *128*(2), 344–355.

Garfinkel, H. (1964). Studies of the routine grounds of everyday activities. *Social Problems*, *11*(3), 225–250.

Garfinkel, H. (1967). *Studies in ethnomethodology*. Englewood Cliffs, NY: Prentice-Hall.

Gass. S. (1979). Language transfer and universal grammatical relations. *Language Learning 29*, 327–344.

Gass, S., & Mackey, A. (2000). *Stimulated recall methodology in second language research*. Mahwah, NJ: Earlbaum.

Gharibeh, S., Mirzaee, M., & Yaghoubi-Notash, M. (2016). The role of instruction in the development of EFL learners' pragmatic competence. *The Asian Journal of Applied Linguistics*, *3*(2), 173–184.

Ghavamnia, M., Eslami-Raseck, A., & Dastjerdi, H. V. (2014). Exploring the effects of input based instruction on the development of EFL learners' pragmatic proficiency. *International Journal of Research Studies in Language Learning*, *3*(7), 43–56.

Gibbs, R. W. J. (1994). *The poetics of mind*. Cambridge/New York: Cambridge University Press.

Gibson, J. J. (1977). The theory of affordances. In R. Shaw & J. Bransford (Eds.), *Perceiving, acting, and knowing*. Hillsdale, NJ: Lawrence Erlbaum Associates.

Gibson, J. J. (1979). *The ecological approach to visual perception*. Boston: Houghton Mifflin.

Gillette, B. (1994). The role of learner goals in L2 success. In J. P. Lantolf & G. Appel (Eds.), *Vygotskian approaches to second language research* (pp. 195–213). Westport, CT: Ablex.

Giltrow, J., & Stein, D. (Eds.). (2009). *Genres in the internet: Issues in the theory of Genre*. Amsterdam: Benjamins.

Giora, R. (2003). *On our mind: Salience, context, and figurative language*. Oxford: Oxford University Press.

Givón, T. (1990). *Syntax: A functional-typological introduction* (Vol. II). Amsterdam: Benjamins.

Gobl, C., & N Chasaide, A. (2003). The role of voice quality in communicating emotion, mood and attitude. *Speech Communication*, *40*(1–2), 189–212.

Godfrey, J., Holliman, E., & Mcdaniel, J. (1992). SWITCHBOARD: Telephone speech corpus for research and development. *In Proceedings of ICASSP-92* (pp. 517–520). San Francisco.

Goffman, E. (1955). On face-work: An analysis of ritual elements in social interaction. *Psychiatry, 18*(3), 213–231.

Goffman, E. (1967). *Interaction ritual.* Garden City, NY: Doubleday.

Goffman, E. (1974). *Frame analysis: An essay on the organization of experience.* Cambridge, MA: Harvard University Press.

Golato, A. (2003). Studying compliment responses: A comparison of DCTs and recordings of naturally occurring talk. *Applied Linguistics, 24*(1), 90–121.

Goldberg, A. E. (2006). *Constructions at work: The nature of generalization in language.* Oxford: Oxford University Press.

González-Lloret, M. (2008). Computer-mediated learning of L2 pragmatics. In Alcón Soler, E. & Flor, A (Eds.), *Investigating pragmatics in foreign language learning, teaching and testing* (pp. 114–132). Bristol: Multilingual Matters.

Goodwin, C. (2007). Participation, stance and affect in the organization of activities. *Discourse & Society, 18*(1), 53–73.

Goodwin, C., & Goodwin, M. H. (2004). Participation. In A. Duranti (Ed.), *A companion to linguistic anthropology* (pp. 222–244). Malden, MA: Blackwell.

Goossens, L. (1982). Say: Focus on the message. In R. Dirven, L. Goossens, Y. Putseys, & E. Vorlat (Eds.), *The scene of linguistic action and its perspectivization by speak, talk, say and tell* (pp. 85–131). Amsterdam: Benjamins.

Gopnik, M., & Crago, M. B. (1991). Familial aggregation of a developmental language disorder. *Cognition, 39*(1), 1–50.

Gorsuch, G., Meyers, C., Pickering, L., & Griffee, D. (2013). *English communication for international teaching assistants* (2nd ed.). Long Grove, IL: Waveland Press.

Gray, B., & Biber, D. (2012). Current conceptions of stance. In K. Hyland & C. S. Guinda (Eds.), *Stance and voice in written academic genres* (pp. 15–33). London: Palgrave Macmillan.

Grainger, K. (2013). Of babies and bath water: Is there any place for Austin and Grice in interpersonal pragmatics? *Journal of Pragmatics, 58*, 27–38.

Gray, B., & Biber, D. (2015). Stance markers. In K. Aijmer & C. Rühlemann (Eds.), *Corpus pragmatics: A handbook* (pp. 219–248). Cambridge: Cambridge University Press.

Green, D. W. (2017). Trajectories to third-language proficiency. *International Journal of Bilingualism, 21*(6), 718–733. https://doi.org/10.1177/1367006916637739

Green, M. (2017). Speech Acts. In E. N. Zalta (Ed.), The Stanford Encyclopedia of philosophy. https://plato.stanford.edu/archives/win2017/entries/speech-acts

Greenberg, J. H. (1956/2010). *Language universals.* Berlin: De Gruyter.

Greenberg, J. H. (1963). Some universals of grammar with particular reference to the order of meaningful elements. In Greenberg, J. H. (Ed.), *Universals of language* (pp. 73–113). MIT Press.

Grewendorf, G., & Meggle, G. (Eds.). (2002). *Speech acts, mind and social reality.* Dordrecht: Kluwer.

Grice, H. P. (1957). Meaning. *The Philosophical Review, 66*(3), 377–388.

Grice, H. P. (1975). Logic and conversation. In P. Cole & J. Morgan (Eds.), *Speech Acts* (pp. 41–59). New York: Academic.

Grice, H. P. (1989). *Studies in the way of words.* Harvard University Press.

Grosjean, F. (2015). Bicultural bilinguals. *International Journal of Bilingualism, 19*(5), 572–586.

Gu, X. (2011). The effect of explicit and implicit instructions of request strategies. *Intercultural Communication Studies, 20*(1), 104–123.

Gu, Y. (1990). Politeness phenomena in modern Chinese. *Journal of Pragmatics, 14*(2), 237–257.

Gudykunst, W. B. (2003). *Cross-cultural and intercultural communication*. Thousand Oaks: Sage.

Gumperz, J. J. (1964). Linguistic and social interaction in two communities. *American Anthropologist, 66*(6), 137–153.

Gumperz, J. J. (1972). Introduction. In J. J. Gumperz & D. Hymes (Eds.), *Directions in sociolinguistics: The ethnography of communication* (pp. 1–25). New York: Holt.

Gumperz, J. J. (1977a). Socio-cultural knowledge in conversational inference. In M. Saville-Troyke (Ed.), *Linguistics and anthropology* (pp. 191–211). Washington, DC: Georgetown University Press.

Gumperz, J. J. (1978). Dialect and conversational inference in urban communication. *Language in Society, 7*(3), 393–409.

Gumperz, J. J. (1982). *Discourse strategies*. Cambridge: Cambridge University Press.

Gumperz, J. J. (1996). The linguistic and cultural relativity of conversational inference. In J. J. Gumperz & S. C. Levinson (Eds.), *Rethinking linguistic relativity* (pp. 374–406). Cambridge: Cambridge University Press.

Gumperz, J. J. (1999). Inference. *Journal of Linguistic Anthropology, 9*(1–2), 131–133.

Gumperz, J. J. (2015). Interactional sociolinguistics: A personal perspective. In D. Tannen, H. E. Hamilton, & D. Schiffrin (Eds.), *The handbook of discourse analysis* (Vol. *1*, pp. 309–323). Malden, MA: Wiley Blackwell.

Gumperz, J. J., & Kaltman, H. (1980). Prosody, linguistic diffusion and conversational inference. In *Annual Meeting of the Berkeley Linguistics Society* (Vol. *6*, pp. 44–65).

Gumperz, J. J., & Tannen, D. (1979). Individual and social differences in language use. In C. J. Fillmore, D. Kempler, & W. S-Y. Wang (Eds.), *Individual differences in language ability and language behavior* (pp. 305–325). New York: Academic Press.

Gundel, J. K. (1975). Left dislocation and the role of topic-comment structure in linguistic theory. *Ohio State University Working Papers in Linguistics, 18*, 72–131.

Gundel, J. K. (1985). 'Shared knowledge' and topicality. *Journal of Pragmatics, 9*(1), 83–107.

Gundel, J. K. (1988). Universals of topic-comment structure. In M. Hammond, E. A. Moravcsik, & J. R. Wirth (Eds.), *Studies in syntactic typology* (pp. 209–239). Amsterdam: Benjamins.

Gundel, J. K., & Fretheim, T. (2004). Topic and comment. In L. R. Horn & G. Ward (Eds.), *The handbook of pragmatics* (pp. 174–196). New York: Blackwell Publishing.

Gundel, J., Hedberg, N., & Zacharski, R. (1997, August). Topic-comment structure, syntactic structure and prosodic tune. In *Workshop on Prosody and grammar in interaction* (pp. 13–15), Helsinki, Finland.

Hall, J. K. (2018). *Essentials of SLA for L2 teachers: A transdisciplinary framework*. New York: Routledge.

Halliday, M. A. K. (1967). Notes on transitivity and theme in English: Part 2. *Journal of Linguistics, 3*(2), 199–244.

Halliday, M. A. K. (1985). *Introduction to functional grammar*. London: Routledge.

Halliday, M. A. K., & Matthiessen, C. M. I. M. (2014). *Halliday's Introduction to Functional Grammar* (4th ed.). London: Routledge.

Halliday, M. A. K., & Hasan, R. (1976). *Cohesion in English*. Longman: London.

Hamilton, K. C. (2009). *Y'all think we're stupid: Deconstructing media stereotypes of The American South*. Unpublished PhD dissertation. Georgia Southern University.

Harris, D. W., Fogal, D., & Moss, M. (2018). Speech acts: The contemporary theoretical landscape. In Fogal, W., D. W. Harris, & Moss, M. (Eds.), *New Work on Speech Acts* (pp. 1–39). Oxford. Oxford University press.

Hassall, T. (2006). Learning to take leave in social conversations: A diary study. In M. DuFon, & E. Churchill, (Eds.), *Language learners in study abroad contexts*, (pp. 31–58). Bristol: Multilingual Matters.

Haugh, M. (2007). The discursive challenge to politeness research: An interactional alternative. *Journal of Politeness Research*, *3*(2), 295–317.

Haugh, M., Kádár, D. Z., & Mills, S. (2013). Interpersonal pragmatics: Issues and debates. *Journal of Pragmatics*, *58*(1), 1–11.

Haviland, S. E., & Clark, H. H. (1974). What's new? Acquiring new information as a process in comprehension. *Journal of verbal learning and verbal behavior*, *13*(5), 512–521.

Hedberg, N. (2006). Topic-focus controversies. In V. Molnár & S. Winkler (Eds.), *The architecture of focus* (pp. 373–397). Berlin: Mouton De Gruyter.

Held, G. (1992). Politeness in linguistic research. In R. J. Watts, S. Ide, & K. Ehlich (Eds.), *Politeness in language: Studies in its history, theory and practice* (pp. 131–153). Berlin: de Gruyter.

Hellermann, J., & Vergun, A. (2007). Language which is not taught: The discourse marker use of beginning adult learners of English. *Journal of Pragmatics*, *39*, 157–179.

Hendriks, H. (2000). The acquisition of topic marking in L1 Chinese and L1 and L2 French. *Studies in Second Language Acquisition*, *22*, 369–397.

Herbert, R. K. (1986). Say "thank you" – or something. *American Speech*, *61*(1), 76–88.

Heritage, J. (2005). Conversation analysis and institutional talk. In K. L. Fitch, & R. E. Sanders, *Handbook of language and social interaction* (pp. 103–147). Lawrence, NJ: Erlbaum.

Hewings, M. (1995). Tone choice in the English intonation of non-native speakers. *IRAL: International Review of Applied Linguistics in Language Teaching*, *33*(3), 251.

Hill, T. (1997). The development of pragmatic competence in an EFL context. Unpublished dissertation, Temple University, Tokyo.

Hill, B., Ide, S., Ikuta, S., Kawasaki, A., & Ogino, T. (1986). Universals of linguistic politeness: Quantitative evidence from Japanese and American English. *Journal of Pragmatics*, *10*(3), 347–371.

Herring, S. (Ed.) (1996). *Computer-mediated communication: Linguistic, social, and cross-cultural perspectives*. Amsterdam: Benjamins.

Herring, S., Stein, D., & Virtanen, T. (Eds.). (2013). *Pragmatics of computer-mediated communication*. Berlin: de Gruyter.

Hockett, C. F. (1963). The problem of universals in language. In J. H. Greenberg (Ed.), *Universals of language*. Cambridge, MA: MIT Press.

Holdcroft, D. (1978). *Words and deeds: Problems in the theory of speech acts*. Oxford: Clarendon Press.

Holmes, J. (2005). Politeness and postmodernism: An appropriate approach to the analysis of language and gender? *Journal of Sociolinguistics*, *9*(1), 108–117.

Horan, G. (2013). "You taught me language": Cursing and swearing in foreign language learning. *Language and Intercultural Communication*, *13*(3), 283–297.

Horn, L. R. (1973). Greek Grice: A brief survey of proto-conversational rules in the history of logic. *Chicago Linguistics Society*, *9*, 205–214.

Horn, L. R. (1984). Toward a new taxonomy for pragmatic inference: Q-based and R-based implicature. In D. Schiffrin (Ed.), *Meaning, form, and use in context: Linguistic applications* (pp. 11–42). Washington, DC: Georgetown University Press.

Horn, L. R. (1990). Hamburgers and truth: Why Gricean explanation is Gricean. In K. Hall, et al. (Eds.)., *Papers from the 16th Annual Meeting of the Berkeley Linguistics Society* (pp. 454–471). Berkeley, CA: Berkeley Linguistic Society.

Houck, N. R., & Fujimori, J. (2010). Teacher, you should lose some weight: Advice giving in English. In D. H. Tatsuki, & N. R. Houck (Eds.), *Pragmatics: Teaching speech acts* (pp. 89–104). Alexandria, VA: TESOL Press.

House, J. (2009). Introduction: The pragmatics of English as a lingua franca. *Intercultural Pragmatics*, *6*(2), 141–145.

House, J. (2010). 12. The pragmatics of English as a lingua franca. In A. Trosborg (Ed.), *Pragmatics across languages and cultures* (pp. 363–390). Berlin: Mouton De Gruyter.

House, J. (2013). Developing pragmatic competence in English as a lingua franca: Using discourse markers to express (inter) subjectivity and connectivity. *Journal of Pragmatics*, *59*, 57–67.

Howard, A. M. (2003) Politeness is More than "Please" In: Bardovi-Harlig, K, Mahan-Taylor, R. (Eds.), *Teaching Pragmatics*. United States Department of State, Washington, DC.

Howarth, P. (1998). Phraseology and second language proficiency. *Applied linguistics*, *19*(1), 24–44.

Hsiung, H.-Y. (2014). A constrastive rhetoric study: The placement of paragraph thesis statements in English and Chinese research articles. Unpublished PhD Dissertation, Texas A&M University-Commerce.

Huang, L. F. (2019). A corpus-based exploration of the discourse marker well in spoken interlanguage. *Language and Speech*, *62*(3), 570–593.

Hübler, A. (2011). Metapragmatics. In W. Bublitz, & N. R. Norrick (Eds.), *Foundations of Pragmatics* (pp. 107–136). Berlin: Mouton De gruyter.

Humphrey, S., & Macnaught, L. (2016). Functional language instruction and the writing growth of English language learners in the middle years. *TESOL Quarterly*, *50*(4), 792–816.

Hunston, S., & Thompson, G. (Eds.). (2000). *Evaluation in text: Authorial stance and the construction of discourse*. Oxford: Oxford University Press.

Hyland, K. (2005). *Metadiscourse: Exploring interaction in writing* (2nd ed.). London: Continuum. (2018).

Hymes, D. (1972). On communicative competence. In Pride, J.B., & Holmes, J. (Eds.), *Sociolinguistics: Selected readings* (pp. 269–293). Harmondsworth: Penguin.

Hymes, D. (1982). Prague functionalism. *American Anthropologist*, *84*(2), 398–399.

Ide, S. (1989). Formal forms and discernment: Two neglected aspects of universals of linguistic politeness. *Multilingua – Journal of Cross-Cultural And Interlanguage Communication*, *8*(2–3), 223–248.

Ide, S. (1992). On the notion of wakimae: Toward an integrated framework of linguistic politeness. In Mejiro Linguistic Society (Ed.), *Mosaic of language: Essays in honour of Professor Natsuko Okuda* (pp. 298–305). Tokyo: Mejiro Linguistic Society.

Ide, S. (2012). Roots of the wakimae aspect of linguistic politeness. In M. Meeuwis, & J-O. Östman (Eds.), *Pragmaticizing understanding: Studies for Jef Verschueren* (pp. 121–138). Amsterdam: Benjamins.

Igboanusi, H. (2008). Changing trends in language choice in Nigeria. *Sociolinguistic Studies, 2*(2), 251–269.

Infantidou, E. (2014). *Pragmatic competence and relevance*. Amsterdam: Benjamins.

Ishida, K. (2007). Developing understanding of how the desu/masu and plain forms express one's stance. In D. R. Yoshimi, & H. Wang (Eds.), *Selected papers from the conference on pragmatics in the CJK classroom: The state of the art* (pp. 181–202). http://nflrc.hawaii.edu/CJKProceedings

Ishihara, N. (2009). Teacher-based assessment for foreign language pragmatics. *TESOL quarterly, 43*(3), 445–470.

Ishihara, N., & Cohen, A. D. (2010). *Teaching and learning pragmatics: Where language and culture meet*. Harlow, England: Longman Applied Linguistics/Pearson Education.

İstifçi, İ. (2009). The use of apologies by EFL learners. *English Language Teaching, 2*(3), 15–25.

Iwasaki, N. (2011). Learning L2 Japanese politeness and impoliteness: Young American men's dilemmas during study abroad. *Japanese Language and Literature, 45*(1), 67–106.

Izadi, A. (2016). Over-politeness in Persian professional interactions. *Journal of Pragmatics, 102*, 13–23.

Jaffe, A. (2009). The sociolinguistics of stance. In A. Jaffe (Ed.), *Stance: Sociolinguistic perspectives* (pp. 3–28). Oxford: Oxford University Press.

Jaffe, A. (Ed.). (2009). *Stance: Sociolinguistic perspectives*. Oxford: Oxford University Press.

Jaffe, A. (2016). Indexicality, stance and fields in sociolinguistics. In N. Coupland (Ed.), *Sociolinguistics: Theoretical debates* (pp. 86–112). Cambridge: Cambridge UP.

Jakobson, R. (1932) [1971]. Zur Struktur des russischen Verbums. In *Charisteria Guglielmo Mathesio*. Prague. 74–84. Reprinted in Jakobson, Roman (1971). Selected writings (vol. II). The Hague: Mouton. 3–15.

Jakobson, R. (1960). Linguistics and poetics. In T. A. Sebeok (Ed.), *Style in language* (pp. 350–377). Cambridge: MIT Press.

Jakobson, R., & Halle, M. (1956). *Fundamentals of language*. The Hague: Mouton.

Jaszczolt, K. M. (2005). *Default semantics: Foundations of a compositional theory of acts of communication*. Oxford: Oxford University Press.

Jay, T., & Janschewitz, K. (2008). The pragmatics of swearing. *Journal of Politeness Research, 4*(2), 267–288.

Jefferson, G. (1979). A technique for inviting laughter and its subsequent acceptance declination. In G. Psathas (Ed.), *Everyday language. Studies in ethnomethodology* (pp. 79–96). New York: Irvington.

Jenkins, J. (2000). *The phonology of English as an international language*. Oxford University Press.

Jiang, X. (2006). Suggestions: What should ESL students know? *System, 34*(1), 36–54.

Jones, L. (1981). *Functions of English*. Cambridge: Cambridge University Press.

Johnstone, B., Andrus, J., & Danielson, A. E. (2006). Mobility, indexicality, and the enregisterment of 'Pittsburghese'. *Journal of English linguistics, 34*(2), 77–104.

Johnstone, B., & Kiesling, S. F. (2008). Indexicality and experience: Exploring the meanings of /aw/- monophthongization in Pittsburgh. *Journal of sociolinguistics, 12*(1), 5–33.

Jordà, M. P. S. (2005). *Third language learners: Pragmatics production and awareness*. Bristol: Multilingual Matters.

Jucker, A. H. (2009). Speech act research between armchair, field and laboratory: The case of compliments. *Journal of Pragmatics, 41*(8), 1611–1635.

Kachru, B.B. (1985). Standards, codification and sociolinguistic realism: The English language in the outer circle. In R. Quirk & H. G. Widdowson (Eds.), *English in the world: Teaching and learning the language and literatures* (pp. 11–30). Cambridge: Cambridge University Press.

Kádár, D. Z., & Culpeper, J. (2010). Historical (im) politeness: An introduction. In J. Culpeper & D. Z. Kádár (Eds.), *Historical (im)politeness* (pp. 9–36). New York: Peter Lang.

Kádár, D. Z., & Haugh, M. (2013). *Understanding politeness*. Cambridge University Press.

Kanik, M. (2012). Reverse discourse completion tasks. In Dupuy, B. & Waugh, L. (Eds.), *Proceedings of the Third International Conference on the Development and Assessment of Intercultural Competence* (Vol. *2*, pp. 85–99). Tucson, AZ: Center for Educational Resources in Culture, Language and Literacy. University of Arizona.

Kaplan, R. B. (1966). Cultural thought patterns in intercultural education. *Language Learning, 16*(1), 1–20.

Kasper, G. (1990). Linguistic politeness: Current research issues. *Journal of Pragmatics, 14*(2), 193–218.

Kasper, G. (1992). Pragmatic transfer. *Interlanguage Studies Bulletin (Utrecht), 8*(3), 203–231.

Kasper, G. (2001). Four perspectives on L2 pragmatic development. *Applied Linguistics, 22*(4), 502–530.

Kasper, G., & Rose, K. R. (1999). Pragmatics and SLA. *Annual Review of Applied Linguistics, 19*, 81–104.

Kasper, G., & Rose, K. R. (2002). Pragmatic development in a second language. *Language Learning: A Journal of Research in Language Studies, 52*, 1–32.

Kasper, G., & Schmidt, R. (1996). Developmental issues in interlanguage pragmatics. *Studies in Second Language Acquisition, 18*(2), 149–169.

Kecskes, I. (2006). The dual language model to explain code-switching: A cognitive-pragmatic approach. *Intercultural Pragmatics, 3*(3), 257–283.

Kecskes, I. (2019). Impoverished pragmatics? The semantics-pragmatics interface from an intercultural perspective. *Intercultural Pragmatics, 16*(5), 489–515.

Keshavarz, M. H., Eslami, Z. R., & Ghahraman, V. (2006). Pragmatic transfer and Iranian EFL refusals: A cross-cultural perspective of Persian and English. *Pragmatics and Language Learning, 11*(2), 359–401.

Kiesling, S. F. (2008). Recasting language and masculinities in the age of desire. Indiana University Linguistics Club working papers. Department of Linguistics, Indiana University Bloomington, IN.

Kiesling, S. F. (2009). Style as stance. In Jaffe, A. (Ed.). (2009). *Stance: sociolinguistic perspectives* (pp. 171–194). Oxford: Oxford University Press.

Kiesling, S. F. (2015). Cross-cultural and intercultural communication and discourse analysis. In D. Tannen, H. E. Hamilton, & D. Schiffrin (Eds.), *The handbook of discourse analysis* (Vol. *2*, pp. 620–638). Malden, MA: Wiley Blackwell.

Kim, C. H. (2012). The process of Korean learners of English in understanding conversational implicatures. *The SNU Journal of Education Research, 21*, 57–79.

Kim, E. Y. A., & Brown, L. (2014). Negotiating pragmatic competence in computer mediated communication: The case of Korean address terms. *CALICO Journal, 31*(3), 264–282.

Kinginger, C., & Blattner, G. (2009). Histories of engagement and sociolinguistic awareness in study abroad: Colloquial French. In L. Ortega & H. Byrnes (Eds.), *The longitudinal study of advanced L2 capacities* (pp. 239–262). New York: Routledge.

Kinginger, C., & Farrell, K. (2004). Assessing development of meta-pragmatic awareness in study abroad. *Frontiers: The Interdisciplinary Journal of Study Abroad, 10*, 19–42.

Kitao, K. (1990). A study of Japanese and American perceptions of politeness in requests. *Doshisha Studies in English, 50*, 178–210.

Koike, D. A., & Pearson, L. (2005). The effect of instruction and feedback in the development of pragmatic competence. *System, 33*(3), 481–501.

Kopple, W. J. V. (1982). The given-new strategy of comprehension and some natural expository paragraphs. *Journal of Psycholinguistic Research, 11*(5), 501–520.

Kopple, W. J. V. (1991). Themes, thematic progressions, and some implications for understanding discourse. *Written Communication, 8*(3), 311–347.

Krämer, N. C., von der Pütten, A., & Eimler, S. (2012). Human-agent and human-robot interaction theory: Similarities to and differences from human-human interaction. In M. Zacarias, & J. V. de Oliveira (Eds.), *Human-computer interaction: The agency perspective* (pp. 215–240). Berlin/Heidelberg: Springer.

Kroskrity, P. V. (2004). Language ideologies. In A. Duranti (Ed.), *A companion to linguistic anthropology* (pp. 496–517). Malden, MA: Blackwell.

Kubota, M. (1995). Teachability of conversational implicature to Japanese EFL learners. *IRLT (Institute for Research in Language Teaching) Bulletin, 9*, 35–67.

Kuno, S. (1972). Functional sentence perspective: A case study from Japanese and English. *Linguistic inquiry, 3*(3), 269–320.

Labov, W. (1963). The social motivation of a sound change. *Word, 19*(3), 273–309.

Labov, W. (1972). *Language in the inner city. Studies in Black English Vernacular.* Philadelphia: University of Pennsylvania Press.

Lakoff, G. (1987). *Women, fire, and dangerous things: What categories reveal about the mind.* Chicago: University of Chicago press.

Lakoff, G., & Johnson, M. (1980). *Metaphors we live by.* Chicago: University of Chicago Press.

Lakoff, R. T. (1973). The logic of politeness; or, minding your P's and Q's. In C.W. Corum, T. C. Smith-Stark, & A. Weiser (Eds.), *Papers from the Ninth Regional Meeting of the Chicago Linguistics Society* (pp. 292–305). Chicago: Department of Linguistics, University of Chicago

Lakoff, R. T., & Ide, S. (Eds.). (2005). *Broadening the horizon of linguistic politeness* (vol. *139*). John *Benjamins* Publishing.

Langacker, R. W. (1987). *Foundations of cognitive grammar. Vol. 1. Theoretical prerequisites.* Stanford, CA: Stanford University Press.

Lane, G. M. (1898). *A Latin grammar for schools and colleges.* New York, NY: American Book Company.

Lantolf, J. P. (Ed.). (2000a). *Sociocultural theory and second language learning* Oxford: Oxford. University Press.

Lantolf, J. P. (2000b). Introducing sociocultural theory. In J. P. Lantolf (Ed.), *Sociocultural theory and second language learning* (pp. 1–26). Oxford: Oxford University Press.

Larsen-Freeman, D., & Cameron, L. (2008). *Complex systems and applied linguistics*. Oxford: Oxford University Press.

Laver, J. (1980). *The phonetic description of voice quality*. Cambridge: Cambridge University Press.

Lee, C. (2003). The use of the discourse marker say in conversational English. *Seoul National University Working Papers in English Language and Linguistics, 2*, 133–156.

Lee, E., & Canagarajah, S. (2018). The connection between transcultural dispositions and translingual practices in academic writing. *Journal of Multicultural Discourses, 14*, 14–28.

Leech, G. (1981). *Semantics. The study of meaning*. Harmondsworth: Penguin.

Leech, G. N. (1983). *Principles of pragmatics*. New York: Routledge.

Leech, G. (2005). Politeness: Is there an East-West divide. *Journal of Foreign Languages, 6*(3), 1–30.

Lepore, E., & Van Gulick, R. (1991). *John Searle and his critics*. Cambridge: Blackwell.

Levinson, S. C. (1979). Activity types and language. *Linguistics, 17*(5/6), 365–399.

Levinson, S. C. (1983). *Pragmatics*. Cambridge: Cambridge UP.

Levinson, S. C. (1992). Activity types and language. In P. Drew & J. Heritage (Eds.), *Talk at Work* (pp. 66–100). Cambridge: Cambridge University Press.

Levinson, S. C. (2000). *Presumptive meanings: The Theory Of Generalized Conversational Implicature*. Cambridge, MA: MIT Press.

Levinson, S. C. (2015). John Joseph Gumperz (1922–2013). *American Anthropologist, 117*(1), 212–215.

Lewis, D. (1979). Scorekeeping in a language game. *Journal of Philosophical Logic, 8*, 339–359.

Li, S. (2012). The effects of input-based practice on pragmatic development of requests in L2 Chinese. *Language Learning, 62*(2), 403–438.

Li, S., & Taguchi, N. (2014). The effects of practice modality on pragmatic development in L2 Chinese. *The Modern Language Journal, 8*(3), 794–812.

Liao, S. (2009). Variation in the use of discourse markers by Chinese teaching assistants in the US. *Journal of Pragmatics, 41*(7), 1313–1328.

Limberg, H. (2016). "Always remember to say please and thank you": Teaching politeness with German EFL textbooks. *Pragmatics and Language Learning, 14*, 265–291.

Liu, D. (2008). *Idioms. Description, comprehension, acquisition, and pedagogy*. New York: Routledge.

Lock, G. (1996). *Functional English grammar: An introduction for second language teachers*. Cambridge: Cambridge University Press.

LoCastro, V. (1997). Politeness and pragmatic competence in foreign language education? *Language Teaching Research, 1*(3), 239–267

Locher, M. A., & Watts, R. J. (2005). Politeness theory and relational work. *Journal of Politeness Research, 1*(1), 9–33.

Looney, S. D. (2019). Co-operative action: Addressing misunderstanding and displaying uncertainty in a university physics lab. In S. D. Looney, & S. Bhalla, (Eds.), *A transdisciplinary approach to international teaching assistants* (pp. 41–62). Bristol: Multilingual Matters.

Louw, K., Derwing, T., & Abbott, M. (2010). Teaching pragmatics to L2 learners for the workplace: The job interview. *The Canadian Modern Language Review, 66*(5), 739–758.

Lucas, T. H., McKhann, G. M., & Ojemann, G. A. (2004). Functional separation of languages in the bilingual brain: A comparison of electrical stimulation language mapping in 25 bilingual patients and 117 monolingual control patients. *Journal of Neurosurgery, 101*(3), 449–457.

Lyons, J. (1977). *Semantics*. Cambridge: Cambridge University Press.

Macken-Horarik, M. (2005). Tools for promoting literacy development in TESOL classrooms: Insights from systemic functional linguistics. *TESOL in Context, 15*(2) 15–23.

Mackenzie, J. L. (2016a). A first history of functional grammar. In C. Assunção, G. Fernandes, & R. Kemmler (Eds.), *History of linguistics 2014: Selected papers from the 13th International Conference on the History of the Language Sciences (ICHoLS XIII), Vila Real, Portugal, 25–29 August 2014* (pp. 233–246). Amsterdam: Benjamins.

Mackenzie, J. L. (2016b). Functional linguistics. In K. Allan (Ed.), *Routledge handbook of linguistics* (pp. 470–484). New York: Routledge.

Mclennan, M. (2018). Differend and 'post-truth.' *French Journal for Media Research, 9*, 1–13.

Malinowski, B. (1923). The problem of meaning in primitive languages. In C. K. Ogden, & I. A. Richards (Eds.), *The meaning of meaning* (pp. 296–336). London: Kegan Paul, Trench and Trubner,

Margolis, J. (1979). Literature and speech acts. *Philosophy of Literature, 3*, 39–52.

Martin, J. R., & White, P. R. (2005). *The language of evaluation: Appraisals in English*. Basingstoke: Palgrave Macmillan.

Martinet, A. (1955). *Économie des changements phonétiques*. Berne: Francke.

Martínez-Flor, A. (2006). The effectiveness of explicit and implicit treatments on EFL learners' confidence in recognizing appropriate suggestions. *Pragmatics and Language Learning, 11*, 199–225.

Martínez-Flor, A. (2007). Analysing request modification devices in films: Implications for pragmatic learning in instructed foreign language contexts. In Alcón Soler, E., & Safont Jordà, M.P. (Eds.), *Intercultural language use and language learning* (pp. 245–280). Dordrecht: Springer.

Martínez-Flor, A., & Fukuya, Y. J. (2005). The effects of instruction on learners' production of appropriate and accurate suggestions. *System, 33*(3), 463–480.

Mathesius, V. (1975). *A functional analysis of present day English on a general linguistic basis*. Berlin: De Gruyter and Prague: Academia. [original Czech edition, 1961].

Matsuda, M. (1999). Interlanguage pragmatics: What can it offer to language teachers. *The CATESOL Journal, 11*(1), 39–59.

Matsumoto, Y. (1988). Reexamination of the universality of face: Politeness phenomena in Japanese. *Journal of Pragmatics, 12*(4), 403–426.

Matsumura, S. (2007). Exploring the aftereffects of study abroad on interlanguage pragmatic development. *Intercultural Pragmatics, 4*(2), 167–192.

Mauranen, A. (2006). A rich domain of ELF – the ELFA corpus of academic discourse. *Nordic Journal of English Studies, 5*(2), 145–59.

McConachy, T. (2013). Exploring the meta-pragmatic realm in English language teaching. *Language Awareness, 22*(2), 100–110.

McDonald, S. (1992). Differential pragmatic language loss after closed head injury: Ability to comprehend conversational implicature. *Applied Psycholinguistics, 13*(3), 295–312.

McDonald, S. (1999). Exploring the process of inference generation in sarcasm: A review of normal and clinical studies. *Brain and Language, 68*(3), 486–506.

McDonald, S. (2017). Emotions are rising: The growing field of affect neuropsychology. *Journal of the International Neuropsychological Society, 23*(9–10), 719–731.

McKay, S. L. (2009). Pragmatics and EIL pedagogy. In F. Sharifian (Ed.), *English as an international language: Perspectives and pedagogical issues* (pp. 227–241). Bristol: Multilingual Matters.

Menjo, S. (2018). The development of L2 prosody in Japanese speakers of English: A quasi-longitudinal study. Unpublished dissertation, Texas A&M-Commerce, Texas.

Mercury, R. E. (1995). Swearing: A "bad" part of language; A good part of language learning. *TESL Canada Journal, 13*(1), 28–36.

Mey, J. (2001). *Pragmatics* (2nd ed.). Oxford: Blackwell.

Miller, G. A. (1956). The magical number seven, plus or minus two: Some limits on our capacity for processing information. *Psychological Review, 63*(2), 81.

Milligan, K., Astington, J. W., & Dack, L. A. (2007). Language and theory of mind: Meta-analysis of the relation between language ability and false-belief understanding. *Child Development, 78*(2), 622–646.

Mills, S. (2003). *Gender and politeness*. Cambridge: Cambridge University Press.

Mills, S. (2005). Gender and impoliteness. *Journal of Politeness Research, 1*, 263–280.

Mirzaei, A., & Esmaeili, M. (2013). The effects of planned instruction on Iranian L2 learners' interlanguage pragmatic development. *International Journal of Society, Culture & Language, 1*(1), 89–100.

Molinsky, S. J., & Bliss, B. (2002). *Side by side: Student book* 3, Audio Cd. Prentice Hall Regents.

Moravcsik E., & Wirth J. (1986). Markedness – An overview. In F. R. Eckman, E. A. Moravcsik, & J. R. Wirth (Eds.), *Markedness* (pp. 1–11) Boston, MA: Springer.

Mori, J. & Nguyen, H. (2019). Conversation analysis in L2 pragmatics research. In N. Taguchi (Ed.), *The Routledge handbook of second language acquisition and pragmatics* (pp. 226–240). New York, NY: Taylor & Francis.

Mugford, G. (2007). How rude! Teaching impoliteness in the second-language classroom. *ELT Journal, 62*(4), 375–384.

Müller, S. (2005). *Discourse markers in native and non-native English discourse*. John Benjamins Pub.

Murdock, G. (1940). The cross-cultural survey. *American Sociological Review, 5*(3), 361–370. Retrieved from http://www.jstor.org/stable/2084038

Murray, J. C. (2011). Do bears fly? Revisiting conversational implicature in instructional pragmatics. *TESL-EJ, 15*(2), n2.

Myers-Scotton, C. (1983). Comment: markedness and code choice. *International Journal of the Sociology of Language, 39*, 119–128.

Narita, R. (2012). The effects of pragmatic consciousness-raising activity on the development of pragmatic awareness and use of hearsay evidential markers for learners of Japanese as a foreign language. *Journal of Pragmatics, 44*(1), 1–29.

Nelson, G. L., Carson, J., Batal, M. A., & Bakary, W. E. (2002). Cross-cultural pragmatics: Strategy use in Egyptian Arabic and American English refusals. *Applied Linguistics, 23*(2), 163–189.

Nguyen, M. T. T. (2008). Criticizing in an L2: Pragmatic strategies used by Vietnamese EFL learners. *Intercultural Pragmatics*, *5*(1), 41–66.

Nguyen, M. T. T. (2011). Learning to communicate in a globalized world: To what extent do school textbooks facilitate the development of intercultural pragmatic competence? *RELC Journal*, *42*(1), 17–30.

Nguyen, M. T. T., Do, T. T. H., Nguyen, A. T., & Pham, T. T. T. (2015). Teaching email requests in the academic context: A focus on the role of corrective feedback. *Language Awareness*, *24*(2), 169–195.

Nguyen, M. T. T., Pham, T. H., & Pham, M. T. (2012). The relative effects of explicit and implicit form-focused instruction on the development of L2 pragmatic competence. *Journal of Pragmatics*, *44*(4), 416–434.

Niżegorodcew, A. (2007). *The role of L2 classroom input in the light of second language acquisition models and relevance theory*. Bristol: Multilingual Matters.

Noonan, N. (1999). Non-structuralist syntax. In M. Darnell, E. A. Moravcsik, M. Noonan, F. J. Newmeyer, K. Wheatley (Eds.), *Functionalism and formalism in linguistics* (pp. 11–31). Amsterdam: Benjamins.

Noveck, I. (2018). *Experimental pragmatics: The making of a cognitive science*. Cambridge: Cambridge University Press.

Núñez, R. E., & Sweetser, E. (2006). With the future behind them: Convergent evidence from Aymara language and gesture in the crosslinguistic comparison of spatial construals of time. *Cognitive Science*, *30*(3), 401–450.

O'Driscoll, J. (2007). Brown & Levinson's face: How it can–and can't–help us to understand interaction across cultures. *Intercultural Pragmatics*, *4*(4), 463–492.

O'Keeffe, A., & McCarthy, M. (Eds.). (2010). The Routledge handbook of corpus linguistics. Routledge.

Ochs Keenan, E. (1976). The universality of conversational postulates. *Language in Society*, *5*, 67–80.

Ogiermann, E. (2009). Politeness and in-directness across cultures: A comparison of English, German, Polish and Russian requests. *Journal of Politeness Research*, *5*, 189–216.

Olshtain, E. (1983). Sociocultural competence and language transfer: The case of apology. In S. Gass, & L. Selinker (Eds.), *Language transfer in language learning* (pp. 232–249). New York, NY: Newbury House.

Ortega, L. (2011). SLA after the social turn. In D. Atkinson (Ed.), *Alternative approaches to second language acquisition* (pp. 167–180). New York: Routledge.

Paige, M., Cohen, A., Kappler, B., Chi, J., & Lassegard, J. (2002). *Maximizing study abroad*. Minneapolis, MN: University of Minnesota.

Parola, A., Gabbatore, I., Bosco, F. M., Bara, B. G., Cossa, F. M., Gindri, P., & Sacco, K. (2016). Assessment of pragmatic impairment in right hemisphere damage. *Journal of Neurolinguistics*, *39*, 10–25.

Pavlenko, A. (2011). Thinking and speaking in two languages: Overview of the field. In A. Pavlenko (Ed.), *Thinking and speaking in two languages* (pp. 237–257). Bristol: Multilingual matters.

Pavlidou, T. (1994). Contrasting German-Greek politeness and the consequences. *Journal of Pragmatics*, *21*, 487–511.

Perani, D., & Abutalebi, J. (2005). The neural basis of first and second language processing. *Current Opinion in Neurobiology, 15*(2), 202–206.

Petruck, M. (1996). Frame semantics. In J. Verschueren, J.-O. Östman, J. Blommaert, & C. Bulcaen (Eds.), *Handbook of pragmatics* (pp. 1–13). Philadelphia: Benjamins.

Pexman, P. M., Glenwright, M., Krol, A., & James, T. (2005). An acquired taste: Children's perceptions of humor and teasing in verbal irony. *Discourse Processes, 40*(3), 259–288.

Pickering, L. (2001). The role of tone choice in improving ITA communication in the classroom. *Tesol Quarterly, 35*(2), 233–255.

Pickering, L. (2004). The structure and function of intonational paragraphs in native and nonnative speaker instructional discourse. *English for Specific Purposes, 23*(1), 19–43.

Pickering, L. (2009). Intonation as a pragmatic resource in ELF interaction. *Intercultural Pragmatics, 6*(2), 235–255.

Pickering, L. (2018). *Discourse intonation: A discourse-pragmatic approach to teaching the pronunciation of English.* Ann Arbor, MI: University of Michigan Press.

Pickering, L., & Bruce, C. (2009). *The AAC and non-AAC workplace corpus (ANAWC) [Collection of Electronic Texts].* Atlanta, GA: Georgia State University.

Pickering, L., & Byrd, P. (2008). Investigating connections between spoken and written academic English: Lexical bundles in the AWL and in MICASE. In Belcher, D., & Hirvela, A. (Eds.), *The oral/literate connection: Perspectives on L2 speaking, writing and other media interactions* (pp. 110–132). Ann Arbor, MI: University of Michigan Press.

Pickering, L., & J. Litzenberg. (2011). Intonation as a pragmatic resource, revisited. In A. Archibald, A. Cogo, & J. Jenkins (Eds.), *Latest trends in ELF*, (pp. 32–55). Newcastle-Upon-Tyne: Cambridge Scholars.

Piller, I. (2002). Passing for a native speaker: Identity and success in second language learning. *Journal of Sociolinguistics, 6*(2), 179–208.

Plonsky, L., & Zhuang, J. (2019). A meta-analysis of L2 pragmatics instruction. In N. Taguchi (Ed.), *The Routledge handbook of SLA and pragmatics* (pp. 287–307). New York: Routledge. https://doi.org/10.4324/9781351164085-19.

Pomerantz, A. (1984). Agreeing and disagreeing with assessments: Some features of preferred/dispreferred turn shaped. In J. M. Atkinson & J. Heritage (Eds.), *Structures of social action* (pp. 57–101). Cambridge: Cambridge University Press.

Pons Borderìa, S. (2001). Connectives discourse markers: An overview. *Quaderns de filologia. Estudis literaris, 6*, 219–143.

Pons Borderìa, S. (2008). Do discourse markers exist? On the treatment of discourse markers in Relevance Theory. *Journal of Pragmatics, 40*(8), 1411–1434.

Portolés, L., & Safont, P. (2018). Examining authentic and elicited data from a multilingual perspective. The real picture of child requestive behaviour in the L3 classroom. *System, 75*, 81–92.

Pratt, L. M. (1986). Ideology and speech-act theory. *Poetics Today, 7*(1), 59–72.

Prince, E. F. (1981). Toward a taxonomy of given-new information. In P. Cole (Ed.), *Radical pragmatics* (pp. 223–256). New York: Academic Press.

Prince, E. F. (1985). Fancy syntax and 'shared knowledge'. *Journal of pragmatics, 9*(1), 65–81.

Prince, E. F. (1992). The ZPG letter: Subjects, definiteness, and information-status. In W. C. Mann, & S. A. Thompson (Eds.), *Discourse description: Diverse linguistic analyses of a fund-raising text* (pp. 295–326). Amsterdam: Benjamins/Philadelphia.

Rapp, A. M., Mutschler, D. E., & Erb, M. (2012). Where in the brain is nonliteral language? A coordinate-based meta-analysis of functional magnetic resonance imaging studies. *Neuroimage, 63*(1), 600–610.

Récanati, F. (1989). The pragmatics of what is said. *Mind and Language, 4*, 295–329.

Récanati, F. (2010). *Truth-conditional pragmatics*. Oxford: Oxford University Press.

Redeker, G. (1991). Linguistic markers of discourse structure. *Linguistics, 29*(6), 1139–1172.

Regala-Flores, E., & Yin, K. (2015). Topical structure analysis as an assessment tool in student academic writing. *3L, Language, Linguistics, Literature, 21* (1). doi:http://dx.doi.org.proxy.tamuc.edu/10.17576/3L-2015-2101-10

Reinhart, T. (1981). Pragmatics and linguistics: An analysis of sentence topics. *Philosophica, 27*, 53–94.

Ren, W., & Han, Z. (2016). The representation of pragmatic knowledge in recent ELT textbooks. *ELT Journal, 70*(4), 424–434.

Renandya, W., & Richards, J. (2003). *Methodology in language teaching*. Cambridge: Cambridge University Press.

Reyes-Aguilar, A., Valles-Capetillo, E., & Giordano, M. (2018). A quantitative meta-analysis of neuroimaging studies of pragmatic language comprehension: In search of a Universal neural substrate. *Neuroscience, 395*, 60–88.

Richmond, A. (2013). https://www.forbes.com/sites/85broads/2013/05/09/what-do-you-mean-by-that-it-just-might-be-your-communication-skills-that-are-holding-you-back-at-work/#2f736d8a67f5

Roberts, C. (2012). Information structure: Towards an integrated formal theory of pragmatics. *Semantics and Pragmatics, 5*, 6–1.

Roberts, C., & Campbell, S. (2006). Talk on trial: Job interviews, language and ethnicity (No. 344). Corporate Document Services.

Roever, C. (2005). *Testing ESL pragmatics*. Frankfurt: Peter Lang.

Roever, C. (2007). DIF in the assessment of second language pragmatics. *Language Assessment Quarterly, 4*(2), 165–189.

Roever, C. (2013). Technology and tests of L2 pragmatics. In N. Taguchi & J. M. Sykes (Eds.), *Technology in interlanguage pragmatics research and teaching* (pp. 215–233). Amsterdam: Benjamins.

Roland, D., Dick, F., & Elman, J. L. (2007). Frequency of basic English grammatical structures: A corpus analysis. *Journal of memory and language, 57*(3), 348–379.

Römer, U. (2006). Pedagogical applications of corpora: Some reflections on the current scope and a wish list for future developments. *Zeitschrift für Anglistik und Amerikanistik, 54*(2), 121–134.

Römer, U. (2011). Corpus research applications in second language teaching. *Annual review of applied linguistics, 31*, 205–225.

Romero-Trillo, J. (1997). Your attention, please: Pragmatic mechanisms to obtain the addressee's attention in English and Spanish conversations. *Journal of Pragmatics, 28*(2), 205–221.

Romero-Trillo, J. (2002). The pragmatic fossilization of discourse markers in non-native speakers of English. *Journal of Pragmatics, 34*(6), 769–784.

Romero-Trillo, J. (2007). Adaptive management in discourse: The case of involvement discourse markers in English and Spanish conversations. *Catalan Journal of Linguistics, 6*, 81–94.

Rosa, J., & Burdick, C. (2016). Language ideologies. In O. Garcia, N. Flores, & M. Spotti (Eds.), *The Oxford handbook of language and society* (pp. 103–123). Oxford: Oxford University Press.

Rose, K. R. (1994). Pragmatic consciousness-raising in an EFL context. In L. F. Bouton & Y. Kachru (Eds.), *Pragmatics and language learning*, (pp. 52–63).

Rose, K. R. (2001). Compliments and compliment responses in film: Implications for pragmatics research and language teaching. *IRAL, 39*(4), 309–326.

Rose, K. R. (2005). On the effects of instruction in second language pragmatics. *System, 33*(3), 385–399.

Rose, K. R., & Ng, C. (2001). Inductive and deductive teaching of compliments and compliment responses. *Pragmatics in language teaching, 145*, 145–170.

Ross, S., & Kasper, G. (Eds.). (2013). *Assessing second language pragmatics*. New York: Springer.

Rutherford, W. (1986). Grammatical theory and L2 acquisition: A brief overview. *Second language research, 2*(1), 1–15.

Sadeghi, B., & Heidaryan, H. (2012). The effect of teaching pragmatic discourse markers on EFL learners' listening comprehension. *English Linguistics Research, 1*(2), 165–176.

Safont-Jordà, M. P. (2003). Metapragmatic awareness and pragmatic production of third language learners of English: A focus on request acts realizations. *International Journal of Bilingualism, 7*(1), 43–68.

Safont-Jordà, M. P. (2005). *Third language learners. Pragmatic production and awareness*. Multilingual Matters, Clevedon.

Safont-Jordà, M. P., & Portolés-Falomir, L. (2015). *Learning and using multiple languages: Current findings from research on multilingualism*. Newcastle upon Tyne: Cambridge Scholars Publishing.

Safont-Jordà, M. P., & Portolés-Falomir, L. (2016). Pragmatic functions of formulaic speech in three different languages: A focus on early L3 learners of English. *Journal of Immersion and Content-Based Language Education, 4*(2), 225–250.

Salsbury, T., & Bardovi-Harlig, K. (2000). Oppositional talk and the acquisition of modality in L2 English. In B. Swierzbin, F. Morris, M. Anderson, C. Klee, & E. Tarone (Eds.), *Social and cognitive factors in second language acquisition* (pp. 57–76). Somerville, MA: Cascadilla Press.

Sampson, G. (1982). The economics of conversation: Comments on Joshi's paper. In N. Smith (Ed.), *Mutual knowledge* (pp. 200–210). London: Academic.

Sankoff, G., Thibault, P., Nagy, N., Blondeau, H., Fonollosa, M.O., & Gagnon, L. (1997). Variation in the use of discourse markers in a language contact situation. *Language Variation and Change, 9*, 191–217.

Sarab, M. R., & Alikhani, S. (2016). Pragmatics instruction in EFL context: A focus on requests. *International Journal of Research Studies in Language Learning, 5*(1), 29–42.

Sardegna, V. G., & Molle, D. (2010). Videoconferencing with strangers: teaching Japanese EFL students verbal backchannel signals and reactive expressions. *Intercultural Pragmatics, 7*(2), 279–310.

de Saussure, F. (1916). *Cours de linguistique générale*. Paris: Payot.
Savić, M. (2016). Do EFL Teachers in Serbia have what they need to teach L2 pragmatics? Novice teachers' views of politeness. *Pragmatics & Language Learning, 14*, 207–231.
Sawyer, M. (1992). The development of pragmatics in Japanese as a second language: The sentence-final particle ne. *Pragmatics of Japanese as a native and target language, 3*, 83–125.
de Swaan, A. (2001). *Words of the world: the global language system*. Cambridge, Polity.
Schegloff, E. A. (2001). Discourse as interactional achievement III: The omnirelevance of action. In D. Tannen, H. E. Hamilton, & D. Schiffrin (Eds.), *The handbook of discourse analysis* (pp. 229–249). Malden, MA: Blackwell.
Schiffrin, D. (1987). *Discourse markers*. Cambridge: Cambridge University Press.
Schmidt, R. (1983). Interaction, acculturation, and the acquisition of communicative competence: A case study of an adult. In N. Wolfson & E. Judd (Eds.), *Sociolinguistics and language acquisition* (pp. 137–174). Rowley, MA: Newbury House.
Schneider, M., & Connor, U. (1991). Topical structure in ESL essays: Not all topics are equal. *Studies in Second Language Acquisition, 12*, 411–427.
Schourup, L. (1999). Discourse markers. *Lingua, 107*(3–4), 227–265.
Schröder, M., Cowie, R., Douglas-Cowie, E., Westerdijk, M., & Gielen, S. (2001). Acoustic correlates of emotion dimensions in view of speech synthesis. In *Seventh European Conference on Speech Communication and Technology*.
Schwarz, F. (2017). Experimental pragmatics. Oxford research encyclopedia of linguistics. Online.
Scollon, R., & Scollon, S.W. (1981). *Narrative, literacy and face in interethnic communication*. Norwood, NJ: Ablex Publishing Corporation.
Scollon, R., & Scollon, S.W. (1995). *Intercultural communication*. Malden, MA: Blackwell.
Searle, J. R. (1969). *Speech acts: An essay in the philosophy of language*. Cambridge: Cambridge University Press.
Searle, J. R. (1979). *Expression and meaning*. Cambridge: Cambridge University Press.
Searle, J. R. (1992). *The rediscovery of the mind*. Cambridge, MA: MIT Press.
Searle, J. R., & Vanderveken, D. (1985). *Foundations of illocutionary logic*. Cambridge: Cambridge University Press.
Seidlhofer, B. (2007). Common property: English as a lingua franca in Europe. In J. Cummins & C. Davison (Eds.), *International handbook of English language teaching* (pp. 137–153). Boston, MA: Springer.
Shifman, L. (2014). *Memes in digital culture*. Cambridge, MA: MIT press.
Shively, R. L. (2011). L2 pragmatic development in study abroad: A longitudinal study of Spanish service encounters. *Journal of Pragmatics, 43*(6), 1818–1835.
Showstack, R. E. (2017). Stancetaking and language ideologies in heritage language learner classroom discourse. *Journal of Language, Identity & Education, 16*(5), 271–284.
Sidgwick, H. (1907). *The methods of ethics*. New York: Macmillan.
Siegal, M. (1994). Looking east: Learning Japanese as a second language in Japan and the interaction of race, gender and social context. Unpublished PhD dissertation. University of California, Berkeley.
Siegal, M. (1996). The role of learner subjectivity in second language sociolinguistic competency: Western women learning Japanese. *Applied Linguistics, 17*(3), 356–382.
Siewierska, A. (1991). *Functional grammar*. New York: Routledge.

Sifianou, M. (1992). *Politeness phenomena in England and Greece*. Oxford: Clarendon.

Sifianou, M. (1993). Off-record indirectness and the notion of imposition. *Multilingua*, *12*(1), 69–79.

Sifianou, M., & Antonopoulou, E. (2005). Politeness in Greece: The politeness of involvement. In L. Hickey & M. Stewart (Eds.), *Politeness in Europe* (pp. 263–276). Cleveland, OH: Multilingual Matters.

Silverstein, M. (1979). Language structure and linguistic ideology. In P. R. Clyne, W. F. Hanks, & C. L. Hofbauer (Eds.), *The elements: A parasession on linguistic units and levels* (pp. 193–247). Chicago, IL: Chicago Linguistic Society.

Silverstein, M. (1992). The indeterminacy of contextualization: When is enough enough. In P. Auer (Ed.), *The contextualization of language* (pp. 55–76). Amsterdam: Benjamins.

Silverstein, M. (1993). Metapragmatic discourse and metapragmatic function. In J. A. Lucy (Ed.), *Reflexive language: Reported speech and metapragmatics* (pp. 33–58). Cambridge: Cambridge University Press.

Silverstein, M. (2003). Indexical order and the dialectics of sociolinguistic life. *Language & Communication*, *23*(3–4), 193–229.

Silverstein, M. (2016). The "push" of *Lautgesetze* and the "pull" of enregisterment. In N. Couplnand (Ed.), *Sociolinguistics. Theoretical debates* (pp. 37–67). Cambridge: Cambridge University press.

Simpson, J. M. (2000). Topical structure analysis of academic paragraphs in English and Spanish. *Journal of Second Language Writing*, *9*(3), 293–309.

Simpson, R., & Mendis, D. (2003). A corpus-based study of idioms in academic speech. *TESOL quarterly*, *37*(3), 419–441.

Singleton, D., Fishman, J. A., Aronin, L., & Ó Laoire, M. (Eds.). (2013). *Current multilingualism: A new linguistic dispensation*. Berlin: de Gruyter.

Soler, E. A. (2005). Does instruction work for learning pragmatics in the EFL context? *System*, *33*(3), 417–435.

Spencer-Oatey, H., & Jiang, W. (2003). Explaining cross-cultural pragmatic findings: Moving from politeness maxims to sociopragmatic interactional principles (SIPs). *Journal of Pragmatics*, *35*(10), 1633–1650.

Sperber, D., & Wilson, D. (1986). *Relevance. Communication and cognition*. Cambridge, MA: Harvard University Press.

Sperber, D., & Wilson, D. (1987). Precis of relevance: Communication and cognition. *The Behavioral and Brain Sciences*, *10*(4), 697–710.

Sprong, M., Schothorst, P., Vos, E., Hox, J., & van Engeland, H., (2007). Theory of mind in schizophrenia: A meta-analysis. *British Journal of Psychiatry*, *191*(1), 5–13.

Stenson, N. (1983). Induced errors. In B. W. Robinett & J. Schachter (Eds.), *Second language learning: Contrastive analysis, error analysis and related aspects* (pp. 256–71). Ann Arbor, MI: University of Michigan Press.

Stevens, S. G. (1989). A "dramatic" approach to improving the intelligibility of ITAs. *English for specific purposes*, *8*(2), 181–194.

Stvan, L. S. (2006). Diachronic change in the discourse markers why and say in American English. In A. M. Hornero, M. J. Luzon, & S. Murillo (Eds.), *Corpus linguistics: Applications for the study of English* (pp. 61–76.) Bern: Peter Lang.

Sulpizio, S., Del Maschio, N., Fedeli, D., & Abutalebi, J. (2020). Bilingual language processing: A meta-analysis of functional neuroimaging studies. *Neuroscience & Biobehavioral Reviews, 108*, 834–853.

Swales, J. (1990). *Genre analysis: English in academic and research settings*. Cambridge: Cambridge University Press.

Swales, J. M. (2004). *Research genres: Explorations and applications*. Cambridge: Cambridge University Press.

Sykes, J.M. & Cohen, A. (2006). Dancing with words: Strategies for learning pragmatics in Spanish. *Regents of the University of Minnesota. Retrieved December 20*, 2019.

Tada, M. (2005). Assessment of EFL pragmatic production and perception using video prompts. Unpublished PhD Dissertation. Temple University.

Taguchi, N. (2002). An application of relevance theory to the analysis of L2 interpretation processes: The comprehension of indirect replies. *IRAL, 40*(2), 151–176.

Taguchi, N. (2005). Comprehending implied meaning in English as a foreign language. *The Modern Language Journal, 89*(4), 543–562.

Taguchi, N. (2010). Longitudinal studies in interlanguage pragmatics. In A. Trosborg (Ed.), *Pragmatics across languages and cultures*, (pp. 333–361). Berlin: Mouton De Gruyter.

Taguchi, N. (2011). The effect of L2 proficiency and study-abroad experience on pragmatic comprehension. *Language Learning, 61*(3), 904–939.

Taguchi, N. (2015). Instructed pragmatics at a glance: Where instructional studies were, are, and should be going. *Language Teaching, 48*(1), 1–50.

Taguchi, N., & Kim, Y. (2016). Collaborative dialogue in learning pragmatics: pragmatic-related episodes as an opportunity for learning request-making. *Applied Linguistics, 37*(3), 416–437.

Taguchi, N., & Sykes, J. M. (Eds.). (2013). *Technology in interlanguage pragmatics research and teaching*. Amsterdam: Benjamins.

Taguchi, N., & Yamaguchi, S. (2019). Implicature comprehension in L2 pragmatics research. In N. Taguchi (Ed.), *The Routledge handbook of second language acquisition and pragmatics* (pp. 31–46). New York: Routledge.

Tajfel, H. (1970). Experiments in intergroup discrimination. *Scientific American, 223*(5), 96–103.

Takahashi, S. (2010). Assessing learnability in second language pragmatics. In A. Trosborg (Ed.), *Pragmatics across languages and cultures* (pp. 391–415). Berlin: Mouton De Gruyter.

Takamiya, Y., & Ishihara, N. (2013). Blogging: Crosscultural interaction for pragmatic development. In N. Taguchi & J. M. Sykes (Eds.), *Technology in interlanguage pragmatics research and teaching* (pp. 185–214). Amsterdam: Benjamins.

Tannen, D. (1984). *Conversational style: Analyzing talk among friends*. Norwood, NJ: Ablex.

Tapper, G., Drzazga, G., Mendoza, M., & Grill, J. C. (2018). Discourse management strategies revisited: Building on Tyler's Early insights regarding international teaching assistant comprehensibility. In L. Pickering & V. Evans (Eds.). *Language learning, discourse and cognition: Studies in the tradition of Andrea Tyler* (pp. 37–62). Amsterdam: Benjamins.

Tatsuki, D. H., & Houck, N. R. (Eds.). (2010). *Pragmatics: Teaching speech acts*. Alexandria, VA: TESOL Press.

Taylor, C. (1989). *Sources of the self: The making of modern Identity*. Cambridge: Cambridge University Press.

Taylor, T. J., & Cameron, D. (1987). *Analysing conversation*. New York: Pergamon Press.

Terkourafi, M. (2005a). Beyond the micro-level in politeness research. *Journal of Politeness Research, 1*(2), 237–262.

Terkourafi, M. (2005b). An argument for a frame-based approach to politeness. In R. T. Lakoff & S. Ide (Eds.). *Broadening the horizon of linguistic politeness* (pp. 99–116). Amsterdam: Benjamins.

Terkourafi, M. (2011). The pragmatic variable: Toward a procedural interpretation. *Language in Society, 40*(3), 343–372.

Terkourafi, M. (2015). Conventionalization: A new agenda for im/politeness research. *Journal of Pragmatics, 86*, 11–18.

Terkourafi, M. (2015b). The linguistics of politeness and social relations. In K. Allan (Ed.), *The routledge handbook of linguistics* (pp. 221–235). New York: Routledge.

Thomas, J. (1983). Cross-cultural pragmatic failure. *Applied linguistics, 4*(2), 91–112.

Thompson, G. (2013). *Introducing functional grammar*. New York: Routledge. 3rd ed. First edition, 1996.

Timmis, I. (2013). Corpora and materials: Towards a working relationship. In B. Tomlinson (Ed.), *Developing materials for language teaching* (2nd ed.) (pp. 461–474). London, UK: Bloomsbury Academic.

Toman, J. (1995). *The magic of a common language: Jakobson, Mathesius, Trubetzkoy, and the Prague Linguistic circle*. Boston, MA: MIT Press.

Trosborg, A. (Ed.). (2010). *Pragmatics across languages and cultures*. Berlin: Mouton de Gruyter.

Trubetzkoy, N. (1939). *Grundzüge der Phonologie*. Gottingen: Vandenhoeck & Ruprecht.

Trudgill, P. (1972). Sex, covert prestige and linguistic change in the urban British English of Norwich. *Language in Society, 1*(2), 179–195.

Tsohatzidis, S.L. (Ed.). (1994). *Foundations of speech act theory: Philosophical and linguistic perspectives*. London: Routledge.

Tyler, A. (1992a). Discourse structure and specification of relationships: A cross-linguistic analysis. *Text Interdisciplinary Journal for the Study of Discourse, 12*(1), 1–18.

Tyler, A. (1992b). Discourse structure and the perception of incoherence in international teaching assistants' spoken discourse. *TESOL Quarterly, 26*(4), 713–729.

Tyler, A. (1994a). The role of repetition in perceptions of discourse coherence. *Journal of Pragmatics, 21*(6), 671–688.

Tyler, A. (1994b). The role of syntactic structure in discourse structure: Signaling logical and prominence relations. *Applied Linguistics, 15*(3), 243–262.

Tyler, A. (1995). The co-construction of cross-cultural miscommunication. *Studies in Second Language Acquisition, 17*(2), 129–152.

Tyler, A., & Bro, J. (1992). Discourse structure in nonnative English discourse: The effect of ordering and interpretive cues on perceptions of comprehensibility. *Studies in Second Language Acquisition, 14*, 71–86.

Tyler, A., Jefferies, A., & Davies, C. E. (1988). The effect of discourse structuring devices on listener perceptions of coherence in non-native university teachers' spoken discourse. *World Englishes 7*(2), 101–110.

Tyler, J. C. (2015). Expanding and mapping the indexical field: Rising pitch, the uptalk stereotype, and perceptual variation. *Journal of English Linguistics, 43*(4), 284–310.

Uffmann, C. (2017). World Englishes and *phonological* theory. In M. Filppula, J. Klemola, & D. Sharma (Eds.), *The oxford handbook of world Englishes* (pp. 63–83). Oxford: Oxford University Press.

Vachek, J. (ed.)(1964). *A Prague School reader in linguistics*. Indiana University Press.

Vachek, J. (1966). *The Linguistic School of Prague: An introduction to its theory and practice*. Bloomington: Indiana University Press.

Vahid Dastjerdi, H. (2012). The impact of explicit instruction of metadiscourse markers on EFL learners' writing performance. *Journal of Teaching Language Skills, 29*(2), 155–174.

Vanderveken, D. (1990). *Meaning and speech acts*, Vols I and II, Cambridge: Cambridge University Press.

Vanderveken, D., & Kubo, S. (Eds.). (2002). *Essays in speech act theory*. Amsterdam: John Benjamins Publishing.

Van Lier, L. (2004). The semiotics and ecology of language learning. *Utbildning & Demokrati, 13*(3), 79–103.

Van Olmen, D. (2013). The imperative of say as a pragmatic marker in English and Dutch. *Journal of Germanic Linguistics, 25*(3), 247–287.

Veblen, T. (1889). *The theory of the leisure class*. New York: The Modern Library.

Vellenga, H. (2004). Learning pragmatics from ESL and EFL textbooks: How likely? *TESL-EJ, 8*(2), n2.

Verschueren, J. (1995). Metapragmatics. In Verschueren, J., Östman, J.-O., & Blommaert, J. (Eds.), *Handbook of Pragmatics: Manual* (pp. 367–371). Amsterdam: Benjamins.

Verschueren, J. (2000). Notes on the role of metapragmatic awareness in language use. *Pragmatics. Quarterly Publication of the International Pragmatics Association (IPrA), 10*(4), 439–456.

Vertovec, S. (2007). Super-diversity and its implications. *Ethnic and Racial Studies, 30*(6). 1024–1054. doi: 10.1080/01419870701599465

Vertovec, S. (2019). Talking around super-diversity. *Ethnic and Racial Studies, 42*(1), 125–139.

Vine, B. (2016). Pragmatic Markers at work in New Zealand. In L. Pickering, E. Friginal, & S. Staples, (Eds.), *Talking at Work: Corpus-based explorations of workplace discourse*, (pp. 1–26). London: Palgrave Macmillan.

Vyatkina, N., & Belz, J. A. (2006). A learner corpus-driven intervention for the development of L2 pragmatic competence. *Pragmatics and language learning, 11*, 315–357.

Vygotsky, L. (1978). *Mind in society: The development of higher psychological processes*. In M. Cole, V. John-Steiner, S. Scribner, & E. Souberman (Eds.). Cambridge, MA: Harvard University Press.

Warga, M., & Schölmberger, U. (2007). The acquisition of French apologetic behavior in a study abroad context. *Intercultural Pragmatics, 4*(2), 221–251.

Washburn, G. N. (2001). Using situation comedies for pragmatic language teaching and learning. *TESOL Journal, 10*(4), 21–26.

Watts, R. J. (1992). Linguistic politeness and politic verbal behaviour: Reconsidering claims for universality. In R. J. Watts, S. Ide, & K. Ehlich (Eds.), *Politeness in language: Studies in its history, theory and practice* (pp. 43–69). Berlin: Mouton de Gruyter.

Watts, R. J. (2005). Linguistic politeness research: Quo vadis? In R. J. Watts, S. Ide, & K. Ehlich (Eds.), *Politeness in Language. Studies in its history, theory and practice* (2nd ed.) (pp. xi–xlvii). Berlin/New York: Mouton de Gruyter.

Watts, R. J. (2010). Linguistic politeness theory and its aftermath: Recent research trails. In M. A. Locher & S. L. Graham (Eds.), *Interpersonal pragmatics* (pp. 43–70). Berlin: Mouton Gruyter.

Wei, M. (2011). Investigating the oral proficiency of English learners in China: A comparative study of the use of pragmatic markers. *Journal of Pragmatics, 43*(14), 3455–3472.

Weil, H. (1844). *De l'ordre des mots dans les langues anciennes comparées aux langues modernes: question de grammaire générale*. Paris: Joubert.

Weissberg, R. (1984). Given and new: Paragraph development models from scientific English. *TESOL Quarterly, 18*(3), 485–500. doi:10.2307/3586716

West, M. (1953). *A general service list of English words*. London: Longman, Green and Co.

Westergaard, M., Mitrofanova, N., Mykhaylyk, R., & Rodina, Y. (2017). Crosslinguistic influence in the acquisition of a third language: The Linguistic Proximity Model. *International Journal of Bilingualism, 21*(6), 666–682.

White, L. (1989). *Universal grammar and second language acquisition*. Amsterdam: Benjamins.

Whorf, B. L. (1956). *Language, Thought, and Reality: Selected Writings of Benjamin Lee Whorf* (Carroll, J. B. Ed.). Cambridge, MA: MIT Press.

Wierzbicka, A. (1985). Different cultures, different languages, different speech acts: Polish vs. *English. Journal of pragmatics, 9*(2–3), 145–178.

Wilkowski, B. M., Meier, B. P., Robinson, M. D., Carter, M. S., & Feltman, R. (2009). "Hot-headed" is more than an expression: The embodied representation of anger in terms of heat. *Emotion, 9*(4), 464–477.

Wildner-Bassett, M. (1994). Intercultural pragramtics and proficiency: "Polite" noises for cultural appropriateness, *IRAL, 32*(1), 3–17.

Wilkinson, S. (2002). The omnipresent classroom during summer study abroad: American students in conversation with their French hosts. *The Modern Language Journal, 86*(2), 157–173.

Wilson, D., & Sperber, D. (2012). *Meaning and relevance*. Cambridge: Cambridge University Press.

Wilson, R. A., & Foglia, L. (2017). Embodied cognition. In E. N. Zalta (Ed.), *The stanford Encyclopedia of philosophy*. https://plato.stanford.edu/archives/spr2017/entries/embodied-cognition

Wodak, R. (Ed.). (1989). *Language, power and ideology: Studies in political discourse*. Amsterdam: Benjamins.

Wood, D. (2010). *Formulaic language and second language speech fluency: Background, evidence and classroom applications*. London: Continuum.

Yabuuchi, A. (2006). Hierarchy politeness: What Brown and Levinson refused to see. *Intercultural Pragmatics, 3*(3), 323–351.

Yamashita, S. (2008). Investigating interlanguage pragmatic ability: What are we testing? In Alcón Soler, E., & Martínez-Flor (Eds.), *Investigating pragmatics in foreign language learning, teaching and testing* (pp. 201–223). Bristol: Multilingual Matters.

Yang, L. (2016). Learning to express gratitude in Mandarin Chinese through web-based instruction. *Language Learning & Technology, 20*(1), 191–208.

Yus, F. (2011). *Cyberpragmatics.* Amsterdam: Benjamins.

Yus, F. (2019). An outline of some future research issues for internet pragmatics. *Internet Pragmatics, 2*(1), 1–33.

Zaferanieh, E., Tavakoli, M., & Eslami-Rasekh, A. (2016). Second language pragmatics development through different instructional techniques: Focus on speech act of criticizing. *ITL – International Journal of Applied Linguistics, 171*(1), 113–141.

Zhao, H. (2013). A study on the pragmatic fossilization of discourse markers among Chinese English learners. *Journal of language teaching and research, 4*(4), 707.

Zipf, G. K. (1949). *Human behavior and the principle of least effort.* New York: Addison-Wesley.

# Name Index



*Pragmatics and Its applications to TESOL and SLA*, First Edition. Salvatore Attardo and Lucy Pickering.

## t



## u



## v



## w

# Subject Index